Getting opera

Getting

opera

a guide for the

cultured but confused

Matt Dobkin

POCKET BOOKS

New York   London   Toronto   Sydney   Singapore

An *Original* Publication of POCKET BOOKS

POCKET BOOKS, a division of Simon & Schuster Inc.
1230 Avenue of the Americas, New York, NY 10020

Library of Congress Cataloging-in-Publication Data

Dobkin, Matt.
    Getting Opera : a guide for the cultured but confused / Matt Dobkin.
       p. cm.
    Includes bibliographical references and discography.
    ISBN 0–671–04139–8
     1. Operas—Stories, plots, etc.   I. Title.

MT95 .D63 2000
782.1—dc21   99–045234

First Pocket Books trade paperback printing March 2000

10 9 8 7 6 5 4 3 2 1

POCKET and colophon are registered trademarks of Simon & Schuster Inc.

Book design by Lindgren/Fuller Design

Cover design by Lisa Litwack

Front cover photo courtesy of the Metropolitan Opera–Winnie Klotz. John Tomlinson as Moses in the Metropolitan Opera production of Arnold Schoenberg's *Moses und Aron;* director Graham Vick; set and costume designer Paul Brown.

Title page photo courtesy of the Metropolitian Opera—Winnie Klotz.

Printed in the U. S. A.

For my parents

contents

getting opera

getting opera

How *I* got it–and why I
decided to write this book

The year is 1983. I'm eleven years
old. I've been singing in the children's choruses of the Metropolitan Opera and the New York City Opera for about a year, but thus
far have only managed to score crappy, low-paying parts: urchins,
schoolboys, that sort of thing. Who is getting all of the meat-and-
potatoes roles: the shepherds, the young princes, the "crippled"
boys? Over the course of the last few months, I have managed to
ingratiate myself with the aging chorus mistress (named Mil-
dred—no joke) and am cast in the Met's production of Wagner's
Tannhäuser as one of eight pages (underage footmen, essentially).
We're only onstage for about three minutes and sing a total of just
nine German syllables, which we learn phonetically. But my name
will be in the program, my fee is jacked up (thirty dollars per performance!), and I can enjoy the satisfaction of having graduated to
"small-ensemble work."

What's more, I'm now in good with the stage director, sharing
my Nerds candy with her during rehearsals. She returns the favor
by designating me "the urn boy." Unlike my seven prepubescent

colleagues, I am entrusted with the care of a prop! The responsibility is tremendous: I have to walk in a circle on an inclined platform and present the metal bowl to various Wartburg Castle song-contest participants, who throw slips of paper with their names written on them into the vessel. I am directed to subsequently march up to Austrian soprano legend Leonie Rysanek and extend the urn in her direction, so that she can pull a name out of the hat, as it were, and inaugurate the Act II competition.

What if I trip while negotiating the ramped stage, scattering the strips of paper everywhere? The opera would be ruined! What if I block Rysanek's sight lines? Will she pull some crazy diva crap and come at me with the intent to cause physical harm? The pressure is considerable, but, like a male adolescent Eve Harrington, I am not about to let anyone stop me on my journey to the upper echelons of boy sopranohood.

Opening night finally arrives and, as luck would have it, I am sick with the flu. But it doesn't matter to me. I'm not about to let a little obstacle like a 102-degree fever thwart my shot at onstage glory. Nothing my parents can say will keep me in my sickbed. "I'll be fine, Mom! Just bring me fluids! Orange juice! Egg drop soup! Now!"

By the time I get to the theater, I'm a mess: white as a sheet, clammy, and sniveling—but determined nonetheless. In the Level 2 children's chorus rehearsal studio, I slip into my costume (a heavy, purplish, dresslike robe, which, having been used for several seasons by a rotating cast of preteen boys, is in urgent need of a trip to the dry cleaner). I am already in a sweat and the garment makes things worse. Feeling increasingly unwell, I think I should perhaps visit the men's room and splash some cool water on my face. Why did I have to become sick on this of all nights?

Forlornly, I shuffle down the cement-floored hallway—its width narrowed by racks and racks of old costumes—toward the men's room. Waves of nausea gain power as I slowly near my destination. It occurs to me that I might not make it, that I will end up hurling all over last season's tunics. But just then, like Violetta in the final act of *La Traviata,* I feel my strength miraculously return-ing. The nausea seems to retreat. I stop sweating. I am going to make it!

Well, if you've seen *Traviata,* you know that Violetta's eleventh-hour recovery lasts about six seconds, at which point she simply drops dead. I, too, come suddenly crashing back to earth. I fall to my knees, retch convulsively, and puke a steady stream of vomit, which splatters along the hallway's concrete floor, soiling the hems of costumes that have been worn by folks like Leontyne Price, Luciano Pavarotti, and Joan Sutherland. The fit lasts only a few sec-onds, and I immediately feel better. But my mortification is sealed when I look up from my prostration, mouth awash in regurgitated filth, and behold the stunned expressions of a crowd of horrified onlookers, engaged at that very moment in a backstage tour. Some-how I don't think the sight of a broken young child, collapsed on the cold, hard cement, heaving uncontrollably, is listed on their tour itinerary. The guide makes a few nervous remarks and hastily leads the group away.

Whenever people ask me about my first time at the opera, I invari-ably recall this incident. Although my entrée into the world of clas-sical singing was relatively smooth, the *Tannhäuser* barfing experience seems apropos as an example of an early dose of opera, since so many operagoers' first time at an opera house is so, well, sickening. It's unfortunate but true. A lot of folks who are perfectly game about giving opera a shot nonetheless don't take the neces-sary steps to prepare for their first time and really figure out which works they're most likely to enjoy. I'd argue that unless you have a strong sense of what to expect when you set foot in the Metropoli-tan Opera House or San Francisco's War Memorial Opera House for the first time, you're going to come away disappointed, if not downright queasy.

Many potential opera lovers don't even get that far. Most of my contemporaries (people in their twenties) wouldn't even dream of going to the opera. It's simply not on their radar. Foreign language.

High ticket prices. General air of elitism. With so many easier, less costly forms of entertainment readily available, why would any savvy urban resident bother with, of all things, an opera?

Well, I am an opera critic. But I am also in my mid-twenties, have all my hair, and am more likely to have the latest Björk CD in my Discman than an obscure 1950s import of *Lucia di Lammermoor*. I don't have a doctoral degree in musicology, I don't stay up nights worrying about the twelve-tone/tonality conundrum, and I'd rather read *Spin* than *Opera News*. These stats combine to make me something of an anomaly among classical-music writers. Most of my colleagues are in their fifties, graying, and wide around the middle. They're also reflective of too large a sector of opera audiences today. Things are definitely changing, with the median age of operagoers steadily decreasing and opera gaining a certain degree of cachet among downtown types. But I still don't see enough people my age in the opera house these days, a fact that worries not just the opera companies, eager to lure new generations of fans, but me, as well.

If I hadn't had the early exposure I experienced as a boy soprano, I probably wouldn't think much of opera, either. But I'd be missing out. Although I'm not going to take the position of most rabid opera freaks, who say that opera is *the* greatest art form of all time, putting all others to shame, I will say emphatically that there is much to appreciate in opera that too many people aren't aware of. These virtues became apparent to me at an early age, because I was immersed in opera from the time I was nine. Several nights a week, I found myself on the Met's stage alongside some of the greatest singers of the late twentieth century. Pavarotti, Domingo, Rysanek, Troyanos, and Caballé are all stars whom I heard up close before I even knew enough to realize that opera was considered a peculiar interest for a small child. As a result, operatic singing seemed like no big deal. The magnificence of opera's grand sets and costumes were commonplace. And a story told in a foreign language was par for the course. The fact that my parents and grandparents were season ticket holders didn't hurt my chances of forming an attachment to opera, either. But most people I know have had limited experience with opera, if any.

About twelve years after my voice changed (sending me into a downward career spiral I'm still reeling from), I found myself, ironically, with a job that once again required my presence at the opera house several nights a week. As the classical-music editor of *Time Out New York* magazine, I was responsible for reviewing all the productions at the Met and New York City Opera. The circumstances had changed drastically, but the experience of witnessing fine performances by world-class artists was the same. But it soon started to bother me that though these companies generally manage to pack their theaters, the audience is primarily made up of blue-hairs, and I don't mean the kind found in the East Village. Of course, it depends on which opera houses you frequent, but opera audiences are, for the most part, a too-elderly lot. And that's a shame, because there's so much about this art form that's vital and potentially of interest to sophisticated young consumers of various other forms of entertainment. It's my belief that people like you— educated, in your twenties or thirties, a fan of theater, film, television, and music—harbor, somewhere deep down, a genuine interest in opera. It's never difficult for me to entice friends to join me when I have a spare ticket. "Yeah, I'd love to go!" is the usual reply to those invitations. "I don't really know anything about opera, but I'd be into checking it out."

After a few months of getting this response from friends, I realized that there was a need for some sort of guide to opera for the educated, urban consumer of culture, pop or otherwise. Most classical-music writing presupposes a fairly substantial knowledge of the material at hand. Opera guides tend to be either overly academic and impenetrable to anyone who's not conservatory-trained, or so unbelievably watered down as to be insulting to your intelligence. To find most writings about opera worthwhile, you must either have advanced musical study under your belt or be a half-wit. It occurred to me that the people I knew and hung out with were well versed in many areas of the arts and could appreciate facets of both "high" and "low" culture. Because opera is (to my mind) the ultimate fusion of the high and the low, it seems as though it should be a potentially compelling art form to those people. That's essentially how the idea for this book came about. It's really geared toward my friends, so that they can accompany me to the opera without being frightened or intimidated by what they perceive to be a mysterious and challenging art, which seems to exist on some almost otherworldly plane.

At a dinner party not long ago, I was seated next to a woman in her twenties, who, I quickly learned, was an opera lover (we youthful opera fans seem to have some sort of radar that enables us to pick each other out of a crowd). We got to chatting about the opera world's state of affairs and how difficult it can be to interest anyone less than seventy years of age in this historically populist art form. She had a pretty good analogy for why some folks are reluctant to check it out. "Opera is like amateur golf," she explained. "Most of the time it's pretty awful, but on those rare occasions when everything falls into place and you make a great shot, it feels amazing." I'm not much of a golfer, but I catch her drift. Opera is not easy to produce, perform, or even attend. There are so many variables adding to the possibility of a failed performance that it can seem like a waste of time and money to someone who's not already enamored of the genre. But I'd argue that even in a flawed performance, there are moments of wonder and beauty that are hard to come by when viewing other forms of entertainment. Opera doesn't always work, but when it does...

Once a popular entertainment, opera has, through the ages, acquired an increasingly rarefied air. To many people, it's an elitist art form that exists to please a small cadre of wealthy benefactors. It's expensive, long, and almost always performed in a foreign language. It takes work to appreciate an opera—work that many aren't willing to put in given the fact that watching TV or going to a movie is so easy. Well, this book is intended to give you all the workout you need to start *getting opera*. In the following chapters, I'll take a look at the state of the opera world today; provide a history of opera through the ages; explain classical singing; and give tips on getting cheap tickets, choosing the right opera to suit your interests, and what to do during intermission. I've tried to strip opera of its aura of elitism and explain how to make a night at the opera as easy to enjoy as an episode of *Friends* or *ER* (depending on the composer). This book is intended to be useful. It's not an academic assessment of musical trends or a love letter to some long-lost golden age. It is meant to guide you through your early experiences with opera. Feel free to write in its margins or share it with friends. Don't feel you need to read straight through. Flip around. Glance at the sidebars. Read what interests or informs you and skip what doesn't. You don't need a degree in musicology to appreciate opera. All you need is to do the basic groundwork. With any luck, you'll find yourself moved to buy a ticket. Opera needs to be reclaimed by young people as a popular, accessible, and moving art form.

The Berkeley, California–based opera critic and scholar David Littlejohn has written a funny and insightful book called *The Ultimate Art: Essays Around and About Opera,* in which he captures perfectly the sensation *I* experience when the right singer is singing the right aria in the right production at the right moment. "For reasons I cannot understand or explain," he writes, "I sometimes find myself staring with unnatural intensity at a performer in an opera who is singing exceptionally well . . . as if we were related in some intimate, emotional way. I catch myself either foolishly beaming or near to tears, *not* because of the joy or plight of the character, but because I have been moved beyond any reasonable, critical response by the simple, sensual fact of the quality and vibrations of a human voice." Obviously, opera is not the only performing art that can have a direct hold on an audience's emotions, but I think the heightened emotional realm of opera and the form's inescapable, over-the-top quality increase the chance that a listener will be seized by one of the rapturous moments that Littlejohn describes. It's kind of like those moments in a rock concert when the artist brings it down a notch and performs a slow jam that seems aimed directly at you. Time seems to stop, and you don't know whether to laugh or cry. Of course, it's important that the narrative of an opera unravel properly and that the musical numbers don't hinder the advancement of the story. But I think opera is essentially about those moments when the singer seems to become some sort of magician, able to make the flaws of a production disappear and reveal certain fundamental human truths simply by opening his or her mouth and letting sound escape.

Okay, it's only the first chapter and I'm already getting all deep, so I'll leave the metaphysical speculation at that. Time for me to get into cheerleader mode. There are a host of reasons why I think you should give this whole opera thing a try. And in the next few chapters I'll see what I can do to pique your interest.

Opera Jokes

As with any field, opera boasts a regular lineup of jokes that poke fun at its main figures. Most of them have to do with the brainlessness of sopranos and tenors and with the arrogance of conductors. Here are a few I've culled from various Web sites.

How do you put a sparkle in a soprano's eye?
Shine a flashlight in her ear.

How many sopranos does it take to change a lightbulb?
Just one. She just holds it in place, and the whole world revolves around her.

What do a conductor and a condom have in common?
It's safer with—but more fun without.

What's the difference between an orchestra and a bull?
The bull has the horns in the front and the asshole in the back.

If you took all the tenors in the world and laid them end to end . . .
It would be a good idea.

Where is a tenor's resonance?
Where his brain should be.

What do you call ten baritones at the bottom of the ocean?
A good start.

What's the difference between a soprano and a terrorist?
You can negotiate with a terrorist.

What's the difference between a soprano and a pit bull?
The jewelry.

What's the difference between a Wagnerian soprano and an offensive lineman?
Stage makeup.

What's the difference between a Wagnerian soprano and a Wagnerian tenor?
About ten pounds.

What's the ideal weight for a conductor?
About two and a half pounds—including the urn.

What do you have when a group of conductors are up to their necks in wet concrete?
Not enough concrete.

What does a contralto say when she gets work?
"Would you like fries with that?"

exploding opera

A look at some myths—
and truths—surrounding opera
(and a few reasons why
you should go)

F or his final opera, *Capriccio,* which premiered in 1942, Richard Strauss turned his attention to the original conundrum of opera: how to reconcile words and music. Which is more important? How do you balance the two so that they complement rather than overwhelm each other? It was an ironic choice of subject matter, because Strauss had endured a notoriously prickly relationship with his primary librettist, Hugo von Hofmannsthal, who defiantly believed himself to be the composer's artistic superior. He was also vocal in his belief that music was *clearly* meant to serve the aims of the poetry to which it was set.

Strauss, however, wasn't so sure about this. The plot of *Capriccio* concerns a countess who must choose between two suitors—one a poet, the other a composer. The opera is somewhat ponderous and slow moving: There are no melodramatic killings or passionate affairs to keep the pace up. But as an important composer's swan song, the work is interesting because its topic returns to the original aims of opera's founding fathers. Indeed, that an opera composed as recently as the mid twentieth century would be fixated on the same problem that troubled composers in the seventeenth century seems to me indicative of the fact that opera is a vexed, contentious, flawed form. That may sound a bit surprising coming from someone who already has flatly stated that his goal is to get you interested in opera. But I think it's important, before we go any further, to point out that from its origins to this day opera, the combination art form (or, to use Wagner's term, *Gesamtkunstwerk*), is a genre made up of warring factions. Opera observer Winton Dean has frequently been praised for his dead-on observation that "opera is a gigantic series of compromises." As a result, there really isn't one perfect, pure, seamless opera. Opera is defined by its relationship to different elements, and, as with any relationship, there's baggage.

Because opera relies on compromise, balance, and reconciliation, it's a form that can't avoid giving rise to certain myths and misconceptions. Since the genre's beginnings nearly four hundred years ago, people have been fighting about it: how it should be staged, how it should be composed, how it should be sung. It's only natural that someone not wholly familiar with opera would be put off by its mysterious, almost mythical qualities. In this chapter, before we really get into the nuts and bolts of operatic history, of classical singing, and of actually taking the plunge, I'm going to take a look at some of those operatic myths. Despite what you've heard about opera's monumental egos, challenging music, irritating fans, and relative costliness, I hope you'll still be persuaded to pick up a recording or, better yet, a ticket. Regardless of what negative impressions you may have gotten, opera is (almost inexplicably) hot these days, and it has a lot to offer even the most skeptical and savvy citizen.

Mixed Media

If only there were just two disciplines to be reconciled in opera. In fact, there are far more. Opera has been called the ultimate combination art form with good reason. It's not just text and music that have to be balanced; opera requires sets, costumes, lighting, and all the other accoutrements of a theatrical performance. Those facets of opera production are accomplished by very specific types of artists versed in the art of the theater. The text is perhaps the second most important element of an opera (after the music), and it is usually written by someone with a very different set of creative talents from the person who, say, puts together the scenic design. Historically, many operas were required to contain dance segments, and even the ones that weren't usually *did* include movement of some kind; thus choreography and dance are often thrown into the opera mix. Then, of course, there's the musical element, inarguably the most important facet of opera. A composer must strive to write a substantial piece of music that is new and fresh, that will bring out the best in operatic singing voices, that musically evokes the work's story through the orchestral writing, and that doesn't get in the way of the plot. Any given opera will incorporate elements of music, poetry, dance, narrative, set design, costume design, and lighting design, as well as the varying sensibilities of the practitioners of each of those arts. That's a lot for any performing-arts organization to get a grip on.

Most fans of opera point to its mix of genres as proof that it is in fact the best of all art forms. Bigger is better, right? By combining all the arts into one overreaching über-art of sorts, opera heightens each individual form on which it capitalizes, right? Poetry is even better when married to music, right? A story with a sound track is better than one without, right? Well, I think that opera's postmodern mix of styles is indeed one of the most interesting of its characteristics. But to get into the vein that opera is better than theater and better than ordinary music seems to foster a competitive spirit that's both immaterial and off-putting. Part of the appeal of opera is its ability to confront all the senses by means of its various artistic factors. But I think the constant assertions of opera aficionados that nothing can compare to their beloved art do nothing to appeal to someone who may not know that much about opera to begin with. Assaulting potential listeners with absolute statements of opera's superiority as a genre because it draws on so many different forms will only turn them off, as far as I can tell. Opera is certainly different from other art forms, but to say it's better only adds to the elitist mystique that keeps most people away.

As someone who wants to convince a young, hip crowd that opera is worth checking out, I'd like to suggest that the "combination" aspect of opera, though fascinating, is in many ways fascinating in the train-wreck sense. Do you know how easy it is for an opera production to be nearly ruined because of all the disparate elements? This grand notion that opera is monumental because it fuses all the arts ignores the fact that it's incredibly easy for an opera production to fall flat *because* of the difficulty in balancing the different elements. A seamless opera production is a rare thing, and once you realize that opera is in fact flawed, that the rhapsodic endorsements of opera queens are immaterial, and that opera is an art form both to be admired *and* to poke fun at, then I think you're more likely to get over any hesitation you may have. Opera brings together many different fields, several of which you may not have mastered or even be interested in. But don't let that scare you. It is those people who essentially think that all art is inferior to opera who are the ignorant fools. God forbid this book should convince you to renounce pop music or action movies because they lack the grandeur of the "combination art form."

The High/Low Country

The myth that opera is an elite, "high" art form is certainly one factor that works to deter newcomers. In fact, opera occupies a sort of dubious place in the firmament of classical music. Many people mindlessly attend the opera in an attempt to get a shot of "class." Enjoying opera is seen by many as proof of being "cultured." But among hard-core classical types, opera is largely viewed as vulgar, and certainly as inferior to the loftier aims of "absolute" music, which aims to affect its listeners without the maudlin, manipulative presence of (egad!) a plot. On the list of bona fide historical

Deconstructing Opera

Racism, Sexism, Classism, Imperialism, Orientalism, Ageism, Animal-Companionism—and More!

Because of its often questionably chosen subject matter and its multitude of different elements to "read," opera has predictably fallen prey to the deconstructionists and poststructuralists who people our nation's universities. Opera is seen as a political and cultural text to be unraveled, and these days there are more sociological studies of opera as a genre on bookstore shelves than there are guides of the kind you have in your hands. I find a lot of this scholarship very interesting, but often can't help but laugh when I read some of the virtually impenetrable prose that these theorists pass off as analysis. Even more than literary works, opera has proven to be the ultimate fodder for this type of "discourse."

Here, for example, is an analysis of the castrati from the introduction to Richard Dellamora and Daniel Fischlin's *The Work of Opera: Genre, Nationhood, and Sexual Difference:* "Castrati were accused of transgressing conventional norms, and [Todd] Gilman contends that the projection of hypervirility upon the figure of the castrato inadvertently called into question not only the sufficiency of the manly stance of the satirist but also a construction of English citizenship that was based upon the conflation of the ideal, in classic republican discourse, of the virile citizen-soldier with the Tory ideal of the country gentleman." You probably already knew that. Later in the same chapter, the writers go on to say: "Opera's erotic fusion of media in the Wagnerian *Gesamtkunstwerk* produces a form of aesthetic *jouissance* that works to contradict the powerful ideological forces that make of opera a microcosmic and imaginary national polity."

I, for one, love this sort of thing. When Carolyn Abbate asserts in her influential and often enlightening *Unsung Voices: Opera and Musical Narrative in the Nineteenth Century* that "the great moments of operatic narrating are those that waver as it were in another domain, adding to the oscillation inherent in the reflexive moment a shift between reflexive and monaural modes," I have no idea what the hell she's talking about. But she sure knows how to turn a phrase. The point is, by getting opera, you'll be potentially exposing yourself to a whole new world of mind-bogglingly abstruse theory of the kind you thought you abandoned for good when you graduated from college.

musical geniuses, the only opera composer who has a firm spot is Mozart (and he of course wrote music in all kinds of nonoperatic vernaculars). As Herbert Lindenberger puts it in *Opera: The Extravagant Art,* "anyone who included Bellini, Bizet, or Puccini [on a list of great 'composers'] would risk intellectual embarrassment."

Now, I'm hardly trying to convince you that opera is low, vulgar, or something to turn up your nose at. I'm simply trying to point out the irrelevance of designating *anything* as an example of high or low culture. No matter how worthy the artistic object of your admiration, there will always be someone who can cite an even more "legitimate" creation. My point is, essentially, screw the whole struggle between high and low. And certainly don't be afraid of opera because some force has foolishly built it up as the ultimate in refinement. Opera has historically been a popular art form that aimed to entertain ordinary people. Don't let that bother you, and don't let some uptight classical geek tell you any different.

I think this blending of the high and low is best represented by the recent staging of the MTV Video Music Awards at the Metropolitan Opera House. I won't soon forget the sight of the teenage Welsh soprano Charlotte Church (the one who, her record label assures us, has "the voice of an angel") presenting white rapper Eminem with his trophy for Best New Artist. I wonder if little Charlotte had ever heard Eminem's hit "My Name Is," with its talk about impregnating Spice Girls and such.

Artists from the pop and opera worlds aren't merely crossing paths these days. They're actually trying their hands at each other's material. Frankly, I'm repulsed by Michael Bolton's recent CD *My Secret Passion: The Arias,* an opera album on which his plaintive rock-soul vocals suggest Al Green doing Donizetti (although *that* would actually not be half bad). Nevertheless, I do place myself in the camp of people who believe that if the newly shorn cheese-pop whiz can somehow bring opera to the masses, well, then, I'm all for it. And as far as Aretha Franklin singing Puccini's "Nessun dorma" on the Grammy Awards is concerned, I can't remember a performance that gave me such pleasure. Most of my classical colleagues were appalled that the Queen of Soul would actually endeavor to sing a tenor aria in public, but I think they're missing the fun of it. First, the aria is habitually sung by the male lead of *Turandot.* It's probably never before been sung by a woman, let alone a soul diva. Right away, it has to be judged by a different set of criteria. What's more, by imposing her considerable chutzpah on the aria, riffing as she's wont to do, Aretha pulled the ultimate diva trick of making the song her own and flouting convention. If you can't get a kick out of the absurdity of an R&B singer interpreting Puccini, then I don't get how you can stomach the even greater stretches that many operas put before the public in earnest. Aretha singing "Nessun dorma" seems no more absurd to me than the gypsy Azucena claiming to have accidentally burned to death the *wrong* infant in *Il Trovatore.* It's all wonderful and it's all ridiculous. There seems no point in valuing some phantom judge's designation of high and low to the point where no one feels safe enjoying anything. If you find yourself drawn to a particular opera, pay no attention to what I or anyone else has to say about its worth. Just go with it.

Social Studies

Opera audiences have historically gone and continue to go to the opera because they think it's "high" or "classy." Although it would be wonderful to claim that most opera audiences come for the music, that's a little far-fetched. The opera is an incredibly social endeavor, and people come to see and be seen as much as they come for the performance itself. It's easy to disparage those opera-goers with minimal musical inclinations, to ridicule someone so shallow as to actually pay money for a ticket to a performance in which he has little genuine interest. But frankly, though it's not my primary MO when attending an opera, I wouldn't miss the absurd offstage action for anything. Going to the opera can be a strictly musical and intellectual endeavor, but for most people it's an event, a treat that demands looking one's best and flaunting one's sense of culture.

When opera first came on the scene in the seventeenth century, it was subsidized entirely by the nobility, who consequently had to have the best seats in the house. This generally meant the center box of the first balcony, and that's still where dignitaries and important guests tend to sit. As opera houses started to pop up all over Europe (starting, in particular, in Venice), other members of society purchased boxes for the season as a sort of display of wealth and position. Those people paid even less attention to the action onstage than their contemporary counterparts do. Going to the opera didn't mean sitting quietly and listening to music in a darkened theater. It meant playing cards, chatting with friends, sleeping, and occasionally looking up when a star performer launched into an aria. Even the cast of operas in the seventeenth and eighteenth centuries was only minimally involved in performances, even going so far as to chat from the stage with friends in the crowd. In the nineteenth century, the opera-as-party concept reached its apex, with the lounges of many opera houses outfitted with gambling tables and roulette wheels.

If I had my druthers, the poker tables would return. Why shouldn't the opera house be a haven of fun and exuberance? Why has it acquired the musty identity of a museum? To be fair, though there's generally no mid-performance conversation (which is a good thing) or gambling, the opera house nonetheless continues to offer a festive and social environment. The middle class hasn't changed much in the last few centuries: It still seeks to puff itself up by means of season tickets to the opera. But opera houses are not just Society (with a capital "s") hangouts, they are a social place for the rest of us as well. I can't think of a better place to pick up a potential love interest. The opera house lounge at intermission is the ultimate cruising ground. Anybody—straight or gay—will appreciate the inevitable dreamy, dazed (and so damned attractive) look that comes from sitting in the dark and being assaulted by music for the duration of an act. Opera's reputation as the domain of the rich and socially connected is true to a certain degree. But it certainly doesn't exclude the average urban fun-seeker, who wants to get dressed up, see some pretty people, and maybe make a few new friends.

Theater of the Absurd

The offstage scene of nouveau riche types jockeying to see who's the classiest is amusing and ridiculous. But *that* spectacle has nothing on the absurdity to be found in an actual opera performance. A frequent complaint I hear from opera novices revolves around how ridiculous and unreal the onstage events are. Opera is over the top; it's not realistic; the way people behave onstage bears no resemblance to the way an ordinary person would go about his affairs in real life. Furthermore, the practice of singing a long aria when one has just been, say, stabbed also pushes the bounds of plausibility. Opera is unrealistic and artificial.

Well, it's impossible to argue with such a statement. And I'm not going to deny that the dramaturgy of opera presents situations in a way that's at odds with reality. That said, so what? Even the most vivid and realistic of arts is, in fact, "fake." No, people generally don't break into song to express themselves in real life. But neither do they necessarily speak a soliloquy of what's going through their heads when left alone in a room, as they would in a play. The linear, narrative arc of most movies provides a cleaner, more entertaining, more streamlined version of events than actual reality, but people don't seem to be bothered by that. All art apes real life and heightens it, freezes it, bestows added importance or resonance to it. Opera just happens to do so in a more lavish and fanciful way.

Have you ever seen clips of a movie before the sound track has been added? It's hard to know what to make of a scene without a score. Similarly, the music of an opera, the primary element of its unreality, signals to the audience what's important, how to feel, which emotions are being experienced by the singers. It may seem absurd for action to come to a standstill because a performer is compelled to burst into song, but this artificial musical factor helps get the composer's and the actor's point across with added conviction. I, for one, don't mind being manipulated by opera's heartstring-tugging artificiality if it enables me to experience a particular feeling or emotion.

Opera can seem absurd because it consciously attempts to heighten experience and sensation. I think the charge of absurdity stems not just from opera's artifice but also from the form's focus on the fundamental essence of humanity. Opera is, for the most part, not subtle. Pictures aren't drawn in miniature, and the nuances of human behavior aren't delicately illuminated. Opera works in broad strokes. Its subjects are love, passion, jealousy, murder, suicide, war, sickness. Those are heavy-duty topics that don't exactly reek of refinement. Most sensible folks would rather stick to the surface and avoid the raw emotionalism these subjects summon. It's easier, more sophisticated, more polite to laugh off these issues and denigrate them as absurd than it is to let down your guard and get into the nitty-gritty. Opera is dismissed as absurd because its characters ceaselessly lie, cheat, steal, and kill—singing all the while, no less. Well, believe it or not, real people lie, cheat, steal, and kill. Grand subjects presented in an over-the-top way can seem undignified and unappealing, but they are not as absurd, or as far from the facts of real life, as opera's opponents would have you believe.

Dead White European Tales

Of course, claiming that opera is absurd, vulgar, and ridiculous isn't quite as harsh as the frequent charge that it's completely irrelevant. Opera is often seen as the Latin of the performing arts: a dead form. There's nothing new, important, or innovative going on in the world of opera, right? It's a museum art form. (In *The Ultimate Art*, Littlejohn addresses this complaint and jokes, "as if museums had suddenly become reprehensible institutions.")

The focus of most opera houses on standard repertory works, on old chestnuts rather than on progressive new pieces, is hard to refute. Classical-music record labels cite the bread-and-butter works of Puccini and Verdi, performed by familiar superstars, as the real moneymakers in their catalogs. A label or an opera company may take an occasional chance on a younger, less established, less conservative composer, but usually that's done to save artistic face rather than out of some deeply felt desire to educate an audience or attract new listeners. Much as I'd love to argue otherwise, opera's overall conservatism is undeniable and certainly works to alienate a younger crowd of potential fans. I think most people under the age of, say, forty would prefer to go to the gallery opening of a hot new artist than to a museum exhibit of Rembrandts. Similarly, an old-school production of *Manon Lescaut* doesn't exactly get the pulse racing the way a fresher, hipper, newer work would.

Now allow me to slip back into upbeat cheerleader mode. Although its focus on the past rather than on the future is indisputable, opera is nonetheless *not* a dead form. New operas by important young composers *are* produced all the time. And most of those composers are mercifully abandoning the conventions that have dominated for so long. Philip Glass and John Adams aren't exactly spring chickens, but they've done a lot to redirect opera's focus from melodrama to quasi-plotless evocations of current events. Thomas Adès and Adam Guettel are two young composers who cite the influence of pop music on their work and whose theater pieces are refreshingly current, both musically and conceptually.

Further evidence that opera is not an entirely dead or (worse yet) boring art form comes out of the fact that opera seems to have shifted in recent years from the realm of the composer, the conductor, and the singer to that of the producer-director. In this decon-structionist era, operas are increasingly viewed as texts to be inter-preted and, sometimes, radically altered. The Metropolitan Opera House, that bastion of tradition, still churns out superlatively opu-lent productions of Italian favorites to appease the geriatric crew. But the company also demonstrates a willingness to try new things with standard repertory operas. Not too long ago, the Met invited avant-garde director (and frequent Philip Glass collaborator) Robert Wilson to do a new staging of Wagner's *Lohengrin*. The minimalist abstraction of Wilson's production didn't go over well with the con-servative Met audience, which let loose with a torrent of boos when Wilson took a curtain call, the violent likes of which I've never heard elsewhere. (Of course, in Paris, where Wilson is revered, they would have been storming the stage in a frenzy.) Whether you liked the Wilson *Lohengrin* or not (I did), at least there seemed to be a dialogue going on. This reinterpretation of a canonical work man-aged to rile thousands of observers and generate a slew of newspa-per editorials on the nature of tampering with classic works. Opera continues to elicit strong reactions from people, which suggests that it is in no way dead. And opera companies across the United States less traditional than the Met stage progressive, challenging productions like that all the time.

Show Tunes and Arias

Opera is certainly more vital and interesting than musical theater these days (unless, of course, *Mulan—Live!* is your sort of thing). Broadway's current lineup of musicals offers exactly zero shows that interest me—and I'm not trying to be pretentious; my tastes are, in general, thoroughly lowbrow. The powers that be in today's musical-theater world are even more intent than their opera coun-terparts on going back in time and exhuming hits from earlier eras. And, somehow, going back to the 1950s for material seems even lamer than retreating to the nineteenth century.

But I think it's worth mentioning that opera and musical the-ater are in fact closely related, and if you enjoy the occasional

Broadway show, chances are there's an opera on the horizon that you'll get into as well. In his hilarious book on opera fandom, *The Queen's Throat,* Wayne Koestenbaum calls enjoyment of musicals a "predictive sign" of impending interest in opera. Indeed, some musicals, but for a few distinguishing technicalities, *are* operas, a fact that might be confusing to the novice. Andrew Lloyd Webber's *Evita,* for instance, because it is sung throughout (its "arias" are connected not by dialogue but by recitative), is in fact an opera. It's not viewed as such, however, because it is performed with amplification and has habitually been staged nightly in Broadway theaters, rather than programmed into the season of a given opera company. Furthermore, Andrew Lloyd Webber is identified as a musical-theater composer, his works generally thought to be insufficiently highbrow to be classified as operas. As you can gather, there really aren't that many hard-and-fast rules governing the separation of opera and Broadway. Mozart's *The Magic Flute* contains spoken dialogue; does that mean it's not an opera? It's fairly slippery terrain. But it doesn't seem to matter much what a piece is labeled. Opera is essentially a heightened, grander, more dramatic version of musical theater. If you like one form, you'll probably like the other.

Opera Queens

One thing that opera and musical theater indisputably have in common are gay fans. The show-tune queen is the not-too-distant cousin of the opera queen, who invariably has a favorite soprano to whom he's devoted with quasi-religious fervor, and who has a store of opera anecdotes and factoids at his fingertips. But too-rabid fans are by no means exclusively gay. There are plenty of straight men and women who have an almost unhealthy attachment to opera and all it connotes. They're opera queens, too. As it appears in this book, the term "opera queen" is in fact synonymous with "opera freak," and says nothing about a fan's sexual identity. Just as in today's world you don't really have to be Jewish to be a JAP, you don't have to be gay to be an opera queen.

I Sing the Body Electric

The popular image of the opera singer as an obese woman with long blond braids and a horned helmet is one that will always be with us. In many cases, it's not an entirely off-the-mark rendering of what some singers (unfortunately) look like. But fat-diva syndrome seems to be subsiding. Right now, there are a slew of women gracing opera's stages who not only can sing but are positively attractive—and know how to accessorize, to boot. And while many tenors tend to be rather short and plump, recent years have seen the arrival of a number of hunky baritones not afraid to go shirtless for a role. Believe it or not, some opera singers are downright hot! And I should point out that the singers listed below are not just nice to look at but extremely talented as well. Any one of the six sex symbols below also belongs on my lists of top singers on pages 73–87.

RODNEY GILFRY

This baritone has been around for several years, working his way up the ranks of the international opera circuit. In 1998, he achieved operatic superstardom when he went shirtless as Stanley Kowalski in André Previn's adaptation of Tennessee Williams's *A Streetcar Named Desire*. He made Brando look positively puny. Who knew that an opera singer could have pecs?

Rodney Gilfry in the
San Francisco Opera's
production of
A Streetcar Named Desire

NATHAN GUNN

Nathan Gunn in *Iphigénie en Tauride*

When the Glimmerglass Opera in Cooperstown, New York, unveiled its production of Gluck's *Iphigénie en Tauride*, soprano Christine Goerke received kudos for her portrayal of the title character. But she was overshadowed by the attention Nathan Gunn received for his bare-chested, homoerotic onstage frolicking. Opera queens everywhere fell instantly in love with the toned and sinewy baritone. Sorry, people: Nathan's married to his high-school sweetheart.

DMITRI HVOROSTOVSKY

When this Russian baritone gave a concert of Italian arias at Carnegie Hall a few years back, I was blown away. He's recorded and performed a lot of Russian material, which, predictably, suits his voice to perfection. But even with eighteenth-century Italian songs, this guy is capable of taking you places with his singing—not to mention with his hunky, silver-haired appearance. He doesn't have the superhigh profile of Bryn Terfel, but along with that singer he's at the very top of his field.

Dmitri Hvorostovsky

SUSAN GRAHAM

Tall, slim, and chic aren't words that are generally applied to divas—but that's how to best describe mezzo-soprano Susan Graham. She's not hot in the *Baywatch* sense of the word, but she looks good in clothes, and in concert she works an effective Armani vibe that wins over audiences before she even opens her mouth.

Mezzo-soprano
Susan Graham

DENYCE GRAVES

It's for good reason that Graves *owns* the roles of Carmen and Dalila. She's by far the sultriest of the world's top singers; costume designers love decking her out in slinky, revealing outfits. And Graves is a mezzo-soprano who knows that being sexy can be accomplished by smiling, not just by writhing around on the floor, as so many misguided singers are wont to do.

Denyce Graves
as Dalila

ANGELIKA KIRCHSCHLAGER

This Austrian mezzo-soprano is the closest thing the opera world has to a supermodel. Tall, thin, and gorgeous, the chick is fierce. Kirchschlager sings a lot of pants roles (young male characters portrayed by women), and the breeches and tunics of those parts work well to give her a sexy, androgynous vibe.

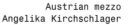

Austrian mezzo
Angelika Kirchschlager

Whatever you call them, those obsessed devotees can be scary, and can certainly turn off the casual fan. I think one reason potential operagoers often skip opera is the idea that enjoying opera means giving up enthusiasm for any other form of entertainment. An opera queen (and you can't set foot in an opera house without encountering at least a handful of them) is probably not something any sane person would strive to be. Koestenbaum talks about following opera with a "vocabulary of addiction." God forbid the average Joe with a passing interest should get "hooked," and turn into a gushy, single-focus opera queen. Opera queens side with certain singers and vociferously boo their rivals. Opera queens make sure that everyone within a twenty-foot radius is privy to their opinions. Opera queens will risk economic impoverishment so that they can travel across the globe to catch a particular lieder, or song, recital. Well, needless to say, this is not what getting opera is about. The too-enthusiastic fan will scare off a newcomer as no other factor can. Rest assured, there are those of us who do not fall into this category of freak, and we don't want to turn you into one, either.

Why Go?

So what kind of fan are you? What about opera gives you pause? Why are *you* the right person to give opera a shot?

If you're like most people, the myths I've addressed so far, though frustrating to encounter, are not the primary stumbling blocks to an appreciation of opera. Most likely, two key factors are preventing you from buying a ticket: the language barrier and the cost. Shakespeare can be tough enough to follow, and that's in English! Why would you expose yourself to a performance you can't even understand? Well, first, I don't think there's a major opera house in the United States that doesn't have some kind of titles system. Most companies use supertitles, which broadcast the English translation of the text onto a screen above the stage. A slight tilt of the head and you can read what the performers are singing. It's like going to a foreign film. The Met has its own interpreting device (called Met Titles), in which the back of every seat is outfitted with a small digital strip on which the translation appears. You can turn the thing on and off at your discretion.

I think the subtitle/supertitle developments of the past ten years or so have been hugely effective in garnering a new audience for opera. But even more than extolling the virtues of a real-time translation, I'd like to suggest that, in opera, the music tells the story. The complaint that it's hard to follow a story in a foreign language is obviously legitimate. But whereas a foreign film only has pictures to convey the sense of the narrative (in addition to the subtitles), opera also has music, which is a powerful tool for directing an audience's attention to certain emotions or sentiments. You may not gather from her Act I aria in *La Bohème* that Mimì loves to make paper flowers. But the music of "Mi chiamano Mimì" conveys that this is a sweet and sensitive girl with simple pleasures. Translations are an enormous plus as far as I'm concerned, but the very nature of opera enables it to get its points across whether you understand the original language or not.

As for the cost, well, it's hard to get around the fact that opera can be expensive. But what isn't these days? Going to a movie can cost as much as ten bucks, and going to the theater is rarely cheap. However, there are ways to get around the expense of attending opera. In chapter 5, I outline some of the practical ways to score cheap tickets. But even more important than scamming your way into a good seat is to embrace the idea that you're not just paying for a few hours of entertainment—you're paying for an experience. Opera doesn't always come cheap, but think of what you're getting. The sets and costumes are more magnificent than anything Broadway has to offer. The music is, for the most part, sublime (once you have a basic understanding of operatic composition). The singing, because it's beautiful and unamplified, can provide one of the most incredible experiences an audience can have. And you can get decked out, feel sophisticated, and have a memorable, complete experience. There's a lot that can go wrong at the opera, but there's even more that can be wonderful and unforgettable. It's not the easiest art form in the world to "get," but once you do, it's one of the most gratifying.

Sound Sites

For more information about opera than this book can provide, your first stop should be the Web. All of the major opera houses have Web sites, with information about schedules, casting, company history, etc. There are also a host of independent sites dedicated to spreading the word about opera. Many have chat areas, where you can meet other fans of opera. But I'd suggest you not jump into this arena until you have some experience under your belt. Opera queens can be vicious, and will gladly rip you to shreds if you give away even the slightest insecurity about the subject. Here are a few of the best sites devoted to opera.

OPERA AMERICA

www.operaam.org
This is sort of the granddaddy of all the opera sites, with general opera stats and factoids, information about opera awareness programs, tips for singers, databases of singers, costume designers, and set designers, and a number of publications available through the site. It's necessary to get a membership to the Washington, D.C.–based organization in order to gain access to some restricted areas of the site. But for the newcomer whose needs are not necessarily all that advanced, this site offers (even minus the membership) just about all the information you could want.

OPERA USA

www.operausa.org
Not to be confused with Opera America (it's kind of like the Miss America versus Miss USA pageants), Opera USA bills itself as a proponent of "opera for the next generation." It too offers quite a few lists and facts regarding singers, production, casting, and the festival circuit.

OPERA MAGAZINE

www.opera.co.uk

Opera magazine is a British publication that's geared toward the opera aficionado. It has reviews of performances from all over the world, as well as CD reviews and feature stories. The magazine's Web site is well designed, and because it contains only excerpts from the magazine (rather than the publication in its entirety) it won't overwhelm the opera novice with information. The magazine may be a little much for someone who's not already a serious fan. But the site will provide a few welcome and insightful tidbits.

OPERISSIMO

www.operissimo.com

The Operissimo site has an international flavor because most of its contents are available in English, French, and German. Like Opera America and Opera USA, this site provides a wealth of information about performers, composers, and opera houses, as well as the expected roundup of the operas themselves. Indeed, the site claims to have listings for 23,000 different operas and includes the names of singers who are famous for their roles in each one. In this area, Operissimo demonstrates that it isn't exactly up-to-the-minute (none of the singers I associate with *The Rake's Progress* was listed with that opera), but it's still a strong resource for information about upcoming productions across the globe.

THE VIRTUAL OPERA HOUSE

www.users.lia.net/dlever/

This site is Cape Town–based fan Dave Lever's one-man over-the-top homage to opera. The site has links, anecdotes, and a wealth of information about singers, conductors, composers, etc. There are even a few not-too-racy "Nudes" of singers brave enough to go topless for the sake of a role. Lever has put together an exhaustive site. He must be a little nutty to have gone to all the effort, but he manages to strike a good balance between enthusiastic fandom and detached bemusement.

OPERA-L

listserv.cuny.edu/archives/opera-l.html

This is the City University of New York's listserv, and it attracts subscribers from all over the world. Indeed, this list boasts more users than any other area of interest among the CUNY sites. Each week, new comments, questions, and requests are posted, and the dialogues can run for months at a stretch. Luckily, the list comprises some relative newbies to opera and not just the dyed-in-the-wool opera freaks who can be so damn terrifying.

tracing opera

A short history of opera from its origins to today

I hope the last two chapters went somewhere toward persuading you that opera is worth checking out. Now that you're on the verge of becoming a bona fide opera queen, you'll want to know a little something about the form's origins and history. I'll spare you the gory details of the less important composers and movements; our little opera history will be taught in broad strokes. Herewith your whirlwind tour of opera through the ages, from its beginnings in Greek tragedy to its current state of affairs.

Orpheus Ascending

As with most of the classical and contemporary arts, opera can be traced back to the Greeks. The Greek tragedies of Sophocles, Euripides, and others from the fifth century B.C. onward were not declaimed but rather chanted or sung in order to best utilize the acoustics of the amphitheaters in which they were performed. It makes sense that the Greeks would naturally ascribe melody to their words because their language was spoken in a singsong way.

Ancient Greek speech relied on particular intonations and shifts in pitch to get its meaning across, not unlike contemporary Chinese, in which words can change definition depending on the tone in which they are uttered. Greek, as a language, was already musical; to take that characteristic one step further in dramatic performance served both to heighten the experience of the action and to make it more audible.

The texts of Greek tragedies, however, were hardly sung in a virtuoso fashion. (Comedies, incidentally, were rarely sung. That was strictly the domain of tragedy.) Actors would sing either unaccompanied or accompanied by one or two lute-like instruments. There was no shape to the notes being sung; they weren't songs so much as an assemblage of sounds. The chorus usually had the most to do in the way of singing, and because tragic choruses generally narrated the action and explained offstage events, their heavy use of chants served to separate the occurrences of each scene from the overall narrative of the play. The choruses inevitably sang in unison; there was no harmony, only the occasional wayward riff of one or two voices to disturb the monotony of the intonation. Obviously, the Greeks had no idea they were planting the seeds of the ultimate multidisciplinary art form, but they did create the foundation upon which a group of Italian Renaissance intellectuals would eventually create opera as it exists today.

Before this group managed to look back at the Greeks and reinterpret their notions of music and drama, a quasi-operatic movement began in the medieval churches of Germany, Italy, France, and England. It seems that some things never change: Even back in the Middle Ages, churchgoers were often bored witless by the sermons they were compelled to endure. Church authorities consequently staged musical performances of narratives that either were based on a religious story or that illustrated an element of religious thought. Suddenly, folks were coming out in droves to attend services. Those liturgical musicals used sets, costumes, and masks, and reflected the important musical developments of the era. The superstatic melodies of the past gave way to new notions of harmony and polyphony. Needless to say, however, the popularity of the church-produced musical dramas began to alarm certain officials of the clergy, who fretted that the crowds were perhaps missing the message in the music. The practice was gradually reined in, but it had made its mark.

With the arrival of the Renaissance, of course, came a mania for all things Greek and Roman. And as one of the chief urban centers of the Renaissance, Florence became a prime site for backward-looking, forward-thinking ideology. The Florentine count Giovanni Bardi was an amateur poet and musician who, caught up in the excitement of his humanistic era, was eager to discuss the future of music and drama. At his well-appointed palace, he assembled a group of local artist types into what became essentially a loosely organized salon. The so-called Camerata convened regularly and found that their primary topic of interest was Greek tragedy and its reliance on sung dialogue. No record of those tragic sound tracks existed at the time, and the group was determined to re-create the phenomenon of words married to music and attached to a plot.

Their success was something of a surprise. It was as if a reading group got together and, with a little effort, came up with a whole new artistic genre. The members of the Camerata were not musical geniuses by any stretch of the imagination, but they were enthusiastic and certainly capable in their musical endeavors. Along with Bardi, the group included Vincenzo Galilei (the astronomer Galileo's father), Florentine musical impresario Jacopo Corsi, the poet and librettist Ottavio Rinuccini, and the composers Giulio Caccini and Jacopo Peri. Peri was the first to try his hand at the new form they'd collectively dreamed up. And in keeping with the focus on the Greeks, his opera, *Dafne,* used Ovid's *Metamorphoses* as source material. Unfortunately, the score to *Dafne* has been lost, but the follow-up still exists. *Euridice,* like its predecessor, had music by Peri and a libretto by Rinuccini, who became the first of innumerable librettists to use the myth of Orpheus and Eurydice. As an operatic fossil, the opera is an amazing piece of work; as a piece of theater, it would bore contemporary audiences to tears. *Euridice* and the other operas of the late sixteenth and early seventeenth centuries were extremely voice-centric; they lacked overtures, and mid-opera instrumental music was kept to a minimum. There were no choruses or ensembles, only solo numbers, and those solo numbers had to get the dialogue across without strong, compelling melodies or vocal fireworks.

Peri and his Camerata cohorts were marvelously successful in their attempt to fuse, as the Greeks did, dialogue and music. Essentially, the true legacy of the Camerata was the creation of recitative, the sung script that in later operas would connect the arias and lead one scene into the next. Indeed, songs (words and music) already existed before the Camerata came around, but a means of connecting songs to each other needed to be invented in order for opera to exist. When the actors were singing, they were—within the context of the opera—speaking. It may seem like a given to anyone who has ever heard an opera, but in Renaissance Italy it was quite a discovery and it caught on like wildfire.

The first major composer to pick up on this trend and turn it into something important and lasting was Claudio Monteverdi of Mantua. If the Camerata kids were ambitious musicians, Monteverdi was an actual genius, the first of many (though not *that* many, despite folks' tendency to throw the word around) to try his hand at opera. Monteverdi was born in 1567 into a wealthy and connected family. He went to good schools, showed a tremendous aptitude for music, and by the time he turned twenty, his works were already being performed and published. Duke Vincenzo Gonzaga of Mantua took notice of the young composer and sent commissions his way (not all of them entirely welcome); it was under his patronage that *Orfeo*, the first bona fide operatic masterpiece, was composed.

Alessandro Striggio was not the first librettist to tackle the tale of Orpheus and Eurydice (in which the former follows the latter—his beloved—into the underworld to save her from premature death, ultimately leaving her there due to a tragic mistake), but he was certainly the best up to that point. Musically, Monteverdi's creation is more than a cut above its predecessors. The work is noteworthy for its compositional symmetry: It opens and ends with a shepherd's song; the second number and the second-to-last number are sung by the chorus; and the symmetry continues in that vein. The instrumental writing is also more complex than had been seen before and is remarkable for its interplay with the vocal parts. The instrumentation and the singing, for the first time, work off each other.

The most important advancement of *Orfeo,* however, is the music's role in advancing the plot and in mirroring the experience of the characters. Peri and the rest of the early composers insisted that melody serve the text. Monteverdi agreed that the poetry came before the music, but he nonetheless augmented the role of the score. Music needed to get out of the way of text, but it could contribute to and heighten the feelings evoked by the plot. You could say that Monteverdi was the first opera composer to infuse his works with passion. *Orfeo* is somewhat slow-moving for modern tastes, but the music is truly gorgeous: simple, restrained, haunting, and moody.

Audiences in Mantua responded accordingly, and Monteverdi found himself inundated with commissions from the duke, a limited number of which survive today. One of these Gonzaga-inspired pieces was *Arianna,* an opera that has been lost except for the title character's superpopular lament, which, in fact, triggered something of a lament trend among a large number of composers. After the duke's death, Monteverdi was free to leave town. In 1613, he quickly hightailed it to Venice, where he took over the musical responsibilities of the San Marco Church. Thanks to Monteverdi's illustrious presence in Venice, many opera houses were erected in that city, the first among them the Teatro San Cassiano, where the composer's operas *Il Ritorno d'Ulisse in Patria* and *L'Incoronazione di Poppea* were both performed. Monteverdi's prominence led in large part to the movement of opera out of the courts and into the public arena. Despite his popularity during his lifetime, Monteverdi (and his operatic ideology) slipped into obscurity relatively soon after his death, when opera seria took over as the popular favorite. Indeed, after the composer's death, *Orfeo* languished unperformed until the early twentieth century. We now know, of course, how influential Monteverdi was, both musically and as a cultural icon. His Orpheus wasn't the first, and it certainly wasn't the last; but, with the possible exception of Gluck's 1762 interpretation, it's the one that matters most.

Let's Get Seria!

As opera began to flourish in seventeenth-century Italy, it also started to spread to other parts of Europe. Jean-Baptiste Lully (1632–1687) may not have brought opera with him to France when he relocated there as a boy, but he was responsible for defining the French school. When he arrived in Paris from Florence in the 1640s, Giovanni Battista Lulli, as he was then called, quickly threw himself into his adopted nationality and became a spokesman for all things French. Musically gifted and profoundly ambitious, he gradually worked his way up the social ladder, entering the world of the French nobility as a court composer and music master. He made it all the way to the top, eventually entering the employ of Louis XIV himself.

Lully was not the first composer of opera in France (that distinction is held by one Robert Cambert, whose name you'll probably never again read in this lifetime), but he was responsible for adapting recitative to the French language. He also beefed up the role of the orchestra and insisted on a rather rigid formality that differentiated French operas from their Italian counterparts. Perhaps most important, he also made sure to insert a ballet sequence in each of his operas, which became the accepted and even required practice in Paris. (Indeed, even Richard Wagner—who didn't appreciate being told what to do—had to rework *Tannhäuser* to include a dance number if he wanted it to play at the Paris Opera.) Lully's *Alceste* (1674) is today the most frequently performed of his operas (but it's not performed all that frequently).

Lully's premier successor in France was Jean-Philippe Rameau (1683–1764), whose most famous opera is *Hippolyte et Aricie,* and who was one of the most accomplished Baroque composers. In

England, Henry Purcell (1658–1695) briefly reared his head and enjoyed a short but explosive career highlighted by *Dido and Aeneas,* the only good opera by an English composer until Benjamin Britten came along in the mid twentieth century. Moreover, Rameau's and Purcell's achievements tend to be overshadowed by the titans of the Baroque period, Bach and Handel—particularly the latter, who, though better remembered for oratorios like *Messiah,* became one of the premier operatic figures of the eighteenth century.

George Frideric Handel was born in Germany in 1685, and traveled extensively as a young man, composing works everywhere he went (which included Hamburg, Rome, Venice, and other musically vital locales). He ultimately settled in London, becoming perhaps the most famous German expatriate in Britain. Despite his multinational exposure, Handel wrote music—like virtually everyone else at the time—in the Italian opera seria style. It was an operatic genre that focused on the heroes of myth and history, and in which dramatic verisimilitude counted for virtually nothing. Opera seria was the quintessential exercise in what's known as number opera, in which showstopping arias are strung together with minimal plot interference. Musicologists writing today tend to get extremely defensive with regard to opera seria, because no one in this day and age can stand it. And while it's true that Handel's operas and those of his contemporaries contain much stunning music and opportunity for impressive singing, they are kind of hard to stomach as pieces of theater. Characters enter, sing, and exit; duets are rare and ensemble numbers nonexistent, which can make for a rather monotonous night at the opera if you're not already enamored of Baroque music.

Having acquired the interest and patronage of King George I of England, Handel was shrewd to engage in the opera seria format, because the genre's various kingly figures appealed to the courtiers for whom most operas of the time were composed. Not that Handel had much say in terms of actually choosing to write in the opera seria vernacular: The public had recently gone mad for vocal virtuosos;

if Handel wanted crowds, he would have to write the songs (and hire the singers) that would attract them. It's no coincidence that opera seria—with its long, florid arias, and the fact that its composers allowed singers to improvise at will—coincided with the rise of the castrati. You've heard all about them: the young boy sopranos whose—ahem—manhood was mutilated in order to preserve their beautiful voices. The idea of an emasculated man singing like a girl may be hard to fathom in today's world, but in the eighteenth century, the castrati were the most popular performers in any field and commanded tremendous fees for their appearances. It was for them that opera seria was tailored, which is one reason the plots of these operas, and even their scores, were viewed as secondary. In his book *Opera in History: From Monteverdi to Cage,* Herbert Lindenberger captures the almost makeshift essence of the genre: "*Opera seria* provides essentially a template that the individual singer would feel free to embellish ... Operatic scores were treated as virtually disposable items: except for Handel's operas, a relatively small percentage of *opera seria* scores was even preserved for posterity."

Would that even fewer had been preserved for posterity! Of course, I'm not being entirely serious. It should be stated that during the heyday of opera seria, composers (Handel in particular) brought about an improvement and deepening of the recitative that the Camerata had originally obsessed over. And many of the arias from Handel's operas (I'm thinking of "Ombra mai fu" and "Lascia ch'io pianga" in particular) are among the most beautiful ever composed, and they may sound even better today when sung by artists who aren't determined to overwhelm the melody with haywire, Mariah Carey–style riffing. Even so, these works are long and dramatically static, and although they are certainly worth experiencing, I would advise the opera novice to get some more accessible operas under his belt before (as they say) going for Baroque.

Fools for Gluck

It wasn't really Handel's fault that singers felt compelled to wreak havoc with his elegant and beautiful melodies. Fortunately, his contemporary and friend Christoph Willibald von Gluck (1714–1787) took the initiative and imposed a number of "reforms," as they've come to be called, onto the opera scene. For part of his career, Gluck composed in the opera seria style of the day, using librettos in a couple of instances by the poet Pietro Metastasio, the predominant librettist of the era and one who was committed to the formulaic scene structure that everyone seemed to favor. Gluck set Metastasio's text to *La Clemenza di Tito* (also used by Mozart later in the eighteenth century) and had a moderate success with it.

But Gluck hated opera's focus on peacock vocal showmanship. He wanted to return to the ideals of the Camerata and recapture the purity of Greek tragedy. When he met librettist Raniero Calzabigi, everything fell into place. Calzabigi shared the composer's disdain for the utter disregard for verisimilitude that characterized opera at the time. Similarly, the pair felt that the over-the-top ornamentation most singers practiced only served to cheapen both the music and the text they were singing. Didn't anyone care about story anymore? Didn't anyone remember that the whole point of opera was to tell a tale through music?

Gluck and Calzabigi's first collaboration yielded *Orfeo ed Euridice* (remember Monteverdi?), and it went gangbusters. The piece marked a return to opera's origins (in terms of both intent and subject matter), and signaled that an audience could be moved by music that was simple and unadorned. *Orfeo ed Euridice* had just three singing characters and a chorus, which was used not as an extraneous commentator but as a participant in the plot. And while the opera shunned the vocal showpieces that had been in vogue, it nonetheless contained memorable tunes that prevented it from becoming one long recitative. Gluck and Calzabigi struck again five years later (in 1767) with *Alceste,* with which they published what essentially amounts to a mission statement, decrying unnecessary embellishment and calling on composers to pay attention to the emotions of the characters they were creating. Opera may be an art form about singers and singing, but Gluck to some degree saved the genre by taking it out of the vocalists' hands.

Scorekeeping

Arturo Toscanini

We've talked a lot about singers, composers, and directors. "What about conductors?" you may be wondering. What exactly do they *do* up there in front? And why do they cop such an attitude?

Basically, you can think of the conductor as the record-producer of the opera performance. He's the guy who chooses the tempos, who decides on the dynamics of the orchestral playing, and who is essentially in charge of shaping the overall musical performance. And because most opera composers are dead, their instructions limited to a few remarks on the score, the role of the conductor is a big one. Conducting opera requires a vast knowledge of the music at hand. What exactly were the composer's intentions? And how important is it to honor those intentions? If you haven't heard a lot of opera, the differences in interpretation from one conductor to the next may strike you as incredibly subtle. But once you've listened to a handful of performances or recordings of a given work, you'll start to notice that Sir Georg Solti, say, keeps things moving along briskly, while James Levine takes his time with a particular work. Arturo Toscanini's orchestra is wildly stirring,

James Levine

but it overwhelms the singers. Herbert von Karajan, on the other hand, elicits great vocal performances but not quite as much excitement. Essentially, it's impossible for a piece of music to sound identical in two different performances. Similarly, it's impossible for two different people to have the exact same response to a piece of music. The conductor is therefore sort of a troubleshooter, who keeps his players and singers on the same page and who influences the general vibe of a given opera rendition.

Wolfgangland

A handful of the operas I've been talking about up to now are still performed occasionally. But the first composer to come around whose works are continually played everywhere, all the time, is Wolfgang Amadeus Mozart (1756–1791). The Camerata's ideas, Monteverdi's originality, Gluck's reforms—it all seems horribly insignificant next to the monumental, almost freakish achievement of the man-child from Salzburg. As an opera composer, Mozart worked in the areas of opera seria, Italian opera buffa (comic opera), and German singspiel (opera with occasional dialogue in lieu of recitative), and he not only mastered all three but wrote the archetypal example of each category.

Mozart was born in Salzburg in 1756; his father was a composer and court musician. He showed promise in music when most children were still playing with rattles, and as a toddler became the quintessential child prodigy, performing for royalty and acting as the primary breadwinner in the family. Mozart's sister, nicknamed Nannerl, was an excellent pianist (though not the bona fide genius on the instrument that her brother was), and along with their father, Leopold, the siblings embarked on a whirlwind tour of Europe, performing for and dazzling all the continent's principal royal figures. Mozart was a truly miraculous kid, who at the age of eleven had composed his first opera; at fourteen, he conducted his own work *Mitridate, re di Ponto* at its premiere in Milan. Supremely talented as a composer of both opera and symphonic works (particularly the piano concerto), he was perhaps the most famous teenager in Europe. Mozart's brilliant career was bound to slow down at a certain point, and as he approached the age of twenty, it did. It's not easy for someone who's eighteen to keep up the whole child-prodigy thing. For several years, Mozart's reputation cooled and his engagements slowed.

However, he continued churning out operas, symphonies, and concertos, improving all the while. In 1781, he unveiled *Idomeneo*, his first mature opera and a landmark in the opera seria genre. The following year, he produced *Die Entführung aus dem Serail,* a singspiel for the Austrian emperor Joseph II. It seems that the child prodigy had managed the relatively rare feat of developing into an adult genius. It makes sense that Mozart, a man born in the mid-eighteenth century, would try his hand at the opera seria format. Much less popular at the time (and viewed as inferior) was opera buffa. Whereas opera seria was concerned with heroes and their lofty endeavors, opera buffa focused on ordinary people. Mozart was drawn to the form, and the three opere buffe he produced with librettist Lorenzo Da Ponte (*Le Nozze di Figaro, Don Giovanni,* and *Così fan tutte*) are the three greatest operas of this type (and among the best of any style) ever written. Indeed, it was Mozart's shifting of opera's attentions to real people with genuine feelings, problems, and relationships that marked him as a greater innovator than Gluck and as the most humanistic of composers either before or since.

In the three Da Ponte operas (most of all in *Figaro,* which I'm not alone in believing to be the best opera ever), Mozart's genius proved to be his ability to mix comedy and pathos. With its identity mix-ups, disguises, and lighthearted deceptions, *Figaro* could be read as a glorified sitcom—if, that is, sitcoms had poignant endings that tore your heart out. But Susanna, Figaro, the Countess, and the others are real people, made vivid by Mozart's music, which, more so than any other that had been written up until that time, illumined the interior struggles of the protagonists. When Countess Almaviva sings about her sadness at the fact that her husband neglects her, she's expressing a sentiment that's familiar to just about everyone. But the melody and mood evoked by "Porgi amor" make her lament sublime despite the ordinariness of the aria's content.

Mozart was able to depict the inner life of his characters not just through arias but in ensemble numbers as well. It is in this area that the guy truly has no peers: In *Figaro*'s ensembles, six people are singing at once, and yet the audience is able to grasp what each is thinking and feeling. Mozart was a contemporary of Jane

Austen, and he reminds me of the novelist in that each created characters that the reader or listener could identify with; each put his or her protagonists into comedic scenarios that revolved around the search for love; and each was able to imbue humor with profundity by conveying the pathos and humanity that underpins even lighthearted comedy. All of a sudden, thanks to Mozart, opera was no longer about noble heroes or mythical royals; it was about us. Mozart died in 1791 at the age of thirty-five.

Vocal Heroes

The term "bel canto" means beautiful singing, and although you'd think such a genre would be highly acclaimed (what is opera supposed to be about if not beautiful singing?), it is in fact one of the most maligned and disparaged of operatic styles—well, at least by reviewers. Like Celine Dion or *Dawson's Creek*, the bel canto operas are generally despised by critics and adored by audiences. My own opinion of the form treads a middle ground: Too frequent exposure to, say, *Il Barbiere di Siviglia* would send me to a sanatorium, but with the knowledge that the operas of Wagner or Strauss exist right around the corner, a night of Rossini can be a pleasure.

Mozart wrote music that could be deemed bel canto; so did Verdi. But the principal composers in this style are Gioacchino Rossini (1792–1868), Gaetano Donizetti (1797–1848), and Vincenzo Bellini (1801–1835). The term has come to be indelibly associated with the comedies of Rossini, which include, most famously, *L'Italiana in Algeri, La Cenerentola,* and, of course, *Il Barbiere di Siviglia.* These operas are fast and funny, and require of singers the kind of high-tech vocalism that recalls the glory days of opera seria. However, bel canto singing is not all tricky fioritura and endless vocal runs. Perhaps the greatest bel canto role is Bellini's Norma, a soprano part that calls on strong musicality and powers of expression more than it does agility and flourish. Indeed, because bel canto has become virtually synonymous with singing, folks tend to forget that, although Rossini was no Wagner, his operas nevertheless employed comparatively advanced orchestration that drew on

45

the composer's study (and worship) of Mozart. Moreover, *L'Elisir d'Amore* and *Don Pasquale* notwithstanding, many of Donizetti's most successful operas (*Lucia di Lammermoor, Maria Stuarda*) lack the frothy light touch that's assumed to characterize all bel canto opera.

Most people do, in fact, attend *bel canto* operas for the singing, and it was up to singers to resurrect the genre in the mid twentieth century, at which point the music of Rossini, Donizetti, and Bellini was essentially swept aside in favor of the inarguably more advanced and impressive music of Wagner and Verdi. Singers like Maria Callas, Joan Sutherland, and Marilyn Horne had the chops, and they wanted to sing bel canto. Producers and audiences responded, and these artists found themselves filling the shoes of legends like Giuditta Pasta, Maria Malibran, and Adelina Patti, superstars who'd ruled the boards about a century earlier. Today's generation of singers is well trained in this style of singing, and obscurities (like, for instance, Donizetti's *Poliuto*) now hit the stage with increasing frequency.

Hey, Nineteenth

The inheritor of the bel canto mantle—and a man who, thankfully (for the sake of music history), went far beyond that form's reaches—was Giuseppe Verdi (1813–1901). Along with Richard Wagner (1813–1883), Verdi is one of the two giants of nineteenth-century opera, which to most observers truly could be called opera's golden age. The two composers could not on the surface be more diametrically opposed: Verdi's operas were (and are) the last word in Italian lyricism; Wagner virtually created a new form of music-drama that focused on narrative continuity and orchestral brilliance rather than on vocal or melodic prowess. And yet, over the course of the century, Verdi and Wagner appear to have moved in the same direction, with Verdi's final works (*Otello* and *Falstaff*) abandoning the number-opera format in favor of dramatic integration.

Even more than Puccini's, Verdi's operas are the perfect place for the newcomer to start, because of their mix of catchy vocal

Divas on (the) Record

Most drag queens are known for their attitudinal, hyperconfident way with a phrase. But before there was RuPaul, there was Maria Callas—and a host of other divas who originated the art of cocky self-promotion. Like the drag queens who read one another, the diva has historically been an expert at turning out bitchy one-liners and assertions of supremacy truly astonishing in their brazenness. Anybody who claims to be sassy needs to pay homage to the prima donnas quoted below. Get out of the way.

Maria Callas to her mother: "Don't come to me with your troubles. I have to work for my money and you are young enough to work, too. If you can't make enough money to live on, you can jump out of the window or drown yourself."

Leontyne Price on her relatively narrow repertoire: "As far as repertoire was concerned, I was never a gambler. I liked the luxury of winning too much. I *adored* to win and make a go of everything I tackled. I got my thrill that way."

Nellie Melba: "I have the voice of a genius. Then why should I not always sing beautifully as long as I take care of it and do not forget what I have been taught? Why should I not sing for a thousand years?"

Adelina Patti on hearing her recorded voice for the first time: "Oh, my God! Now I understand why I am Patti. What a voice! What an artist! Finally I understand everything!"

Leontyne
Price

Shirley Verrett on her performance of Carmen: "It was marvelous—the body was lovely, and I had a lovely voice."

Maria Callas

Maria Callas: "Every time a taxi driver recognizes me it astonishes me. It irritates me. You know, I don't go out very much. I don't put myself on exhibit. I am wild. Very."

Maria Malibran in a letter to her idol, Giuditta Pasta: "If I were near you, you would have neither face nor body, because I would eat all of you."

Adelina Patti on the Russian royal family: "Do you remember how the dear old empress used to make tea for me between the acts? God bless her! And that grand old gentleman, the czar, who used to let me call him Papa. Ah, me! How I shall miss them both. They were so dignified and yet so gentle with little me."

Luisa Tetrazzini at the end of her career: "I am old, I am fat, I am ugly—but I am still Tetrazzini."

Leontyne Price: "I think I've had one of the most beautiful lyric soprano voices I've ever heard. I'm *mad* about my voice. It was *gorgeous*. I loved it so much that from time to time I used to take out one of my best crystal glasses, sip a little champagne, and toast it."

hooks and irresistible melodrama. Verdi's first opera, *Oberto*, made its debut at La Scala in 1839 and was well received. The follow-up was a comic opera called *Un Giorno di Regno;* it was a complete disaster. The opera flopped at around the same time that Verdi's wife and two young children died from a variety of tragic causes. The composer wouldn't try his hand again at comic opera until *Falstaff,* his final work, which premiered when Verdi was eighty. Verdi hit his stride in the early 1840s with successful operas like *Nabucco, Macbeth,* and *Luisa Miller,* with which the composer moved away from the relative confines of bel canto to beef up his standing as a dramatist. In the following decade, Verdi's genius for melody and for eliciting emotion from his audiences was in full evidence, with *Rigoletto, Il Trovatore,* and *La Traviata* making him one of the most famous and beloved figures in Italy. Indeed, with opera the dominant performing-arts form of the mid nineteenth century, audiences waited breathlessly for the unveiling of each new Verdi work.

The composer stirred the interest of his country not just for the lush beauty of his opera scores, however. Verdi became popular during the Italian Risorgimento, and his almost single-handed sustenance of the Italian opera tradition (in the face of more progressive movements in Germany) made him a figure of tremendous pride. He was appalled by the Bourbon influence in Italy, and his enthusiasm when King Victor Emmanuel II of Piedmont regained control of Italy marked him as a nationalist not just musically but politically.

Above all, however, it was the music and nothing else that truly made Verdi's reputation. The scope of Verdi's operas gradually increased over the course of his career. From the melodramatic but rather narrow works of the 1850s, Verdi moved on to the monumentality of operas like *Aida* and *Don Carlo* in the 1860s and 1870s. In the 1880s and early 1890s (at which point he resumed composing after a period of self-imposed retirement), the grandeur of his music served not as an attraction in its own right but as a means to heighten the human drama he focused on so sharply. All the while Verdi's commitment to the dramatic possibilities of his gorgeous ensemble numbers and to developing a richer orchestral language cemented his reputation as the nineteenth-century king of Italian opera. I can't think of a single composer who doesn't at some point or another garner criticism for some perceived shortcoming, and Verdi certainly has his detractors. Except for *Otello* and *Falstaff,* which are universally hailed as unassailable masterpieces, Verdi's operas are often disparaged for being shallow, emotionally manipulative, melodramatic, and focused more on catchy tunes than on complexity of plot. But most opera audiences drag themselves to the theater primarily for a musical experience rather than a theatrical one. Most folks are content to sit through the dull patches of *Il Trovatore* in anticipation of arias like "Stride la vampa" or "Di quella pira." And, frankly, there's nothing wrong with that.

Of course, Richard Wagner would be appalled by the idea of an operagoer who wanted only to hear pretty arias. Wagner so hated the idea of the number opera that he refused to call his works operas at all, preferring the term "music-drama." As you'd imagine, Wagner favored the Gluckian ideal of taking back opera from the singer and refocusing it on the dramatic power of the orchestra. The heroes and heroines of Wagnerian opera are hefty roles that require singers with voices of tremendous power and expression. However, in Wagner's overall conception of opera, the singer becomes almost incidental, a tool for telling the story, which is evoked more powerfully by the orchestral work than by vocalism.

If Verdi picked up and moved on where the bel canto composers left off, Wagner was a child of Beethoven. (Ironically, both Wagner and Verdi confessed to being influenced by the composer Giacomo Meyerbeer, who was a master of the overblown sentimentality of French grand opera, and who is now regarded as a minor composer.) Beethoven composed just one opera, the stirring and powerful *Fidelio,* of which Wagner was a fan. Indeed, there is an often told story of how teenage Wagner was moved beyond expression by the performance of one Wilhelmine Schröder-Devrient in the title role of the Beethoven work—a portrayal that had a lasting effect on the young composer's ideas about the powerful dramatic potential of opera. Beethoven, of course, is known primarily as a symphonic composer, and his sole opera has all the traces of a man who knows how to use an orchestra to the best possible advantage. Telling a story and evoking feeling through the orchestra was, in part, what Wagner also sought to do. And all Wagner's operas, including early works like *Rienzi* and *Der Fliegende Holländer,* demonstrate his ability to do just that.

Wagner was the inheritor of the German Romantic opera tradition, which had previously been dominated by the one-hit wonder Beethoven and by Carl Maria von Weber, who, most notably, produced the operas *Der Freischütz* and *Oberon,* which anticipate Wagner in their orchestral sweep. Wagner proved himself the able spokesman for Romantic opera with *Tannhäuser* and *Lohengrin,* which are probably the two most affecting examples of this genre by any composer. But egomaniac Wagner was not content to merely improve an area already established by other composers: He wanted to create his own form. And, of course, he did. The four-part *Ring* series is the greatest achievement in the history of opera and illustrates Wagner's notion of the *Gesamtkunstwerk,* the total work of art that encompasses music, poetry, drama, scenic and lighting design, and dance. Of course, from its very beginnings opera has aimed to be the art form that marries all art forms. But Wagner didn't want to merely make sure the text and the music complemented each other. He sought to pile on as many different artistic disciplines as he could think of and fuse them into a magnificent and monumental whole that had the power not just to entertain (God forbid) but to affect the culture at large. By bringing together these various forms, Wagner believed each individual element would be heightened. Poetry is even more poetic when married to sublime music. Music is even more affecting when it's telling the story of mythical heroes and of the fundamental essence of the human condition. Wagner's operas are characterized by the use of leitmotivs, in which characters and themes are represented by musical phrases that recur throughout the opera. This technique was used most prominently in the *Ring* operas.

Wagner didn't trust anyone to help him in the creation of his vast music-dramas. He was a control freak who, in addition to composing all the music, wrote his own librettos. Indeed, Wagner was so intent on controlling every aspect of his productions that he had his own theater built in the town of Bayreuth (constructed in large part thanks to the generosity of the Bavarian king Ludwig II), which could accommodate his various theatrical needs. It was at the Festspielhaus in Bayreuth that Wagner instituted many of his innovations, including the placement of the orchestra under the stage so that it wouldn't distract the audience from the action

Opera on Film

For whatever reason, opera doesn't often work well on film. Videos of actual performances are for the most part boring as all get-out: It's like watching someone's VHS recording of a school play. Actual film versions of operas, with a genuinely cinematic mise-en-scène, work better, but still only appear in theaters every so often. Perhaps it's the age-old problem of reconciling all of opera's disparate elements, but no film version of an opera has ever (to my knowledge) generated either box-office or Oscar® buzz. However, viewing opera movies is a great way to prepare for watching a live performance. Hell, it may even be better than the real thing, since you can pause and fast-forward. The following movies can be kind of hard to track down, but they're worth taking a look at as part of your ongoing quest to get opera.

CARMEN

By Georges Bizet. Directed by Francesco Rosi. 1984
This picture opens with a horrifying bullfight torture scene but quickly turns into a well-done take on the perennial favorite. Julia Migenes-Johnson made her reputation with her sexy turn as the kittenish gypsy. Plácido Domingo (who stars in just about every opera film) is his usual solid self as Don José, and Ruggero Raimondi makes a daunting challenger in the person of the bullfighter Escamillo.

DON GIOVANNI

By Wolfgang Amadeus Mozart. Directed by Joseph Losey. 1979
This is one of the best operas on film. Ruggero Raimondi makes a seductive Don Juan, and the trio of ladies (Edda Moser, Kiri Te Kanawa, and Teresa Berganza) bitch and moan appropriately.

THE MAGIC FLUTE

By Wolfgang Amadeus Mozart. Directed by Ingmar Bergman. 1974
Known in Sweden as *Trollflöjten*, this Swedish-language film of the Mozart fable is one of the best filmed operas ever. It's vintage Bergman minus the gloomy depression factor.

THE MEDIUM

By Gian Carlo Menotti. Directed by Gian Carlo Menotti. 1951
Anna Maria Alberghetti is not a genuine opera singer, but here in her film debut she gives a winning performance as the daughter of the titular psychic (played by the able Marie Powers).

OTELLO

By Giuseppe Verdi. Directed by Franco Zeffirelli. 1986
Zeffirelli followed up the successful (and better) *La Traviata* with this straightforward but compelling take on the Verdi-Boito-Shakespeare opera. Plácido Domingo gives a great performance in the title role.

PARSIFAL

By Richard Wagner. Directed by Hans Jürgen Syberberg. 1982
Having directed the six-hour film *Hitler*, Syberberg knows a little something about length. He's well suited to Wagner's epic final opera.

LA TRAVIATA

By Giuseppe Verdi. Directed by Franco Zeffirelli. 1982
Zeffirelli's Met productions of this opera are truly ghastly in their over-the-top opulence. But this screen version works, in large part due to the searing performance of Teresa Stratas as the titular fallen woman.

onstage. Wagner also invented the ritual dimming of the lights so that the audience sat in the dark. Of course, no theater event is presented nowadays without the theater lights being dimmed; the practice originated with Wagner. The composer's many innovations influenced not just his immediate twentieth-century successors (most prominently Strauss) but all subsequent opera composers and producers.

All Natural(ist)

Mozart's great operas focused on the ordinary folk of opera buffa. Wagner, on the other hand, chose mythical gods, giants, and other supernatural beings for his huge productions. In the late nineteenth and early twentieth centuries, a movement in Italian and French opera placed the ordinary people that had previously dominated comic opera in tragic circumstances. This genre was meant to explore the passions and problems of average folks enduring hardship, and it was known as verismo, from the Italian word for realism.

The genre has become associated primarily with Italian composers like Pietro Mascagni (1863–1945) and Ruggero Leoncavallo (1857–1919), whose *Cavalleria Rusticana* and *Pagliacci,* respectively, are archetypes of the form. Perhaps the first true verismo opera, however, is Bizet's *Carmen*. Although Bizet's *Les Pêcheurs de Perles* is sometimes produced today, for the most part the Parisian composer is something of a one-hit wonder, which makes *Carmen* sort of hard to classify. It came along at a time when verismo was not yet the rage, and it explored musical and dramatic terrain unlike the French grand opera that had dominated for some time. Don José was an ordinary army officer; Carmen, your garden-variety gypsy. Her death at his hands, however, was a novel spectacle on the opera stage, and audiences were shocked and outraged. It didn't take long for them to get used to it, however, and by the time *Cavalleria Rusticana* and *Pagliacci* (which are often referred to as *Cav* and *Pag,* and are usually performed together, since they're both so short) arrived on the scene, audiences were ready and willing to digest the real-people violence contained within them. Naturalistic, nonmusical drama was popular at this time, and it only made sense that composers would follow the lead of their theater counterparts.

The greatest verismo composer was undoubtedly Giacomo Puccini, who wasn't an innovator but an accomplished artist and an unbelievable crowd-pleaser. Indeed, his modern-day doppelgänger would have to be Andrew Lloyd Webber, whom critics loathe but who manages to be successful even when he puts singing roller skaters on the stage. It's a shame that so many critics deride Puccini, because despite the undeniable schmaltz factor of his operas, they're really very moving and beautiful. Joseph Kerman, one of the best known and respected opera critics of the twentieth century, hates Puccini and has famously labeled the composer's *Tosca* the "shabby little shocker." Will it surprise you, then, that I think *Tosca* should be just about your first stop on the opera circuit? It's true that Puccini has not changed the course of opera the way, say, Verdi or Wagner has, but he nevertheless did an awfully good job of synthesizing Verdi's knack for vocal hooks with Wagner's genius for dramatic tension and orchestration. I have to say, I love *La Bohème*. It's got terrific melodies, rousing crowd scenes, a charming love story, and the heroine dies in the end. *Tosca*, similarly, contains love, jealousy, lust, murder, and suicide. Puccini's works have all the elements we have come to expect from opera (and Italian opera in particular), and as a representative of all the form has to offer, the composer shouldn't be dismissed.

Strauss Case

Puccini wanted to align himself with Wagner and that composer's avant-garde theatricality. But ultimately, Puccini's reputation rests firmly within the canon of Italian opera. Wagner's true heir turned out to be Richard Strauss, who never attempted anything as overwhelmingly ambitious as the *Ring* cycle, but who shared his predecessor's orchestral gifts. Strauss had an incredible technical ability and was able to elicit a tremendous range of sounds and moods from his orchestra. Many of his operas can be tough sledding, musically, for a newcomer, although most of them contain at least one lush, romantic outpouring of melody to grasp onto.

In a certain sense, Strauss embodies the two divergent paths of twentieth-century opera. When he first achieved a measure of acclaim with *Salome,* adapted from Oscar Wilde's play, Strauss was seen as a modernist. The opera dealt explicitly with female sexuality and it portrayed the horny teenage girl's carnality with a powerful, dissonant, and explosive score. Salome's famous "Dance of the Seven Veils" is the only moment in the opera when the almost assaultive tone lets up. Strauss's subsequent endeavor, a musical updating of Sophocles's *Electra,* was even more explosive and cemented the composer's reputation as an uncompromising purveyor of aurally disturbing musical tragedy. *Elektra* was Strauss's first collaboration with poet and playwright Hugo von Hofmannsthal, who became the composer's regular partner in crime; the two paired up for a total of six operas. But if the initial product of the Strauss-Hofmannsthal partnership built on the avant-garde ferocity of *Salome,* their subsequent effort signaled a significant turn toward conservatism. *Der Rosenkavalier* is a wonderful opera, musically complex and with several unforgettable characters and set pieces: The final trio, for three female voices, is out of this world. But the work could hardly be called progressive, especially in light of Strauss's savage earlier achievements. And, as it turned out, the opera was not an anomaly. All of Strauss's subsequent operas eschewed the horrific dissonance of *Salome* and *Elektra.* All of a sudden, it seems, Strauss was a Romantic, throwback composer.

Because of this dichotomous musical identity, Strauss can be seen as the father of the two distinctive schools of composition that characterize twentieth-century opera. Strauss's earlier, avant-garde period marks him as a forerunner of Alban Berg and Arnold Schoenberg, who together explored the possibilities of dissonance and atonality. Berg's masterpiece, *Wozzeck,* is an adaptation of Georg Büchner's play, and the opera exhibits the same dramatic

Opera in Film

Opera is an extremely visual medium, with its over-the-top sets and costumes, ornate theaters, and overall sense of grandeur. So scenes containing operatic moments often come off well on film. Here are a few fairly recent releases that use opera to further the narrative or just to provide visual exuberance.

AMADEUS

Director: Milos Forman. 1984

Forman's Oscar winner, based on the stage play by Peter Shaffer, can be a little heavy-handed at times. But its interpretation of Mozart's working methods is undeniably fun to watch. Tom Hulce essentially disappeared after his turn as the Salzburg genius. And F. Murray Abraham hasn't exactly entered the Tom Cruise–Tom Hanks Hollywood pantheon. But with *Amadeus,* they had their moment, and it's one that still holds up well on video.

ARIA

Various directors. 1987

A number of well-known film auteurs (including Nicolas Roeg, Julien Temple, Robert Altman, Ken Russell, and Derek Jarman) each directs a short film set to a particular opera aria or passage. The two most interesting are Franc Roddam's Vegas "Liebestod," with Bridget Fonda, and Jean-Luc Godard's piece about a pair of horny cleaning women who worship the muscleheads at a California Gold's Gym to the strains of Jean-Baptiste Lully.

CARMEN JONES

Director: Otto Preminger. 1954

Her voice dubbed by a young Marilyn Horne, Dorothy Dandridge sounds like she's never even heard of the ghetto, let alone set foot in one, when she sings the dubiously Ebonicized "Dat's Love" in this African-American adaptation of the Bizet favorite. This is the part that (rightfully) made Dandridge a star, and in the role of the latter-day Don José, Harry Belafonte exudes his patented Belafonte charm.

DIVA

Director: Jean-Jacques Beineix. 1982

The premise of this film (an opera star has never heard her own voice because she refuses to be recorded) is fascinating. And the high-kitsch performance of American Wilhelmenia Wiggins Fernandez as the diva and the whole 1980s Frenchness of the affair don't hurt the terrific tale of intrigue set against the backdrop of an opera house, either.

FARINELLI

Director: Gérard Corbiau. 1994

Those freaks of nature, the castrati, are endlessly fascinating, but Corbiau's biopic about the most famous of the female-voiced men has its ups and downs. There's really no way to recreate the long-dead castrato sound, so the full effect of those singers' power is hard to grasp. Still, the share-and-share-alike bedroom practices of Farinelli and his brother make for some sexy moments.

THE FIFTH ELEMENT

Director: Luc Besson. 1997

The high point of this futuristic Bruce Willis action flick comes when an enormously tall blue alien diva gives a recital in which she sings the beginning of

Lucia di Lammermoor's mad scene before the number is transformed into an upbeat techno song. In my fantasy world, this is what the lieder recital of the future will be like.

THE HUNGER

Director: Tony Scott. 1983

Okay, so there's really not much in the way of true opera content in this bisexual vampire picture. But Catherine Deneuve and David Bowie play undead classical musicians. And when Deneuve endeavors to seduce an unwitting Susan Sarandon, she does so by playing the title character's big aria from Delibes's *Lakmé* on the piano. Hot!

MEETING VENUS

Director: Istvan Szabó. 1991

This film is in English, but it was made by a team of Europeans and has a distinctly transatlantic vibe. Glenn Close is the only familiar actor; she plays a famous opera singer starring in a nearly doomed production of Wagner's *Tannhäuser* (Kiri Te Kanawa dubs her vocals). The cast's conviction that all they need is passion and chutzpah to pull off an under-rehearsed production is a little bit of a stretch. But for the most part this film's look at the vexing inner workings of an opera house is dead-on.

MOONSTRUCK

Director: Norman Jewison. 1987

"It was awful. Sad. She died!" What were you expecting, Cher? This is *La Bohème*. A night at the opera is pretty much all it takes for Nicolas Cage to secure Cher for life. He's sensitive; she's passionate. This is what we're told by the lovebirds' successful visit to the Met. For the rest of the movie, *La Bohème* serves as the sound track and as a reminder that the opera house is the ultimate spot for a date.

PHILADELPHIA

Director: Jonathan Demme. 1993
Tom Hanks finally gets Denzel Washington to see what it's like to be gay and have AIDS when he sings along with Maria Callas in "La mamma morta" from Giordano's *Andrea Chénier*. Gays just *love* opera, Hollywood reminds us. A lot of observers cite this scene as the clincher that won Hanks his Oscar.

PRETTY WOMAN

Director: Garry Marshall. 1990
Julia Roberts loves *La Traviata*. Clearly, she's too good for a life of hooking on the streets.

leanness and musical intensity of Strauss's initial offerings. Schoenberg's *Moses und Aron* and *Erwartung* similarly mine challenging musical terrain and engage in vivid and straightforward storytelling. However, another set of twentieth-century composers looks backward for inspiration, just as Strauss looked to update *Le Nozze di Figaro* with *Der Rosenkavalier*. Igor Stravinsky's one operatic triumph is *The Rake's Progress,* which utilizes harpsichord-accompanied recitative and plot-furthering arias of great beauty; the opera is clearly meant to evoke a Mozartean sensibility. *The Rake's Progress* sounds nothing like *Rosenkavalier,* but it has a similar musical and dramatic vibe. Benjamin Britten is another of the most popular and able of twentieth-century composers, and he, too, is relatively conservative in his musical tastes. Indeed, the romantic nature of his music stigmatized the composer of *Peter Grimes, Billy Budd,* and *The Turn of the Screw* at a time when Schoenberg's atonality was all the rage among intellectual musician types. This struggle between newness, progressivism, and dissonance versus retrospection, tradition, and melody is not only representative of the twists and turns of Strauss's career, it also characterizes the tenor of twentieth-century opera as a whole.

Here Today, Gone Tomorrow?

So where are we now? Where has the continuum from Greek tragedy to the Camerata to Gluck to Mozart to Wagner to Schoenberg taken us today? Who are opera's current movers and shakers? What reforms are they implementing now? Where is the art form headed? Well, I wish I could say that the latter half of the twentieth century has seen drastic steps forward, but there have been, unfortunately, no reforms of the Gluckian or Wagnerian variety of late. Even so, more and more composers of contemporary classical music are turning to opera as a viable (and not shameful) outlet for their talents. "Serious" classical composers have historically viewed opera as inferior to "absolute music," a designation that connotes music for music's sake, without the allegedly corrupting element of a story or narrative. Opera has been seen as a second-class citizen, particularly to the musical elitists who seem much more prominent in the twentieth century than in earlier eras. Nowadays, however, there's no shame in composing for the opera stage. And while there doesn't seem to be an abundance of composers with an innate sense of theatricality, there are certainly a few, and the others are content to try their hands at opera as an experiment.

I would argue that the two most important opera composers of the past few decades are Philip Glass and John Adams. They are the two who are creating an original and accessible new musical language, and who are committed to dramatic novelty. In the case of Adams, the conceptual advances of his two important works, *Nixon in China* and *The Death of Klinghoffer,* are in large part the result of the composer's collaboration with director Peter Sellars. Whereas the creation of opera had historically been the domain of a composer and a librettist, these days a conceptually inclined director can be as closely involved in the development of a new piece as the composer. Philip Glass is another case in point: His monumental *Einstein on the Beach* was the result of his work with avant-garde director Robert Wilson. If the opera seria days were the age of the singer, and if the nineteenth century is notable for the contributions of iconic composers like Wagner and Verdi, the current scene is characterized by a focus on productions and concepts rather than just the score.

For the most part, however, contemporary operas stick to the tried-and-true poetry/music fusion. Thomas Adès is an important young British composer whose exuberant *Powder Her Face* draws on a multitude of musical styles and ideas. It's an impressive work, but not one that subverts any accepted opera practices. That's why a composer like Glass is so important. *Einstein on the Beach* is progressive and new in many respects, but perhaps most so in its avoidance of a linear narrative. The opera really has no plot; the figure of Einstein and his life and work is evoked through the music and through the various theatrical tableaux of its many scenes. This may be the perfect solution to the perpetual conundrum of words versus music: Avoid the topic altogether. There will always be a place for operas that tell a story through beautiful music. But the future of opera just may rely on disregarding the original aims of the Camerata. Most people's conceptions of opera revolve around the form's grandeur, the heightened emotions, and the stirring, almost otherworldly music. At this point, it seems to me that this end can be achieved without fixating on the problem of how to tell a linear story and still make the music matter. Certainly, the opera world is due for a change; there are many observers who argue that not a single development has occurred since the late nineteenth century. This seems a bit extreme, if you ask me. But the message that something needs to change, that a drastic overhaul of our notions of what opera is and should be is overdue—this all seems painfully obvious. If the art form is to move ahead in the twenty-first century, mild developments aren't needed. Drastic reforms and a complete rethinking of the genre are.

singing opera

An explanation of the classical voice

Whenever I mention to a friend that I'm going to the opera, I invariably receive a reply sung in faux-operatic head voice. *The opera! Mi-mi-mi-mi! La!* Most people's instinct is to make fun of the kind of singing that you find in an opera house. Even well-educated, seemingly intelligent people like to affect momentarily the voice of a diva and sing a few notes, after which they generally break into hysterics. Operatic singing seems like a joke, or, at the very least, a mystery. "Why do they sing that way?" I'm often asked. "Why can't they sing normally?" It's not a bad question, because operatic vocalism *is* weird. Not long ago, I saw soprano Renée Fleming being interviewed on *60 Minutes*. Mike Wallace asked her about classical singing, and she replied that, basically (and I'm paraphrasing), "We're screaming in a very cultivated fashion." She's right. The sensations and production of everyday, around-the-house singing are completely different from the way in which opera singers spend years learning to sing. With a little luck, it'll take less time for you to learn to appreciate operatic singing than it did for the stars to learn how to perform it.

The New York City Opera recently found itself in an uproar of sorts over a decision to install a new amplification system in the New York State Theater, which the company calls home. The plan calls for several hundred small microphones to be placed at various points throughout the theater, which will not so much amplify sound as improve the hall's admittedly inferior acoustics. Opera purists are going out of their minds over this development. The whole point of operatic singing is that it's natural, unamplified. I generally hate to side with purists of any kind, but I have to say that I'm a little concerned about this development. While I'm pleased to hear that the new system is intended to affect acoustics rather than volume, to a certain degree I find myself agreeing that if opera is amplified, it won't take long for it to turn its back on tradition (even though this is only rarely a bad thing) and enter the realm of the Broadway musical.

The primary reason that opera singers "sing that way" is that they need to in order to fill with sound a house that seats four thousand people. Certainly, there are soul divas (Chaka Khan comes to mind) who could stand center stage in an opera house and be heard wailing in the back of the theater. But could they sing softly and be heard? No. Pop singers rely on mikes in order to project over the sound of backup bands and to be able to perform dynamic shifts in tone without losing resonance. If Jewel sang one of her little folk ditties in the Metropolitan Opera House without amplification, she wouldn't be heard past the third row. Opera singers, however, have to be heard singing a pianissimo phrase over an orchestra, all the way to the back row of the Family Circle. The seemingly "strange" way they sing allows them to do this. Moreover, singing a five-hour Wagnerian marathon several nights a week requires tremendous vocal stamina. If a singer wants to be heard and wants to still have a voice after a few hours of shrieking at the top of his or her lungs, he or she must learn how to use the voice properly, and employ a technique that has existed for centuries. This method is tricky and involves many different components, which is why it takes so long before an opera singer is actually ready to hit the stage. Opera singers are like athletes in that they need to train and strengthen certain parts of the body in order to perform their "sport" the best they can. You certainly don't need to know every gory detail of operatic vocal production, but here are what I would consider to be the three most important elements that allow opera singers to combine volume, stamina, flexibility, and beauty.

Breath Control

There is simply no more important aspect of singing than being able to ration breath in order to produce long, seamless musical phrases. And I don't mean inhaling deeply as if you're about to do an underwater dive. Most opera singers inhale almost imperceptibly (if they're doing it right), but manage to gather a large repository of air in a movement that originates in the diaphragm. If a singer inhales in such a way that his shoulders rise up under his ears, all the breath will emanate from the lungs and throat, which is not a good thing. Essentially, when a singer prepares to let loose with a note, she wants to create a column of air that extends from the diaphragm up through the chest. An opera singer's shoulders will never rise due to an intake of air, but his stomach will seem to expand. By forming this column of air within the body, a singer is much more adept at controlling how much breath is emitted with a single note. Certain phrases in opera are extremely long and require a dolphin-like capacity to hold breath. You don't want to blow all your air in the first few notes. Once a singer has created an air column, voice projection becomes much easier. The voice simply rides the wave of the breath. Instead of shouting from the throat to be heard, a singer essentially gets out of the way and lets the breath do all the work.

Open Throat

People often refer to the "golden throat" of a talented singer. But, in fact, the throat is almost an impediment to beautiful singing. I've just mentioned that the breath is all-important, and for the breath to escape most effectively, a singer must keep the throat open as much as possible. Since stamina is so important for opera singers, a strained throat is something to avoid at all costs. This is what I mean when I say that a singer needs to get out of the way of the breath. It makes sense that if the throat is at all closed, air will have a more difficult time escaping. An opera singer wants the throat to be almost in the same state it would be if it were engaged in a yawn. That way, the breath has plenty of room to ease out of the body, and the sound can come out round and warm. Because they frequently have to blast out loud phrases, opera singers tend to run their throats ragged. Singing properly involves singing from the diaphragm and relying on breath—not singing from the throat, which will only hurt the vocal cords.

The Mask

Okay, so I've made a big deal about open throats and heavy breathing, but if you think this technique sounds like it promotes an unfocused, uncontrolled wash of noise to spill out of the singer's mouth, you're not entirely wrong. Breath control and an open throat need to be balanced or harnessed by a focused tone. Many voice teachers make a lot of fuss about what they call "singing in the mask," which refers to the singer's facial passages and resonating cavities. This is tricky to explain, but basically a singer wants to summon his reserves of breath, allow the breath to exit freely through an open throat, and train the sound to come together in a focal point. It's kind of like aiming the breath through a small target where the sinuses come together. The rush of air that has traveled through this rounded tunnel and exited freely through the open throat is focused into a point at the singer's lips just as it exits the body. Essentially, what this does is prevent the voice from sounding breathy. There may be a lot of breath involved, but you don't want the sound to be airy and open; it needs to be focused and precise if it's going to carry through the auditorium and possess a range of expressive colors. Does any of this make sense? Probably not at first reading. But if you keep these things in mind as you listen to the great singers, either on record or in performance, you'll start to get what I'm talking about.

When these aspects of operatic singing are well balanced, a singer is able to project to the last row and sing for hours with no apparent strain. The technique also supplies the singer with tremendous vocal flexibility. The tricky roulades and vocal runs that Rossini and Handel are known for would be impossible for an ordinary, nonoperatic singer to perform. Even if a pop singer managed to squeak out the notes of a Rossini flourish, he certainly wouldn't be able to do it with control over the volume or with a smooth transition from note to note. Opera singing demands total control over the voice and adherence to certain old-school notions of vocal production. What makes a given opera singer great is the ability to infuse this technique with genuine emotion, feeling, and sensitivity. Indeed, just because an opera singer has an incredible technical capacity does not guarantee a compelling stage presence. At the opposite end of the spectrum, a singer with a faulty technique could still possess interpretive gifts and an innate musicality that would make a performance memorable, if not vocally perfect. If you do in fact turn into a true opera fan, you'll at one point or another have to wrestle with this conundrum. Perfect singing? Or deep feeling? Fans of operatic singing historically have been a particularly vociferous lot on this subject, with only a few levelheaded aficionados recognizing that, in fact, there are merits and drawbacks to both vocal styles.

The mind-boggling success of the Three Tenors concerts has, to a certain degree, shifted the focus of the opera fan's attention away from the soprano in today's scene. The absence of a tempestuous, headline-grabbing diva like Maria Callas has also perhaps led to a slight decline in the soprano worship that has characterized opera fandom for generations. But whether the object of adoration is a soprano or a tenor, neither one can claim the affection of the public the way the castrati did in the eighteenth century. The castrati, male sopranos whose testicles were removed in boyhood, were opera's all-time singing masters. We're going on hearsay of course, because only a few recordings exist of the last of the castrati, and these recordings are of singers who were by no means at the top of their field. But all reports seem to confirm that the castrati had unparalleled breath control, which allowed them to sing enormously long, difficult passages with no apparent effort. As I've mentioned, the opera serias in which the castrati starred were written to accommodate vocal improvisation. And the castrati certainly seized the opportunity, spinning out ridiculously long, complicated riffs that left their audiences slack-jawed. The castrati are often described as having the voices of women and the lungs of men, and the result was a voice of amazing power. If a dramatic soprano like Deborah Voigt can cut through a powerful Wagnerian orchestra, she's still got nothing on the castrati, who could sing so loudly that some listeners allegedly put cotton in their ears when attending performances.

The most famous of the castrati is undoubtedly Farinelli, who was born Carlo Broschi and who turned into the most famous singer in Europe. Farinelli spent a large part of his career in London and Paris, where he developed immense followings and earned a fortune. In 1737, when he was in his early thirties, he up and left for Spain, where for more than twenty years he served as King Philip V's personal singer, performing the same four songs for the monarch every single night. Needless to say, he was well paid for this perverse service, but the fans were devastated by the disappearance of a man who was certainly one of the most well loved singers of all time. Gasparo Pacchierotti and Senesino (castrati loved the whole one-name thing, apparently) were two other tremendously successful eighteenth-century castrati, but neither achieved the renown of Farinelli.

In the early nineteenth century, castrati were still performing, but the neutering practice was gradually abandoned, to the huge relief of talented boy sopranos everywhere, who must have been scared witless by the possibility of a not-so-pleasant (but allegedly painless) operation. As a result, the fans' ardor turned to the next best thing: sopranos. And it has pretty much remained there ever since. It's hard to pinpoint exactly why high singing voices have such power over the masses (is it that they're louder? more flexible?). Regardless, the key opera figures of the nineteenth and twentieth centuries have for the most part been sopranos.

Much of the early nineteenth century was the era of bel canto, and the superstars of the day were women who could deal with the technical demands of composers like Rossini, Donizetti, and Bellini. But not every singer handled the repertory in the same way, and different modes of expression elicited different kinds of devotion in the fans. Giuditta Pasta (1798–1865) and Maria Malibran (1808–1836) were contemporaries and quasi-rivals, and were similar in that neither had a perfect voice but both were able to conquer audiences by means of tremendous theatricality and fierceness of interpretation. Both were known for their kick-ass portrayals of Norma, and many historians argue that their equal in the part was not seen until Maria Callas came along in the 1950s. Malibran, in particular, sounds like a really good time. She was always the life of the party wherever she went, smart and witty and always ready to entertain a gathering, accompanying herself on the piano. Bellini himself is reported to have found her Norma ideal. But shortly after a riding accident, Malibran died at the age of twenty-eight.

These women, as well as figures like the Russian bass Fyodor Chaliapin and the German soprano Wilhelmine Schröder-Devrient, were compelling actors instrumental in advancing opera as a dramatic, rather than just a musical, form. But, of course, there were numerous vocal superstars who were known for the profound beauty of their voices and emphatically *not* for the conviction of their acting. The archetypal diva and one of the early twentieth century's greatest sopranos was the Australian Nellie Melba, whose name and fame inspired both peach melba and melba toast. Like her contemporary Enrico Caruso (perhaps history's best-known tenor, along with Pavarotti), Melba was able to spin out elegant musical phrases with a flawless technique. Nothing she sang ever sounded forced or unnatural, and her voice was large enough to easily fill any theater with crystalline sound. That said, she was an utter bitch, the supremely confident diva of lore, who, consequently, didn't really feel she needed to expend much effort acting. Caruso, too, while a little more game at the whole acting thing and possessing undeniable charm, was not always the most convincing actor, in part due to his portly frame, which made the romantic heroes he played something of a stretch in terms of verisimilitude.

No one would argue that when an opera singer gives a concert performance or a lieder recital, vocal beauty is at the top of everyone's wish list. But in the opera house, the struggle to balance lovely singing with convincing acting remains a huge issue among singers. This debate reached its apex in the 1950s and 1960s, when Maria Callas endeavored to revive the popularity of the bel canto operas after a period of dormancy. It's funny to think that Callas would even want to go near a bel canto opera, because her voice was so much better suited to more dramatic operas. Callas was an extremely intelligent musician and had tremendous stage presence, but as a technical singer, she was nothing special (to put it kindly). You have to live in a cave not to be aware that the Greek-American soprano remains (more than twenty years after her death) the most worshiped and revered of all the opera stars of the past hundred years. But I frankly find listening to her recordings painful. Her high notes are shrill as all get-out, and her overall sound is abrasive, without the warmth of tone that so many lesser known sopranos are capable of. Still, I would kill to have seen her in performance as Norma, which became her signature bel canto role. Her intensity and dramatic conviction are generally considered to be top-notch, and judging from the videos I've seen, I have to agree.

Callas may have inspired the bel canto revival, but she was certainly not its only exponent. Dame Joan Sutherland, an Aussie three years Callas's junior, acquired a reputation as a technical magician who could easily navigate the most difficult coloratura passages as well as handle heavier, more dramatic music. Sutherland on record (which is the only way I've heard her) is fabulous: Her technique and control are amazing, and she's able to pour forth washes of lovely sound. But her diction is pretty miserable, and the first sign that a singer is not going to be a strong actor is when the artist has little commitment to the integrity of the text. Sutherland, like Callas, sang the title role in *Norma,* but whereas Callas was fiery and compelling, Dame Joan was stiff. Audiences marveled at her vocalism, but she never seemed to get under the skin of the character she portrayed. She didn't serve as Callas's actual rival (that distinction was held by Renata Tebaldi, an Italian soprano with a truly gorgeous voice), but she serves as the Callas antithesis. Together, Callas and Sutherland demonstrate the different extremes of what it means to be an opera singer, with each valuing different elements of vocal production.

In today's opera scene, I think this conundrum has become slightly less of an issue, although there are still (and always will be) practitioners of each style of performance. You couldn't drag me to a concert performance of German soprano Hildegard Behrens; after years of use and abuse her voice is a nightmare. But I'd love to see her as Marie in *Wozzeck,* a role that allows her dramatic flair to shine through. And while I admire, say, English soprano Jane Eaglen's vocal ability, I had to walk out of her Met performance of *Turandot,* because it was impossible for me to accept in any way this massive woman as a teenage Chinese vixen. But these days, most opera singers are incredibly well trained, and, what's more, they *want* to try and act, whether they have innate ability in that field or not. Folks perpetually rhapsodize about opera's so-called golden age, when singers supposedly really knew what they were doing. But I would argue that today's singers are comparably equipped vocally, and they are not content to rest on their reputations for cranking out high notes or for staging a convincing death scene after three hours of virtual screaming. The top performers today generally recognize that ideal operatic singing combines lush sound and an ability to express feeling, both through the singing and through the overall performance. Today's superstars are people like Plácido Domingo and Cecilia Bartoli, both of whom sound incredibly good at the same time as they draw you into the world of the drama. I'm not saying that either of them can match Callas for onstage intensity, or that they have the equivalent vocal skills of Adelina Patti, the turn-of-the-century soprano who's often hailed as the greatest singer ever. But it seems to me that fastidiously employing the technique I've outlined above, and adding to that technique a sense of drama and true feeling, is exactly what the great singers aspire to do. It's certainly a lot for a novice to think about when attending a performance, but it won't take long for you to be able to discern between mere technique, however great, and truly wonderful operatic singing.

And if it takes some time for you to pick up on the nuances of various singers' techniques, you'll surely recognize the power and uniqueness of his or her operatic voice right away. A well-sung portrayal elicits a more sublime sensation (in me, at any rate) than any other kind of performance. In *The Ultimate Art*, David Littlejohn describes the unstoppable force of a tremendous voice: "The awesome emotional power of great voices brilliantly used . . . is, I believe, potentially far greater than that of any organ or violin, any orchestra or synthesizer, more compelling than colors on a canvas or words on a page. There before you is a body, like yours, with a throat and a larynx, like yours, drawing out of itself (as you may dream of doing, but cannot) sounds that vibrate and seize beyond the power of any nonsinging actor. It seems to me the most captivating and beautiful thing that a human being can do on a public stage in living time."

Pro Voice: Sopranos

The soprano voice is the highest in the female vocal range and the one that inspires the most rabid and devoted fans. With their high, loud, flexible, and potentially beautiful voices, sopranos manage to garner a lot of attention for themselves. Some of them also garner attention by adopting the bitchy, egomaniacal, diva poses of legends like Maria Callas (a holy terror) and Nellie Melba (probably worse). These days, most opera singers pride themselves on their professional behavior; as a result, the haughty, old-school prima donna has to some degree fallen by the wayside (although a few, admirably, try to keep the flame burning). This is a shame, because the opera world could use some headline-grabbing women among its ranks. Here are a few of the sopranos I consider tops these days. In all of these roundups, I've stuck mainly with singers whom you're likely to hear at houses in the United States. The Russian soprano Galina Gorchakova, for example, is extremely talented, but I've left her off because she doesn't appear all that often in the United States, and when she does, she appears only at the Met.

JANE EAGLEN

It's a shame that Eaglen is physically so wrong for the parts at which she excels vocally. The English soprano fits perfectly with the image of the enormous diva casting a literal shadow over her costars. Fittingly, Eaglen's voice is a powerhouse. She may not look like the teenage Asian vixen of Puccini's *Turandot*, but she sure can launch a ferocious aria like "In questa reggia" with enough force to put the fear of God in any listener. Recently, Eaglen and tenor Ben Heppner created a sensation in the title roles of Wagner's *Tristan und Isolde*. Dramatic realism is nowhere in evidence at these gigs, but if you close your eyes and just listen to the singing, it becomes apparent why Eaglen is the Wagnerian soprano the world's producers and artistic directors are all desperate to book.

LAUREN FLANIGAN

Flanigan is that rare creature: an opera star who has built a major reputation without setting foot in the Metropolitan Opera House. She's the New York City Opera's resident superstar, and has done a lot to drum up interest in that company, which has traditionally (and shamefully) been viewed as the Met's less-significant cousin. Flanigan has a fiercely powerful voice (she's a terrifying Lady Macbeth), but she never sacrifices expression for volume. This woman simply cannot get a bad review, because she's just about the best actress working in opera today. You won't hear the creamy tones that some of the other sopranos produce, but Flanigan's performances are so dramatically gripping that she could trade in her career as a singer for one as a stage actress.

RENÉE FLEMING

To my mind, Fleming is the finest soprano singing today—the one who will surely achieve (along with Deborah Voigt) a lasting reputation of greatness. Fleming excels in roles like the Countess in *Le Nozze di Figaro*, a part she snatched out of the hands of Kiri Te Kanawa, a predecessor to whom many listeners compare the soprano. She's also made the title role of Dvořák's *Rusalka* her calling card. At the time of this writing, she was even working on a jazz album, which she planned to sing in a nonoperatic style. Whatever she's performing, there's a richness to Fleming's voice that's hard to come by: The sound is fuller than many lyric sopranos and prettier than most Wagnerians. Peter Davis of *New York* magazine has described Fleming's instrument as "deluxe," and I agree—that's the term that best suits her fabulous voice.

Renée Fleming as
Blanche DuBois in
A Streetcar Named Desire

ANGELA GHEORGHIU

Gheorghiu has garnered a reputation as a real pain in the ass—a diva of the old school who expects the royal treatment at all times. She's married to "Fourth Tenor" Roberto Alagna, and together the pair has carved out a career as opera's in-demand First Couple, leaving a path of fear and destruction in their wake. This clever marketing strategy has been immeasurably important in making the couple a favorite with audiences, but it should be added that they're not bad singers, either. Gheorghiu's flexible, attractive soprano was impressive enough to attract the attention of the late Sir Georg Solti, the legendary

Angela Gheorghiu

conductor who recorded *La Traviata* with Gheorghiu not long before his death. The Romanian soprano cannot be depended on (like, say, Voigt or Fleming) to give near-flawless performances all the time. But she's nonetheless a major talent whose career would be substantial even without the added luster of her superstar marriage.

RUTH ANN SWENSON

Ruth Ann Swenson is one of those singers who has a lovely voice, but you don't always feel like there's much intensity behind the singing. I heard her in a Met *Lucia di Lammermoor* not long ago, and, granted, she was working in a production that had absolutely zero redeeming value. But Swenson, too, seemed out of sorts: She made some very pretty sounds but seemed kind of spaced out throughout the whole opera (which, to be fair, is not entirely out of keeping with the character). Even so, you couldn't ask for a more beautiful sound. Swenson's clear yet velvety tone makes her a natural for the bel canto operas and early Verdi in which she specializes. For sheer vocal beauty, Swenson is absolutely among the top handful of American sopranos.

DAWN UPSHAW

Upshaw has emerged as one of the most important sopranos of her generation, not just for the beauty of her crystalline voice but because of her commitment to unearthing neglected repertoire and trying new things. When most divas are content to release CDs of opera arias that everyone's heard a thousand times too many, Upshaw devotes her talents to underheard contemporary American composers and to modest gems like Canteloube's *Songs of the Auvergne*. I'm not crazy about some of Upshaw's recent forays into the realm of pop standards

Dawn Upshaw

and cabaret (her voice on these records is so girlish and clear that she ends up sounding like an irritating Shirley Jones impersonator), but I admire her desire to tread new ground. Upshaw is also a terrific actress (a rarity on the opera stage), one of the few capable of delivering performances of real poignancy.

DEBORAH VOIGT

Despite the current mania for Jane Eaglen, Deborah Voigt is *the* premier Wagnerian soprano singing today. The Illinois native has an enormous voice capable of overwhelming just about any orchestra. Her fondness for heavy, romantic music has made her a natural to play the heroines of Strauss and Wagner. She pretty much owns the title role of the former's *Ariadne auf Naxos*, and in a recent, controversial, Robert Wilson–helmed Met production of the latter composer's *Lohengrin*, even opponents of the direction agreed that Voigt sang a superb Elsa. I've never heard Voigt give a bad performance, and I've also never seen a negative word written about her. If you come across her name on the bill, ignore everything else and buy a ticket—at the very least you'll be guaranteed a spectacular vocal display.

OVERRATED

CATHERINE MALFITANO AND SYLVIA MCNAIR

Malfitano gets mad props for having reinvented herself as a dramatic soprano after a career of singing lighter works. And while it's true that she customarily gives until it hurts in operas like *Salome* and those of Janáček, I still don't get what all the fuss is about. Her singing is all right, and her acting is better than most, but I'm still confounded by the kudos she gets for her relatively ordinary interpretations. And as for McNair: Why does this woman have a career? Her singing is so cutesy and affected it makes you want to scream. As opera singers go, she's cute looking, but that's not really enough to overcome the blandness of her technique.

Pro Voice: Mezzo-Sopranos

We are just now in the midst of the era of the mezzo-soprano, the female vocal category that's lower than the soprano range but higher than that of contraltos (who are seldom heard in the opera house). Traditionally relegated to roles of whores and housekeepers, mezzos have, in the past few years, begun to give sopranos a run for their money as audience favorites. Of course, there have always been fabulous mezzos (Marilyn Horne, Christa Ludwig, Frederica von Stade, and Tatiana Troyanos come to mind), but they have seldom enjoyed the kind of record-label and opera-house marketing muscle used to push a singer like Cecilia Bartoli, who is in greater demand right now than any other singer of any category. All the mezzos mentioned here have major (and hugely deserved) careers.

CECILIA BARTOLI

SASHA GUSOV/DECCA

Cecilia Bartoli

Because Bartoli is so overwhelmingly popular, the inevitable backlash has occurred: "Her voice is so small, her repertoire so narrow!" Well, it's true that she doesn't exactly have an overpowering instrument and she only sings a handful of operas from a fairly specific era. But apart from that, I can't really come up with a single criticism of the Roman mezzo. Her technique is unstoppable, her way with language unsurpassed, and her dusky tone rich and beautiful. I must confess to being one of the crazed Bartoli worshipers.

STEPHANIE BLYTHE

Blythe is probably the least-known singer on this list. And that's too bad, because with her incredibly loud, powerful voice, she truly kicks ass. I think part of the problem is that she's a rather large woman, and if you're going to be a superstar mezzo, you need the looks that allow you to sing the pants roles and debutante parts like Cenerentola. But Blythe has a massive voice of virtually Wagnerian proportions: I've never heard a mezzo with the ability to project so powerfully. Fortunately, Blythe has begun to make the occasional recital appearance, in which she can display her gifts more prominently than in the supporting roles she usually gets in the opera house.

OLGA BORODINA

Bartoli is by far the most famous these days, but Borodina is my personal favorite. The Russian mezzo also has a warm, dusky tone, but whereas Bartoli has a southern Italian vibe to her singing, Borodina adds a Slavic

NICK BRIGGS/PHILIPS CLASSICS

Olga Borodina

intensity to all her portrayals. Her voice is extremely versatile: She can sing Dalila and bel canto as capably as she can the standard Russian works. A star of the famed Mariinsky Theatre of Saint Petersburg (run by firecracker conductor Valery Gergiev), Borodina hasn't taken long to conquer the States as well. She is definitely not a singer to miss.

VESSELINA KASAROVA

This young Bulgarian mezzo hasn't performed much in the United States. She sang in Mozart's *Idomeneo* in Chicago, but her Met debut was canceled due to illness, and she has yet to sing at the house. She has, however, had her New York debut, singing the title role in a concert performance of Rossini's *Tancredi* at Carnegie Hall. I've never heard anything like it. Whereas her voice can sound a bit insecure on record, the tall, striking woman was riveting in live performance, both as a singer and an actress. The crowd (including me) went nuts for Kasarova, and we can only hope that her profile increases in this country soon.

JENNIFER LARMORE

The Georgia-born Larmore has been pitted as Bartoli's chief rival, because they sing much of the same repertoire and are relatively close in age. But although this mezzo is well respected and a top choice of many opera houses around the world, I'm sort of lukewarm about her. One minute she sounds terrific, and the next her singing is not quite so forceful. Still, she's one of the top American mezzos working today, and her recent album of American tunes (*My Native Land*) is a fabulous recording. I'm not sure why exactly I have a block against her, so you should probably just ignore me and accept the general consensus of her excellence.

SUSANNE MENTZER

Mentzer is one of the strongest singing actresses working today and can be relied on to crank out solid performances night after night. As a personality, she doesn't generate the kind of excitement that some of her colleagues do, so she doesn't necessarily have the status she deserves. She's the sort of singer you can kind of forget about when she's singing alongside the big names—until the end of the performance, when it dawns on you that Mentzer gave a far better performance than anyone else on the stage. Mentzer will never have throngs of crazed fans waiting for her at the stage door, but she'll probably also never give anything less than an exceptional performance.

ANNE SOFIE VON OTTER

D. GRÖNSTEIN/DG

Anne Sofie von Otter

There's something kind of attitudinal about this Swedish mezzo's persona, but she's an undeniably exquisite artist of the absolute highest level. The tall blonde can seem sort of glacial and unreachable as a human being, but there's nothing cold about her singing. Von Otter has a wide repertory of opera roles and lieder favorites, and she cites Octavian in *Der Rosenkavalier* as perhaps her favorite part (a role for which she's truly ideal). Other singers are capable of drawing in the casual listener more effectively, but I can't think of anyone (including Bartoli) who possesses von Otter's musical intelligence, taste, and evenness of tone.

DOLORA ZAJICK

The first word that comes to mind when I think of this Nevada-born mezzo is "kick-ass." No one can match this woman for onstage ferocity. And whereas most singers thrill audiences with their high notes, Zajick gets better and better the lower she goes. Her superpowerful chest tones hit you like a punch. She's ideal in the mezzo roles of Verdi operas, like Azucena in *Trovatore* and Princess Eboli in *Don Carlo*. Indeed, any time I've heard her in these parts she's completely stolen the show. At a Zajick performance, be prepared to be blown out of your seat.

Pro Voice: Tenors

Luciano Pavarotti and Plácido Domingo together make the tenor a figure of even greater admiration than the sopranos, who have historically captured the public imagination. These men are still singing, and have been joined by a roster of relative newcomers who demonstrate considerable potential, if not always the star quality that characterizes their forebears. The tenor is the highest male voice (except for the countertenor, who is experiencing a revival but is usually only used in supporting roles). And, as a result, tenor is the vocal category assigned to opera's heroes and leading roles. You'll seldom see a villain whose part has been written for a tenor. Unfortunately, luck would have it that tenors—those heroes—often come plumper and shorter than their lower-voiced friends, which can make them sort of hard to buy as the objects of the ladies' ardor. Still, there are of course exceptions to that rule. Indeed, most of the fellows I've chosen here have escaped that fate, and manage to strike a balance between quasi-heartthrob and vocal wizard.

ROBERTO ALAGNA

It's impossible to talk about the French-Sicilian tenor without referring to his high-profile marriage to soprano Angela Gheorghiu. But before this pair started wreaking havoc on the opera circuit, Alagna had already been tapped (or, rather, anointed by his record label) as the Fourth Tenor, the man who would inherit the mantle from Carreras, Domingo, and Pavarotti. While Alagna lacks the phenomenal tonal beauty of Pavarotti or the power of Domingo, he does possess a genuinely lovely voice that's

MIKE OWEN/EMI CLASSICS

Roberto Alagna

81

well suited to the Italian repertoire of Donizetti, Puccini, and middle-period Verdi. He occasionally has missteps in performance, perhaps because of the pressures that accompany his bona fide and rapidly attained star status. Still, if you ignore the hoopla that surrounds him, you'll be treated to a voice of warmth and charisma.

IAN BOSTRIDGE

DAVID THOMPSON/EMI CLASSICS

Ian Bostridge

Tenors are perpetually maligned for being stupid. Bostridge, however, is the exception. An extremely intelligent singer, this young Brit brings a strong textual incisiveness and subtly shaded tonal beauty to his singing. So far, Bostridge has not made much of an impression on the opera stage, reserving most of his energies for works in the lieder arena, both on CD and in concert. His voice is not particularly weighty, but it is noteworthy for its crystalline beauty and range of colors. Bostridge has made a strong impression in the title role of a recent recording of *The Rake's Progress*. Perhaps he'll follow that up with more frequent live appearances in opera.

JOSÉ CURA

This young Argentine tenor has basically been handpicked by Plácido Domingo as that legendary tenor's successor. Indeed, young tenors are inevitably divided into Domingo or Pavarotti camps, depending on the nature of their instrument. Cura is the perfect successor to his mentor: He's got a voice of tremendous power and is able to convincingly portray characters (like Samson or Otello) that lesser singers often have a hard time making persuasive. By opera's somewhat lax standards, he's also relatively hunky, which is always a welcome change.

PLÁCIDO DOMINGO

This guy is like the Energizer Bunny. After a thirty-plus-year career, he's still going strong and shows no signs of reducing his jam-packed schedule.

In addition to being perhaps the most sought after male singer working today, he's got a regular lineup of conducting gigs, he's the artistic director of the Washington Opera, and also holds a post at the Los Angeles Opera. And after years of near-constant use, his voice still sounds terrific. Needless to say, Domingo is always compared to his chief rival and friend, Pavarotti, who in his heyday undeniably had the more beautiful tone to his voice. But I'd rather see Domingo in performance any day: He's a smarter musician, an infinitely greater actor, and his repertory is vast. He's not an up-and-comer, but he's certainly a singer you should seek out.

JERRY HADLEY

Years ago, Hadley was hailed as the possible successor to Domingo and Pavarotti, but it never really happened. Despite the prophecy of observers, his career never really took off the way folks hoped. But Hadley has carved out a smart and interesting career for himself, one that has made him tops on everyone's lists for various roles. I've already mentioned Ian Bostridge's recent claims on the role of Tom Rakewell in *The Rake's Progress*. But if he's going to own that part, he's going to have to seize it out of the hands of Hadley, who has proven himself to be perhaps the world's premier interpreter of that character. Hadley also excels in the bel canto operas but, thankfully, is committed to trying out more daring and unusual repertoire as well.

BEN HEPPNER

Great Wagnerian heldentenors (heroic tenors who can handle the punishing heights of the composer's music) come around about once in a generation, answering the prayers of opera producers everywhere, who are desperate to find a singer who'll enable them to stage *Tristan* or *Lohengrin*. As a result, folks are nuts for this Canadian tenor because he's genuinely got the goods. Many tenors who specialize

Ben Heppner as Lohengrin

WINNIE KLOTZ/METROPOLITAN OPERA

in Heppner's repertoire actually started life as baritones but have managed to push their voices upward to create a high yet dark-sounding tone. Heppner, however, is a true tenor whose high notes come easily and brilliantly. In addition to pretty much owning the part of Tristan these days, he's also a renowned Peter Grimes, as well as a strong lieder interpreter.

LUCIANO PAVAROTTI

At this point, Pavarotti is probably a more recognizable name than Caruso. It would certainly be hard to imagine anyone's voice being the equal of Pavarotti's in his prime. Unfortunately, the Italian tenor is in a sorry state these days. He shows up for appearances unprepared, is physically unable to handle the demands of live performances (he's always being helped up steps and such by extras), and he sings the same old stuff over and over again. That said, you should run to your record store to pick up Pavarotti CDs from the 1970s, when his voice was unspeakably gorgeous. He's still an important singer, because he has an uncanny ability to sell tickets. Occasionally, traces of his former glory emerge. But for the most part, this is an artist best experienced nowadays on CD.

OVERRATED

ANDREA BOCELLI AND JOSÉ CARRERAS

José Carreras is by no means overrated by critics: They all realize that his voice is shot to hell. But his endeavors as the least famous of the Three Tenors have made him a household name and the idol of many unsuspecting newcomers to operatic singing. Trust me, although he was once an important tenor with a lovely voice, right now he's pretty much past it. And as for Bocelli, the blind Italian superstar who can't sing without a microphone: While he's the only "opera" singer who can sell records in the millions, he'd be laughed off an opera stage by anyone in the know, as he was in his recent performances as Werther in Detroit.

Pro Voice: Baritones and Basses

Baritones and basses have it rough. They inevitably play either best friends or bad guys. Only in the Mozart operas and a handful of others do they have the opportunity to really take center stage. However, they're often very interesting singers, since they get to portray characters that avoid the whole one-dimensional hero thing. Baritones are kind of like the character actors of the opera world: They get all the interesting parts but none of the glory. Many, though, are able to conquer their second-class-citizen status by means of great singing and artistry. Here are a few who do just that.

DWAYNE CROFT

"Solid" is perhaps the best word to describe this New York native. He's not the most electrifying performer the world has ever known (a fact he himself freely admits), but thanks to several years of serious training in the Metro-politan Opera's Young Artists program, he's developed into a smart and dependable singer. His full, rich tone makes him a natural for the baritone roles of the Mozart repertory.

THOMAS HAMPSON

If Ian Bostridge is the resident smarty-pants of the tenor set, Hampson is his baritone coun-terpart. This is an extremely intelligent singer, who invariably brings a measure of taste and refinement to his portrayals. Hampson has a lovely baritone that he uses effectively not just in the expected parts (Count Almaviva in *Figaro*, Rodrigo in *Don Carlo*) but on less familiar turf as well. Last season he sang the

Thomas Hampson

almost-never-heard baritone transcription of *Werther,* and a recent CD took on not the chestnuts of the baritone rep but art-song settings of Walt Whitman poems.

SIMON KEENLYSIDE

In a certain respect, Keenlyside is like a younger version of Thomas Hampson: a smart and talented singer who also manages to be dashing and nice to look at. This young British singer is a relative newcomer to opera-star status, but in performance and on disk, he's already shown himself to be a strong singing actor and an able interpreter of the lieder literature.

Simon Keenlyside
(*center*) in *Capriccio*

SAMUEL RAMEY

Ramey has been around forever and has made a specialty of portraying the devil. Mephistopheles (both the Gounod and the Boito creations) and Nick Shadow in *The Rake's Progress* are parts in which virtually no one can touch him. Boito's Mefistofele, in particular, is the Kansas-born bass's signature part, one in which he regularly thrills audiences with his semi-clothed performances. He's also an important interpreter of Boris Godunov, a fact that has Ramey frequently compared to the legendary Russian bass Fyodor Chaliapin.

BO SKOVHUS

If Dolph Lundgren were an opera singer, he'd be Bo Skovhus. Put the tall, blond Danish baritone in fatigues and stuff a machine gun in his hands, and he'd be ready to take on Stallone. Skovhus recently made his Met debut, and he has a recording contract with Sony Classics, so his profile should only continue to rise in the next few years.

BRYN TERFEL

This bearlike Welshman has rightfully garnered a reputation as the premier baritone of his generation. Terfel's voice is truly fabulous: large, warm, attractive. He's also a strong actor who knows the value of acting with the voice. He's the best Figaro singing today and is also capable in Wagnerian works, his Wolfram in *Tannhäuser* being particularly noteworthy. His recorded output is rapidly increasing and contains a wide range of material, including the show tunes of Rodgers and Hammerstein.

Bryn Terfel

JORDAN DONER/DG

attending opera

Your start-to-finish guide to a fun and worthwhile night at the opera

So now that you know everything you need to about the history of opera, classical singing, and the current state of the opera world, you're all set to pick up a ticket. But attending the opera is not like seeing a film. When you go to a movie, you don't want to know what's going to happen. You slap down your money and you're in. But to get the best experience at an opera, you can't just decide on the spur of the moment to buy a ticket and show up. Opera requires preparation, and while it may seem counterintuitive to already know how a theatrical performance ends before you arrive at the theater, when it comes to opera, you want to know in advance as much about the show as possible. To that end, I've put together a short, start-to-finish guide to help you get the most for your money (opera doesn't come cheap, after all, and you don't want to feel gypped). You've made the decision to check out this whole opera thing. Here's all the information you need to do so.

Housebound

Before you even choose an opera to go to, it's a good idea to figure out which opera house will best satisfy your musical and dramatic interests. Now, depending on which city you live in, the pickings could be kind of slim. If you live in or around, say, Houston, you've pretty much got one option. Lucky for you, the Houston Grand Opera has a comparatively young general director who's into programming interesting works in progressive and novel productions. They also manage to attract top singers, which makes for good odds that you'll have a fun night.

In New York, needless to say, your opera options are much broader. If it's the singing you're interested in, there's really no better place than the Met—the legendary Metropolitan Opera House, which could probably claim to have the best casting in the world. None of the top singers would consider skipping an opportunity to sing at the Met. Even the second-string casts offer some great vocalism. But the Met is notorious for its stodgy productions of the most standard operas (although they're getting better about going for more interesting stagings), a strategy to appease the blue-haired benefactors, who clamor for obvious, ostentatious spectacle rather than innovation. For more compelling productions of works you wouldn't have expected to encounter, the New York City Opera is the place to go. The company doesn't attract the superstars that the Met does, but its roster of young singers is strong and, for the most part, they can act (which is a welcome change). If you hanker for avant-gardism, get on the train and head out to Brooklyn, where the Brooklyn Academy of Music regularly stages operas both brand new and ancient in Euro-style, artsy productions. The Met may have unleashed the world premiere of Philip Glass's *The Voyage,* but it's BAM that can claim to best reflect the aesthetic of Glass and other important contemporary composers. The crowd is also way hotter than you'll find at any other house.

The point is, not all opera houses offer the same kind of experience. While you may not have all that many companies to choose from, it's wise to start off your new life as an opera fan at a company that's in sync with your personal sensibility. For a description of the major U.S. houses, check out "House Music" on page 90.

House Music

There are hundreds of small and worthy opera houses across the United States. And sometimes a modest production at a smaller, semiprofessional company can be more rewarding than an evening of Italianate opulence at the Met. The companies I've listed below, however, are the big poppas of this country's opera scene, the ones where you're most likely to hear great singing in compelling productions.

HOUSTON GRAND OPERA

Wortham Theater Center

www.houstongrandopera.org

HGO is perhaps the most progressive of our nation's opera houses, thanks in part to the forward-thinking sensibility of general director David Gockley, who's comparatively young for someone in such a post. It was under him that the world was given John Adams's *Nixon in China* in 1987, and his commitment to presenting world premieres hasn't dimmed since then.

LOS ANGELES OPERA

www.laopera.org

As far as opera companies go, the Los Angeles Opera is just a baby. It's been around since 1986, and since then general director Peter Hemmings has tried and succeeded in making it a hot destination for the city's young hipsters. At the L.A. Opera's next performance of *Samson et Dalila*, for example, you may just find yourself sitting next to Drew Barrymore.

LYRIC OPERA OF CHICAGO

www.lyricopera.org

The Chicago Lyric, under William Mason, has been one of the top three companies in the United States for years. They attract singers of the highest caliber and are not afraid to balance the traditional operas that Chicago society types clamor for with more progressive (and even naughty) productions.

Civic Opera House

Metropolitan Opera Grand Staircase

METROPOLITAN OPERA

www.metopera.org

The Met is the true granddaddy of opera companies, not just in this country but perhaps the world. They don't pay their artists as well as the European houses do, but no singing career is complete without a stint at the Lincoln Center institution. The Met boasts undoubtedly the best casting in the world; it's a shame that a lot of its productions are overly grand, geared to please the benefactors in the audience rather than the artists.

NEW YORK CITY OPERA

www.nycopera.com

Since Paul Kellogg took over the reins of City Opera a few years ago, the company has developed a close relationship with the summertime Glimmerglass Opera (of which Kellogg is also the helmsman). That has been a good thing. More than most companies, NYCO aggressively seeks out a younger crowd by means of various creative initiatives, and also offers compelling stagings of unusual and seldom heard operas.

SAN FRANCISCO OPERA

www.sfopera.com

Don't let the fact that the San Francisco Opera House is a West Coast society favorite deter you. Under the guidance of general director Lotfi Mansouri, the company is dedicated to producing new works as well as old chestnuts. San Francisco was the site of the premiere of André Previn's *A Streetcar Named Desire*, and will be home to an operatic adaptation of the film *Dead Man Walking* later this year.

SEATTLE OPERA

www.seattleopera.org

Thanks to nightly post-show audience question-and-answer sessions with general director Speight Jenkins, the Seattle Opera has developed a close relationship with its community. The programming leans more toward the traditional than the avant-garde, but its regular staging of *Ring* cycles appeals to audiences of all stripes.

WASHINGTON OPERA

www.dc-opera.org

Washington, D.C.'s Kennedy Center is not just the site of the annually bestowed Honors. It's also the theater the Washington Opera calls home. Superstar tenor Plácido Domingo is the artistic director; Patricia Mossel is the executive director. The pair makes sure to present newer operas (like *Les Liaisons Dangereuses*) alongside the familiar faves.

These are the top opera houses that any opera fan should be aware of. But also keep in mind the numerous summer-season opera and classical music festivals; many of them put on fabulous productions with stellar singers. There is probably no greater place to hear opera than under the stars at the Santa Fe Opera. The Glimmerglass Opera in Cooperstown, New York, also offers a terrific experience, and opera can often be encountered at the Caramoor Festival in Katonah, New York, and at the Ravinia Festival in Chicago.

Sound Decisions

Advising the opera newcomer to check out this or that opera can be tricky. There are no foolproof guidelines for matching an individual with a particular opera. Just because you majored in, say, German Expressionist film in college doesn't mean that a progressive production of a Wagner opera is the thing for you. What's more, getting into opera is not a one-shot deal. If you really want to give this art form a chance, you'd better be prepared to check out a few different works in various styles. You may find Puccini to be torture one evening, but the next night Verdi could provide you with a near-ecstatic experience. Strauss's *Elektra* could have you running for the aisles; his *Ariadne auf Naxos* you might find terrific. I've listed below a few different operatic categories, and I'd recommend picking one or two from each style to get a fairly complete taste of what's out there. No one said getting opera would be easy (although maybe for you it will be). You'll probably need to make at least a few visits to your local opera house before you become someone who seeks out hard-to-find imported recordings of obscure rarities. There will be plenty of time for that sort of thing once you've been properly initiated.

Sitcom Operas

Only the hardest of hearts finds nothing to laugh at during an episode of *Cheers* or *Three's Company*. Similarly, it's not easy to sit stone-faced through Rossini's *Il Barbiere di Siviglia*. Indeed, there's a fairly substantial group of what I call sitcom operas, works that are about six times longer than what Must See TV has to offer but that share television comedy's minimal intellectual requirements. Any idiot can enjoy *Friends*. Said idiot will also probably like certain operas.

The most obvious example of this type of frothy opera buffa is, indeed, *Il Barbiere di Siviglia*. Mozart's *Le Nozze di Figaro*, based on the same Beaumarchais trilogy as the Rossini favorite, is another sitcom opera, but it brings to mind those sitcoms that aren't pure fun but convey some sort of deeper message during the final minutes of the broadcast. The difference is that when *Will & Grace* gets all deep in the last two minutes, it's irritating; when Mozart reconciles the Count and Countess at the end of *Figaro,* it's sublime. Comedy in opera tends to be hokey and obvious—old-fashioned to today's sarcastic and cynical audience. But the buffa works are nevertheless a fairly easy way into the world of opera, since they don't place the kind of demands on a listener that the operas of Strauss or Berg do. I can't imagine anyone being satisfied by a strict diet of sitcom operas only, but these works are a good way to ease into your new status as opera lover. Other sitcom operas include Donizetti's *L'Elisir d'Amore,* Rossini's *L'Italiana in Algeri,* and Mozart's *Così fan tutte.*

Historical Operas

Of course, comedy (and particularly comic opera) is not everybody's cup of tea. Perhaps you're more interested in history and politics. Well, there are operas for you, too. If I had to pick just one, I'd argue that Mussorgsky's *Boris Godunov* is the greatest historical opera ever. The music is quintessentially Russian: rousing, grand, based on native folk tunes. I think the fact that the lead character is a bass (and not some sissy soprano or tenor) is potentially attractive. And the overall spectacle of this huge opera adds to its luster with the novice. The student of Russian history will have a lot to admire and interpret at a performance of Mussorgsky's great work about the usurping czar who goes nuts. The composer also wrote another great historical opera, *Khovanshchina,* which is programmed much less frequently but which has a similar panoply of emotions, characters, and scenarios. A word of warning, though: Both are long.

Verdi, too, tried his hand at the historical opera, most successfully with *Don Carlo,* which premiered in 1867. The opera depicts the political and amorous rivalry between King Philip II of Spain and his son, Carlos. *Don Carlo* anticipates the dramatic integration and grandeur of Verdi's later works, and if you're prepared for a long evening (it's either four or five acts, depending

Opera Rocks

Just because you're devoted to rock and pop music doesn't mean you can't be an opera fan as well. In fact, the similarities between the genres might surprise you.

If you like . . .	You'll love . . .	Why?
KMFDM	Boito's *Mefistofele*	Devil-worshiping teens will get off on Boito's homage to Satan
The Artist Formerly Known as Prince	Saint-Saëns's *Samson et Dalila*	Samson grapples with the same sex/religion dilemma that the Purple One has explored in his career
Björk	Strauss's *Elektra*	Freaky Icelandic chick, freaky Greek chick
Radiohead	Wagner's *Ring* cycle	The ultimate 1990s art-rock band has a lot in common with the big-sound *Gesamtkunstwerk* ethos of the German master
Michael Jackson	Britten's *Peter Grimes*	Like the hero of *Grimes*, Jackson has a reported and oft-denied fondness for young boys
Madonna	Bizet's *Carmen*	Stevie Nicks may be your gypsy, but more than anyone Madonna shares Carmen's sexy independence and bravado

If you like...	You'll love...	Why?
Sean "Puffy" Combs	Anything by Rossini	Rossini was a purveyor of pastiche, which means that he often lifted elements from other works (sample-style) for his operas. The difference is that Rossini usually stole from himself.
Barry White	Mussorgsky's *Boris Godunov*	With that deep bass voice, Barry himself ought to play the role of the Russian czar
Alanis Morissette	Bellini's *Norma*	The angry young woman from Canada has a lot in common with the angry young woman from Gaul
Korn	Berg's *Wozzeck*	The group's angry, assaultive rock shares a similar aesthetic with Berg's atonalism
Rufus Wainwright	Tchaikovsky's *The Queen of Spades*	Gay composers of the world unite!
Missy Elliot and Timbaland	Anything by Philip Glass	The complex, percussive synth sound that Timbaland favors recalls Glass's keyboard polyrhythms

on which version is presented) the work offers the ultimate in epic, multi-thematic opera. For lighter fare on the historical tip, try one of Donizetti's three "Tudor" operas: *Anna Bolena, Maria Stuarda,* and *Roberto Devereux.* They're nowhere near as impressive either musically or dramatically as *Boris* or *Don Carlo.* But if you like the tunes of bel canto without the corny humor, you may like these operas.

Familiar Adaptations

I've mentioned that it's important to be familiar with the story of any opera you plan to see. One way to ensure this without spending countless hours reading synopses and librettos and listening to lengthy recordings is to choose operas that are based on familiar sources. The most obvious of these are the Shakespeare operas of Verdi, who was a lifelong fan of the Bard. His first Shakespearean endeavor was *Macbeth,* dating from 1847. This opera is not as acclaimed as Verdi's later Shakespeare adaptations, but it is staged often, and with the right soprano as the fierce Lady Macbeth, the opera can be kick-ass. *Otello* and *Falstaff,* Verdi's two final works, are almost universally hailed as his masterpieces, thanks in large part to the sensitively reworked text by Arrigo Boito. Any high school graduate knows the story of Othello and his highly sexed relationship with Desdemona. Consequently, when you hear *Otello,* you won't need to stress out about catching every line of dialogue or sussing out the meaning of each individual scene.

A lot of composers have turned to the classics for subject matter, often in an attempt to recapture the original spirit of opera as it relates to Greek tragedy. Strauss's *Elektra* is not something I would ever send a novice to (the score is horrifyingly dissonant and hard for the uninitiated to take), but if you're a rabid fan of Sophocles, you may just like it. Stravinsky's *Oedipus Rex* is a peculiar work, in that it's sung in Latin (of all things) and works more like an oratorio than a true opera. Nevertheless, it's a musically gratifying piece of work, and classics types will love its retelling of the mother-loving hero's story. Folks who love the classics (the *Iliad* in particular) might also take a shine to Berlioz's *Les Troyens* (his take on the Trojan War and its aftermath); Pushkin aficionados will find much to admire in the operas of Tchaikovsky, especially the melodic romanticism of *Eugene Onegin*. Benjamin Britten has written a fabulous short opera version of Henry James's ghost story *The Turn of the Screw*. And, believe it or not, there's even an opera (by Carlisle Floyd) based on John Steinbeck's *Of Mice and Men*. Careful with those puppies, Lenny!

Opera as Drama

This rubric happens to be the title of a famous book on the subject by Joseph Kerman, which was itself a play on Wagner's influential tract *Opera and Drama*. As I've mentioned virtually ad nauseam, the ongoing obsession of composers throughout the ages has been with reconciling opera's status as a piece of theater with the audience's yen for catchy tunes. A few composers have managed to fuse perfectly (or nearly perfectly) the musical and dramatic needs of particular works. For the operagoer who demands that the plot of an opera be unimpeded by showy melodies or action-halting arias, there are a handful of impressive works to choose from. Perhaps the greatest opera of the twentieth century is Alban Berg's *Wozzeck*. Musically, the work can be a bit difficult for some because the composer's commitment to Schoenbergian atonality makes for a noticeable dearth of hooks. But the opera is based on a terrific play: Georg Büchner's *Woyzeck* (see Werner Herzog's film version to get a sense of the opera's source material). And *Wozzeck* maintains *Woyzeck*'s Aristotelian unraveling of plot. From the moment we set eyes on the title character, we know he's doomed, and over the course of three perfectly paced acts, we witness this demise. Because the work is fiercely modern both musically and in terms of subject matter (the dispossession and despair of the lower classes), *Wozzeck* is the kind of opera that attracts strong directors, who seek to do more than just tell a group of overweight singers where to stand. You may need a minute or two to adjust to the opera's musical language, but you're more likely than not to encounter a progressive production that will sweep you up into the drama.

Schoenberg's *Moses und Aron* is like *Wozzeck* in that its odd musical vernacular will be strange to some ears. But it, too, eschews the melodrama that characterizes so much opera in favor of a streamlined, intellectual tale of faith and brotherhood. Czech composer Leoš Janáček was also adept at producing lean musical dramas. *Kát'a Kabanová* and *Jenůfa*, in particular, are two of his operas whose compelling female protagonists and troublesome dramatic situations can seize a theater fan's attention.

Contemporary Opera

Opera administrators everywhere are under the impression that audiences want world premieres. New works by hot composers are surely the perfect lure for a younger crowd. I agree that the prospect of a world premiere, the notion that opera is still evolving and still matters, is attractive to a hipper, younger crowd. But I think it's important to be wary of which new or recent operas to check out. There's a sad truth that most new operas hit the scene to tremendous fanfare, record crowds, and, often, positive reviews. But then they languish unrevived for years, making an adequate assessment of a work's lasting value a tough task. At this writing, the Met has just presented the premiere of John Harbison's *The Great Gatsby*, based, of course, on the F. Scott Fitzgerald novel. New opera. Familiar subject. Great cast. Respected composer. It sounds like all the makings for a terrific new piece. But it will be nearly impossible to make a final judgment of the opera based on its initial run. *The Great Gatsby* will have to appear in a few different opera houses several times before its true worth can be determined.

As a result, you should view new operas as an opportunity to get caught up in the excitement of a new work of art seeing the light of day for the first time. And stick with new works by composers you've heard of. I'll go to anything that Philip Glass releases, and would recommend that you do, too. Similarly, John Adams has proved himself with *Nixon in China* and *The Death of Klinghoffer*.

It's a safe bet that anything new these composers put out there will have something in them to appreciate. I don't mean to sound like I'm down on contemporary opera. I think it's crucial that the form continue to develop and churn out vital new pieces. But for the novice operagoer, recent compositions can sometimes prove rocky terrain. Unless, of course, you're a progressive avant-garde type with a downtown sensibility: If so, by all means ignore my advice and check out all the latest operatic action.

Quintessential Operas

Our final category is the one I think many of you will find the most helpful. There are certain operas, most of them Italian (although *Carmen* fits the bill as well), that somehow define the form as a whole. These operas play into the layperson's notion of what opera is. They possess showstopping arias that require virtuosic singing; predominant story elements include jealousy, love, revenge, murder, suicide, and loyalty; and the heroine dies in the end. These are the kind of operas that inspire hackneyed sayings about it not being over till the fat lady sings. These not-so-subtle, passionate works often leave musical elitists and many critics profoundly disappointed, even disgusted. But the crowds go wild. And despite what classical theorists tell you, most of these archetypal operas have a lot to admire. I think these operas can be the ideal place for the newbie to start.

No composer is as iconic a representative of opera as a genre as Puccini. I can't imagine anybody, except perhaps the Unabomber, who hasn't heard snippets of his pieces at some point, even if unwittingly. I have a personal block against *Madama Butterfly:* The plot betrays the ultimate in racist, imperialist stereotyping; and the role of a teenage geisha girl is usually sung by a white woman old enough to be the character's grandmother. In spite of this, people flock to it all the time (Glenn Close loved it in *Fatal Attraction*). *Butterfly* aside, I think there is a wealth of material from Puccini that's the perfect starting point, particularly *La Bohème* and *Tosca*. The former is the quintessential love story: Poor poet meets cute but sick girl, they fall in love, she gets sicker, they break up, and they get back together just as she falls dead. The opera formed the basis of the Broadway musical *Rent*, and Lord knows folks turn out in droves for *that* show. *Tosca* is even more quintessentially representative of Italian opera. The title character is a ferociously jealous diva. She lies, she kills, she repents, she flings herself off a roof. Exactly what one would expect from an opera. More important than the love story of *Bohème* and the trashy melodrama of *Tosca* are the tunes that each opera includes. Most stalwart fans go to the opera to hear terrific singing, and these two works offer some of the best opportunities for it: "Che gelida manina," Musetta's Waltz ("Quando m'en vo'"), and "Donde lieta uscì" from *La Bohème;* "Recondita armonia," "Vissi d'arte," and "E lucevan le stelle" from *Tosca.*

Puccini was not alone, however, in his mastery of the emotion-stirring possibilities of opera. His predecessor, Verdi, was an even greater composer, and to a large degree he created the style that Puccini ran with. I've mentioned Verdi's *Otello* and *Don Carlo* in earlier categories. As for quintessential representatives of the form, I'd steer you to *Rigoletto* and *La Traviata*. *Rigoletto* possesses all opera's requisite intrigue, murder, and lust, and is remarkable for its seemingly unending string of catchy tunes, particularly "Questa o quella" and "La donna è mobile," both of which you've heard in countless TV commercials whether you realize it or not. The first work that ever really seized my attention and made me get into opera was *La Traviata,* which is still one of my favorites. What could be more heartwarming than observing a selfless prostitute give up the man she loves, only to drop dead when he tries to get back together with her? From the simple but moving opening prelude to Violetta's long, Act I mindboggler of an aria ("È strano! . . . Sempre libera") to Alfredo's rousing "De' miei bollenti spiriti" to the last-act death scene, this opera has one ravishing piece of music after another. Okay, so it lacks the dramatic plausibility of *Wozzeck*. What can you do? Sometimes it's fun to get maudlin and listen to sad songs.

Opera Stars

As I've mentioned, matching an individual with the right opera can sometimes be tricky. There's really no way to determine what a given listener will take to, even if you know that person inside out. The only truly foolproof method for determining which opera a newcomer will love? Astrology. Let your sign direct you to an opera you'll appreciate.

CAPRICORN

You Capricorns have a good sense of humor, but you nonetheless tend to be conservative and are fixated on keeping up appearances of respectability. As a result, you won't want an opera that would cause much of a stir. The simple refinement and conventionality of Handel's operas, like *Giulio Cesare, Serse,* or *Ariodante* won't ruffle any feathers.

AQUARIUS

There's a strong humanitarian streak in you, as well as a sense of fun and nostalgia. All of this should point you toward that most human of composers, Mozart. *Le Nozze di Figaro,* in particular, will satisfy your high regard for truth, loyalty, and originality.

PISCES

You're very imaginative and have a strong need to dream and escape from routine. I'd recommend some of the fantasy operas, like Ravel's *L'Enfant et les Sortilèges* or Strauss's *Ariadne auf Naxos*, both of which will take you to fabulous, otherworldly realms.

ARIES

Passionate, adventurous, impatient, and competitive, you're likely to be enamored of operas with a lot of action and with a strong hero at the story's center. There's no better opera for you than Wagner's *Siegfried*, the third installment of the *Ring* series.

TAURUS

You're very fond of the natural world and enjoy spending time outdoors. You also need your environment to have a calming effect. The relaxing pace and softness of tone (as well as the forest locale) of Debussy's *Pelléas et Mélisande* will suit you just right.

GEMINI

With your changeable and adaptable nature and your need for novelty, it's hard to pin down just one opera that will keep you interested. I'd suggest, therefore, checking out the operas of Strauss, which run the gamut from fiercely modern (*Salome*, *Elektra*) to charming and nostalgic (*Der Rosenkavalier, Ariadne auf Naxos*).

CANCER

Emotional, clingy, and with a profound love of wild parties, Cancers might like Verdi's *La Traviata*. Your moody, romantic side will identify with the heroine, Violetta, while the cautious protector in you will admire her would-be father-in-law, Germont.

LEO

Leos tend to be broad-minded but a bit bossy, and they absolutely love the pomp and circumstance of grand ceremonies and pageantry. The spectacle of Mussorgsky's *Boris Godunov* should do the trick for you.

VIRGO

A stickler for order and perfectionism, you're someone who'll appreciate the near-mathematical precision of Monteverdi's score for *Orfeo*. The work is not overtly passionate, and the wholesomeness of Orfeo's affection for Euridice will strike you as appropriately simple.

LIBRA

You're a hopeless romantic, an incorrigible flirt, and extremely idealistic. You'll undoubtedly be moved by the simple passion and doomed hopefulness of Puccini's *La Bohème*, the favorite opera of lovebirds everywhere.

SCORPIO

How would I describe Scorpio? Emotional, charismatic, jealous, impetuous, and persuasive. Just like the title character of Bizet's *Carmen*.

SAGITTARIUS

Sags are good-humored, enthusiastic (albeit superficial) types who love to travel. They also like to unearth the hidden meanings in ordinary events. Offenbach's *Les Contes d'Hoffmann* is the perfect place to start: The protagonist hangs out with friends in a tavern, regaling them with stories of his travels and the women he loved in each place. Sound familiar?

Prep Talk

Okay, you've finally decided which opera to see and where to see it. Now you've got some homework to do. If you really want to get the most out of your operagoing experience, you need to read up. Your first stop? The back of this book. I've put together a roundup of fifty operas, with synopses of each and short biographies of the composers. Before you show up at the theater, it's helpful to have a sense of the composer's intention with a given piece of music, and absolutely crucial that you have some grasp of a work's plot. No one said getting into opera would be simple. I know it's easier to just flip on the TV, sit back, and be entertained. But I can guarantee that a night at the opera has way more to offer than even NBC's fall lineup. It's worth doing a little research for.

Get your hands on anything you can that will provide information about the composer whose work you're seeing, about singers appearing in the show, and about the production concept. Many opera companies publish newsletters or magazines, which contain write-ups of a given season's repertory. These publications can be enormously helpful in preparing you for the big night. Scanning the opera's libretto is also a good idea, and not nearly as time-consuming as you'd think. Verdi's *Otello,* for example, which is not a particularly short work in actual performance, contains just one-third the lines of Shakespeare's original. Reading through it wouldn't take more than an hour, and you'll be notably more relaxed when you're sitting in your seat looking at the supertitles, gazing with disbelief at the absurdity of the translations. At the very least, arrive at the opera house with enough time to peruse the program, which will invariably have a synopsis of the work, as well as (in most cases) an article about the opera's origins.

Even better than reading up is finding time for a listening session. Even extremely accessible operas like *La Bohème* or *Rigoletto* lack pop music's ability to take up residence in the brain at a moment's notice. Having a sense of the musical character of an opera beforehand is invaluable; being able to anticipate certain arias or ensemble numbers will also make the experience much more pleasurable. Box sets of complete opera recordings cost a fortune, and I'm not recommending that you drop huge wads of cash at the record store. Most libraries lend recordings of operas: Borrow one, and don't feel you have to listen straight through. Skip around, fast-forward to sections that appeal to you, and check out the first few minutes of each act. Just do something to familiarize yourself with an opera's score. CDs of opera highlights cost the same as any rock album. Pick one up, listen to it, and, if you don't like it, sell it back to a used-record store. But whatever you do, listen to the music of an opera before you get to the theater, or you could be in for a very long and frustrating evening.

Film versions of operas generally don't do blockbuster business at the theater (certainly no movie studio would headline a Memorial Day weekend with Zeffirelli's latest celluloid Verdi adaptation). But as a preparation tool, they can be great. Franco Zeffirelli's hyperopulent productions repulse me in live performance but are quite effective on film. His movie versions of *La Traviata* and *Otello* will help you decide if it's worth shelling out cash to see an actual production of those operas. For more information on film adaptations of operas, check out "Opera on Film" (page 52).

Actual film versions of opera are generally more compelling than the rather static videos (available at many libraries as well as for rent or sale) that are simply VHS recordings of actual opera productions in houses around the world. These videos, however, can be a good way to experience an opera cheaply in the comfort of your own home, before trekking to your local movie complex.

Finally, many opera companies organize pre-performance lectures and discussions to shed light on an evening's performance. I know it's not easy finding time to sit through an entire three- or four-hour opera, let alone arriving early to listen to some classical-music educator pontificate. But I have to say that there's no better way to prepare for an opera performance than by listening to an expert chat casually and answer questions. You'll know what to look and listen for when the curtain goes up, and the tricky, confusing bits will have already been explained. From all I've just said, it seems like preparing for a simple opera performance is virtually a full-time job, but you don't need to do everything I've suggested. Pick one or two possibilities. Read the synopsis and listen to a recording. Leave work a little early to get to the pre-performance chat. It really doesn't matter how you prepare, as long as you put in a little effort toward getting acquainted with the opera you've chosen to attend.

Ticket Mastery

Next stop? The ticket window. Much as I'd like to inform you that going to an opera is as cheap as a movie, there's simply no getting around the fact that it's an expensive endeavor. To stage something like *Aida*—with its enormous pyramid sets, huge chorus procession, and (on occasion) menagerie of animals—costs a fortune, and necessitates that opera companies keep orchestra-seat ticket prices high. Fortunately, more and more opera companies are recognizing the importance of attracting the next generation of fans, and they've instituted various programs to help you get the most for your money.

The Los Angeles Opera, for example—because it's a relatively new company (its first production premiered in 1986), and because it exists in a city with no ready-made network of arts contributors to cater to—focuses a lot of energy on the twenty- and thirtysomething crowd. The company has instituted a program called U.F.O., or Urbanites for Opera, which offers tickets to four different operas for one reasonable price. For something like one hundred dollars, you can catch four performances, two of which are followed by a party at a specified L.A. venue. U.F.O. also hooks you up with discounts at bookstores and record stores, as well as a subscription to the company newsletter. To me, this seems like a good hook to get new blood into the theater. I spend more than one hundred dollars on a pair of shoes; to get four performances and a couple of parties for roughly that price is something I can't afford *not* to do!

The L.A. Opera is not alone with this initiative. Coincidentally, both the Seattle Opera and the San Francisco Opera have programs called Bravo! in which young subscribers are entitled to discounted tickets, pre- and post-show lectures, and the all-important cocktail mixer. In a similar vein, the Houston Grand Opera adds on extra performances of successful productions and reduces the ticket price for those performances. If you've decided that you want to give opera a significant shot at finding a permanent place in your cultural life, it's worth participating in one of these multiperformance, single-fee programs.

Of course, you may not want to go to all the effort of finding a suitable initiative and handing over a check that requires your repeated presence at the still-dubious opera house. If you're still too skeptical to pay up, there are cheap tickets to be had at any opera house—you just won't be able to see much. The Met's cheapest ticket is twenty-five dollars, about the same as the cheap seats at a Broadway show. The problem is that the Met's cheap seats are in a section that's about seven stories high. Opera singers know how to project, so you'll be able to hear what's happening. But any subtle facial expressions or dramatic movements will go unnoticed. I think it's a better idea to go in for standing-room tickets, which can be as little as ten dollars. You'll almost always be able to score a seat at the intermission. Many people go to the opera out of a sense of social necessity, but they have no intention of staying all the way through. Enjoy the first act from your standing position. Then watch like a hawk for fugitives, and plant yourself in their empty seats. Just be forewarned: Most opera-house ushers frown on this sort of thing. I've seen more than a few skirmishes between an usher and a standing-room interloper. If you choose this tactic, be discreet.

Big Night

The big night has finally arrived. You've got your ticket, you've chosen just the right opera, and you're well prepared. Basically, there's nothing more for you to do but sit back and enjoy the performance. But there are a few last-minute "night-of" tips you should keep in mind.

1. Only half-wits wear black tie. This is a hard and fast rule with me. Unless you've been invited to a post-performance gala reception with the mayor, do not think that the opera is the right time to drag that tux of yours out of the closet. I know that in the movies, black tie is de rigueur at the opera, but I assure you that you'll regret being overdressed. Sure, there are inevitably a handful of men, trying to look dashing, who wear

tuxes to an ordinary night at the opera. I laugh at those people. Operas are long, and you don't want to feel fidgety or uncomfortable in a constraining outfit. I wear jeans to the Met all the time, and while that may be pushing it a little, I haven't yet been ejected. Needless to say, opera *is* the perfect opportunity to get dressed up, and you should by all means deck yourself out and try to look your best, if you feel so inclined. But too formal is not a good thing. Leave the monkey suit at home. And ladies, keep the sequins to a minimum.

2. A few important personal items are absolutely necessary, in my opinion. I wouldn't dream of going to the opera without breath mints. Sitting silently for long stretches inevitably makes your breath go rank. And God forbid the person sitting next to you should lean over to ask the time and you've got a dead animal in your mouth. There's nothing worse than turning to your neighbor when the curtain falls and saying, "Wasn't that great?" only to be greeted with a look of horror at the stench emanating from your person. Cough drops, too, are a must. Although the primary sources of mid-performance disruptions these days are cell phones and beepers, there are still far too many heavy coughers, who start hawking up loogies in the middle of "Nessun dorma." Don't be one of these people. Coughing fits strike without warning; be prepared for one just in case.

3. One of the most enjoyable elements of going to the opera (indeed, it can be the best part of the evening, depending on the performance) is intermission. There are a few rules of intermission etiquette that you should be aware of. First, run—don't walk—to the concession stands at halftime. Opera audiences can be ferociously impatient when it comes to queuing up for a glass of champagne. Try with all your might to beat these people to the front of the line. Second, bring plenty of cash. Opera companies are desperate to get funds in any way they can. The concession stands at most opera houses make the food prices at Disney World seem cheap. Finally, keep in mind

that intermission lounges are just about the ultimate cruising ground. You better be sure to have a few cute and witty opinions of the performance to share just in case you get picked up.

4. Before a performance begins, figure out where the rest rooms are. Excusing yourself in the middle of a performance to pee is absolutely out of the question. Go before the show starts or be prepared to hold it in. At the opera, the lines for the men's room can be as long as those for the ladies' room. The second the curtain goes down, there's invariably a mad rush to the toilet. A good way to avoid the rest-room throngs is to wait until the end of the intermission to go. When the theater staff starts chiming bells to signal it's time to get back to your seats—that's the moment you should rush to the bathroom. There will only be a few other stragglers in there with you, and you'll be able to pee in peace.

5. Opera is perpetually maligned for being boring. And even opera lovers will tell you that not every second of every opera can sustain your interest. It happens to the best of us on occasion: Folks fall asleep during performances. And my attitude is, hey, if you're not snoring, don't sweat it. If it's at all possible to be fresh and well rested before you show up at the theater, please try. But sometimes you're coming straight from work and it's not easy to keep your eyes open. For a while, I violently fought off the urge to sleep: pinching myself, poking, physically holding my eyes open, you name it. Finally, I realized that when sleep starts approaching, it's best to just go with it. Don't fight it. I often find myself drifting off in the first act, even during operas that I love. What I've learned is that after a few minutes of slumber, I wake up refreshed and able to concentrate on the rest of the piece. If it's the final act and you can't keep your eyes open, chances are it's late, the performance is dull, and you're just wiped out. If it's early on, there's still time to rally and get into it. Allow yourself to take little naps, as needed, so that you can appreciate the later acts when you're wide awake. There's nothing worse than forcing yourself to stay

awake for hours, risking that you'll be too weary to enjoy what's going on.

Well, there you have it. All the necessary tools to enjoy a night at the opera (pay particular attention to the bathroom insights). If it all goes well, your first visit won't be your last. And if you've already been to a performance and found yourself confused, maybe next time you'll have better luck. As I've said, opera takes some getting used to. The tidbits above are intended to ease you into it, but they are by no means a substitute for repeated listenings. When I first tasted beer, I didn't like it. Now I'm considering getting a "Budweiser" tattoo. It's the same thing with opera. You need to test the waters and stick with it. Take it slow, try a wide variety of styles, and make sure you're prepared for each production you attend. Pretty soon you'll be arguing with the rest of the nutcases about how Amelita Galli-Curci kicks Adelina Patti's ass, or how Samuel Ramey has nothing on Fyodor Chaliapin. You'll be a fanatic in no time.

111

fifty operas

Fifty operas may seem like a lot of ground to cover, but in fact it wasn't easy narrowing the field to this number. I could very easily have discussed the operas of Mozart, Wagner, Puccini, and Verdi, and the tally would have reached fifty. But I wanted to include a wide range of different operatic styles and periods. There are a few omissions, which I'm sure will have certain observers appalled. How, for example, could I have included Verdi's *Il Trovatore* but not his *Don Carlo*? Well, believe it or not, these choices were not made arbitrarily. I felt that the tunes of *Trovatore* and the legend of its absurd plot made its inclusion more important and useful than that of the admittedly superior *Don Carlo*. And why did I choose Monteverdi's *Orfeo* over Gluck's more frequently staged interpretation? It was important to me to go all the way back to opera's origins, and the Monteverdi work is the first true masterpiece of the form. And it didn't make sense to waste space listing two operas with the same plot. The point is, there are many worthy operas that you won't find on this list, and several you *will* see on the list that aren't staged all that often. I tried to create a good mix, based on historical diversity, frequency of performance, and personal preference. These fifty operas will get you started, and please, by all means, check out any opera you can get to, whether I've discussed it or not.

JOHN ADAMS 1947–

The strangest thing about *Nixon in China* is not the then-progressive choice of current events as subject matter but the fact that the inspiration for the opera was the director's rather than the composer's. It was Peter Sellars, the diminutive one-time bad boy of opera, who conceived the production and brought his idea to the composer. Over the years, Sellars has been a vexing figure on the opera scene, alternately intriguing and dismaying audiences and critics with his bizarre modernizations of classic works (he set *Le Nozze di Figaro* in Trump Tower and made the title character of *Don Giovanni* a homeless heroin addict and rapist). But with *Nixon in China*, Sellars hit the bull's-eye: The stars were clearly aligned when the team of Adams (composer), Alice Goodman (libretto), and Mark Morris (choreographer) was enlisted.

John Adams may not have come up with the initial concept for the opera, but his musical contribution certainly made it a lasting and important work. A minimalist of the Philip Glass/Steve Reich school (which is to say, his music is compositionally complex while remaining accessible to the lay listener), the New Hampshire–born composer made his operatic debut with *Nixon*, which was enthusiastically received at its Houston premiere. His follow-up, *The Death of Klinghoffer*, similarly focused on a then-recent historical event: the hijacking of the *Achille Lauro* cruise ship by Palestinian terrorists. Subsequently, Adams composed a quasi-operatic song cycle based on the 1993 Northridge earthquake outside Los Angeles. As yet, neither of these works has proven to have the staying power of his first foray into opera.

Nixon in China

Libretto by Alice Goodman
Premiere: Houston Grand Opera, 1987
Scene: Beijing, February 1972

ACT I Chinese military await the arrival of the *Spirit of '76*, the aircraft carrying President Richard Nixon to China for a political summit. The president and first lady are greeted by Premier Chou En-lai, who presents the Nixons to various Chinese diplomats. Nixon sings an aria about the importance of the visit. Later, Nixon and his secretary of state, Henry Kissinger, are introduced to Chairman Mao Tse-tung, with whom the dis-

Nixon in China

cussion quickly turns from superficial chitchat to weightier ethical matters. But that night, at a banquet in the Nixons' honor, the American president makes a toast to a shared and fruitful future, restoring a sense of calm to the potentially heated proceedings.

ACT II The second act opens with Pat Nixon on a sightseeing tour of Beijing. She heads all over town, visiting a school, the Great Wall, and the Ming Tombs, among other locales. The aria "This is prophetic" is Pat's big showstopper. Pat's day of sightseeing concludes with her husband and the Maos at the Peking Opera, where the ballet *The Red Detachment of Women* is performed. The ballet depicts the torture of a female prisoner; Pat becomes particularly wrapped up in the drama, even going so far as to try and help the girl. Madame Mao becomes similarly agitated by the ballet when, in a later scene, a group of revolutionaries comes to the aid of a small village's working-class poor. She storms the stage and sings her main number, "I am the wife of Mao Tse-tung."

ACT III It is the final day of the Nixons' Chinese sojourn and everyone has had enough. The stage is split to reveal two bedrooms. In one, the Nixons consider the significance of their dealings with China. In the other, the Maos contemplate the history and future of U.S.–Chinese relations. Premier Chou once again takes the stage to ponder the relevance and the success or failure of the mission.

LUDWIG VAN BEETHOVEN 1770–1827

Everyone knows the iconic short-short-short-long motif of Beethoven's Fifth Symphony (even if only from the disco interpretation on the *Saturday Night Fever* sound track). Most are probably familiar with the "Ode to Joy" finale from the Ninth Symphony and the *Moonlight* Sonata. Along with Mozart, Beethoven remains possibly the most famous and respected composer in the history of music. But despite his monumental successes in the realm of symphonic music, the German composer also sought to make his mark in the world of opera, an arena that proved tough going. Beethoven ended up producing just one opera—*Fidelio*, which was a reworking of the composer's unsuccessful *Leonore*. When it premiered in 1805, *Leonore* received a tepid response, but nine years and four overtures later, Beethoven finally had on his hands the theatrical hit he yearned for.

Although the composer produced just a single musical drama, it was nonetheless an important one. Opera seria was dead and buried with Mozart in 1791, and that composer's comic operas (which have generally proved more influential) failed to inspire Beethoven, who was concerned with weighty ethical matters, which he sought to address through music. Beethoven was the link from the Classical period (epitomized by Haydn and Mozart) to the Romantic era, of which he, Beethoven, was the premier figure. *Fidelio*'s comic opening scene is a bit peculiar in an opera about a political prisoner, but things quickly turn serious as the composer works his way into a plot intended more as moral education than as entertainment. Addressing ethical and political dilemmas, Beethoven infused the opera with an orchestral heft not previously heard in the opera house. *Fidelio* became music's first influential Romantic opera, ultimately affecting the styles of other composers like Weber, Wagner, and Verdi.

Fidelio

Libretto by Joseph Sonnleithner, based on the play *Léonore* by
   Jean Nicolas Bouilly
Premiere: Theater an der Wien, Vienna, 1805 (as *Leonore*);
   Kärntnertortheater, Vienna, 1814 (as *Fidelio*)
Scene: Seville in the 1700s

ACT I In a Seville prison, Marzelline, daughter of the warden, Rocco, is ironing, while Rocco's assistant, Jaquino, hits on her. Smitten with another assistant—Fidelio—Marzelline rebuffs Jaquino, who is called off to perform a task for Rocco. Marzelline sings an aria of love for Fidelio, who promptly arrives with Rocco and Jaquino. Rocco has become fond of his new employee and subtly encourages a potential romance with Marzelline. But Fidelio is actually a woman in disguise, namely, Leonore, the wife of Florestan, a nobleman who is suspected of being held in Rocco's jail. Fidelio avoids the talk of marriage and offers his/her services in dealing with the dungeon inmates. Rocco, however, has been forbidden by the governor, Don Pizarro, from allowing anyone into the dungeon; but he does let slip that there is a prisoner down below with whom he could use a little help. He agrees to ask Pizarro for permission.

Don Pizarro enters and expresses concerns over the discovery that the minister, Don Fernando, is looking into charges of false imprisonment. He decides to kill Florestan and turns to Rocco for help in perpetrating the crime. Leonore (Fidelio) has overheard these dealings and sings an angry aria ("Abscheulicher!") denouncing Pizarro. When Rocco returns, "Fidelio" suggests that they let out the other prisoners for some fresh air, to which the warden agrees. Fidelio is then told that s/he must help dig a grave for the man in the dungeon. Pizarro returns, annoyed about the prisoners strolling about the courtyard, and angrily sends the folks back to their cells, their few moments of "freedom" cut short.

ACT II The second act opens in the dungeon, where Florestan, in chains, sings of the misery of his confinement—a misery that is nonetheless assuaged by visions of Leonore, whom he imagines coming to his rescue. A few moments later, Leonore/Fidelio and Rocco enter as Florestan sleeps. Leonore approaches with food and water; she's still unable to tell for sure if the prisoner is her husband until he awakes and accepts her offering of nourishment. Florestan remains unaware that the jailer's assistant is in fact his wife. With the grave prepared, Pizarro enters, wielding a knife. As he moves to pounce on the prisoner, Fidelio intercedes, blocking the villain's path and exposing herself as Leonore. Needless to say, everyone is stunned, but that doesn't faze Pizarro, who now simply has two murders to commit. Leonore, however, pulls out a gun, which stops Pizarro in his tracks. A trumpet sounds in the distance, announcing the arrival of the minister, Don Fernando. When other officers arrive on the scene, Rocco and Pizarro withdraw to greet the minister. Florestan is astonished at what his wife has endured on his behalf.

Outside, on the prison grounds, Florestan and Leonore are led to Fernando, who is amazed that Florestan, an old friend he believed dead, is among the living. The other prisoners and the townsfolk on the scene rail against the nasty Pizarro, who begs Fernando for mercy. But the minister is having none of it. He instructs Leonore to unlock her husband's bonds and places Pizarro under arrest. The ensemble sings in praise of the wifely fidelity Leonore has demonstrated.

VINCENZO BELLINI   1801–1835

The operas of Bellini, Donizetti, and Rossini, who comprise the superstar triumvirate of bel canto opera, are often dismissed for being frothy and orchestrally simplistic. They're sort of like the sitcoms of opera: cute, diverting, and with a few memorable moments, but fundamentally without a whole lot of depth. Nevertheless, despite the charge of being "light," much of these composers' music can be hard on singers. The literal translation of "bel canto" is "beautiful singing," and it's a style that relies on virtuosic vocal runs and tricky flourishes. Add to the mix the complexity of a heavy-duty dramatic heroine like Norma, and you've got an extremely challenging, practically Wagnerian responsibility on your hands.

Bellini was thirty when he composed *Norma,* and he had already had a success with *La Sonnambula* earlier the same year. But whereas *Sonnambula* is an easy-to-digest comic opera, *Norma* deals with loftier themes, such as the balance of carnality and religion. Unlike most of the bel canto operas, *Norma* can pose huge problems to stage, chiefly due to the general dearth of sopranos capable of handling the role's vocal feats and dramatic requirements. This was a part that Maria Callas seized and made her own in the 1950s. Joan Sutherland has also sung it with success, but no one has been able to escape the specter of Callas, who to this day owns the role of the Druid priestess. Consequently, performances of *Norma* (really good ones, at least) are relatively rare and should only be attended when the title role is portrayed by a soprano of serious talent.

Bellini was a genius with melody—he was a fabulous and prolific songwriter—so despite the challenges *Norma* presents to producers, it offers listeners a significant degree of beautiful and accessible music.

A
B
C
D
E
F
G
H
I
J
K
L
M
N
O
P
Q
R
S
T
U
V
W
X
Y
Z

Norma

Libretto by Felice Romani, based on the play by Alexandre
   Soumet

Premiere: La Scala, Milan, 1831

Scene: Gaul, around 50 B.C.

ACT I   In a sacred woodland area, Oroveso, the chief Druid priest, leads the Druids and the Gauls in a prayer for victory over the Roman army. Roman officers Pollione and Flavio appear in another part of the forest, where Pollione confides to his friend that he is no longer secretly in love with the Druid priestess Norma (Oroveso's daughter). Instead, he's turned his affection to Norma's priestess protégé, Adalgisa. Norma has had two children by Pollione, a fact that's kept under wraps due to the inimical relationship between the couple's respective people and because of Norma's religious responsibilities. Pollione avows his love for Adalgisa and sings of his fear of Norma's rage.

Norma and her entourage of priestesses enter at the other edge of the forest, where she counsels her people to avoid war with the Romans, who, she claims, are headed downhill already. She sings an aria to the goddess of the moon (a famous and beautiful number known as the "Casta Diva"—the definite article added by opera queens for no apparent reason). The song stirs the people, and Norma turns aside to sing of her love for Pollione, who, she fears, has begun to lose interest in her.

Everyone exits and Adalgisa appears, lamenting the fact that she is not permitted to return the affection offered her by Pollione. The man himself enters and reiterates his words of love. Adalgisa acknowledges her feelings and agrees to meet again with her man the subsequent evening.

Back at the Druid homestead, Norma and her sons' nanny, Clotilde, are discussing the priestess's conflicted feelings toward her children, whom she loves as a mother but who nevertheless serve as a constant and irritating reminder of her betrayal of her people and of the priesthood. Adalgisa shows up, hoping for some girl talk regarding her budding relationship with Pollione; she's unaware of Norma's ties to the man. Norma is at first understanding of Adalgisa's woes—until, that is, she discovers who exactly the younger woman is kicking it with. Pollione arrives on the scene and Norma furiously lets him have it. The signal for Norma to come rally her people is heard in the distance. Pollione determines to leave with Adalgisa, but the young priestess sends him away alone. Her sisterhood with Norma takes priority over any lustful urges.

ACT II Insane with jealousy and rage, Norma watches her children sleep and decides, Medea-like, to kill them in order to get back at Pollione. She's got the dagger in hand but finds she can't go through with the act. She sends Clotilde to fetch Adalgisa, who arrives shortly. Norma asks her friend to take the kids, join Pollione, and start a family. Norma, in the meantime, plans to kill herself. Again, Adalgisa displays priestess team spirit, convincing Norma that she must be a mother to her children and vowing eternal friendship. The women close the scene with a duet of female solidarity, "Sì, fino all'ore estreme," which could have served as the inspiration for the Aretha Franklin–Annie Lennox hit "Sisters Are Doin' It for Themselves."

Back in the forest, Oroveso and the Gauls are preparing themselves for a possible battle with the Romans. The priest asserts, though, that they must wait for the go-ahead from Norma before they engage in combat. Not far off, at the Druid temple, Clotilde breathlessly arrives to inform Norma that Pollione, undeterred, still intends to drag Adalgisa off to Rome. Livid, Norma sounds the battle cry, galvanizing her people in the chorus "Guerra, guerra!" Within moments, it is ascertained that a single Roman has been captured: Pollione, of course. Norma is on the verge of bludgeoning him to death but holds off, feeling the tug of former affection. She demands that Pollione return to her, threatening the murder of their children and of Adalgisa. Pollione won't budge, so Norma determines that they should both die. She instructs her lackeys to build a sacrificial fire, stating that a wayward priestess is to be immolated. When they learn that the victim is to be Norma herself, everyone is up in arms. The strength and steadfastness of his former ladyfriend reawakens Pollione's love for the suicidal Druid and he expresses his renewed devotion. Norma gets assurances from her father that her kids will be taken care of, and, with Pollione at her side, walks into the flames.

ALBAN BERG 1885–1935

Berg wasn't as aggressively abstract or musically antiestablishment as his mentor, Arnold Schoenberg. Nevertheless, his operas, *Wozzeck* and *Lulu*, can be difficult to swallow for the opera newcomer. Schoenberg's legacy was the creation of the twelve-tone system, a method of composition that

A B C D E F G H I J K L M N O P Q R S T U V W X Y Z

threw to the winds accepted ideas of melody and key in favor of an atonal, often dissonant new brand of music. Indeed, much of the twentieth-century classical-music debate centers on the tonal/atonal conundrum: It's only relatively recently that contemporary composers who tried to create melodic, accessible works weren't deemed backward and anti-intellectual.

Berg's feet were planted firmly in the progressive musical ideology of his teacher. But whereas Schoenberg's few operas focused on broad concepts—rather than finely drawn characters—Berg was a true man of the theater, whose two musical-dramatic works are masterpieces of narrative intensity. If your experience in the world of opera is limited, Berg's music will give your ears little to latch on to. But *Wozzeck* and *Lulu* are both attractive to directors and designers committed to a progressive style of theatricality. Consequently, the experience of a live performance of either piece can be particularly gripping and allow the listener to enter a new harmonic world that, at first, might seem accessible only to classical-music academics. The soprano Constance Hauman once told me of a Copenhagen *Lulu* she did that had throngs of young Danish hipsters in the audience. At a coffeehouse the day after a performance, she saw teenage girls wearing jeans with the words "Ich liebe Lulu" (I love Lulu) written on them in magic marker. The music may be tough to take at first, but once you catch the momentum of one of Berg's operas, you may even start to find it beautiful.

Wozzeck

Libretto by Alban Berg, based on the play *Woyzeck* by Georg
   Büchner
Premiere: Staatsoper, Berlin, 1925
Scene: Leipzig, 1820s

ACT I SCENE I Wozzeck, a poor soldier who works for extra money at a variety of odd jobs, is administering a shave to the Captain, who starts rambling about various philosophical issues, including illegitimacy. Wozzeck, who has a bastard child with the wanton Marie, asserts that his son is as entitled as anyone to religious salvation. This doesn't sit well with the Captain, who claims that bearing children out of wedlock is immoral. Wozzeck protests that poor folks like him have no time for that kind of morality.

SCENE 2 Wozzeck and his soldier buddy, Andres, are chopping wood on the outskirts of Leipzig. Increasingly worn down by poverty and responsibility, Wozzeck starts hallucinating; he thinks the field is haunted. Andres tries to distract him by singing until they are called back to the officers' quarters.

SCENE 3 Marie, holding her young son, stares out the window of her apartment at a group of soldiers marching past. Her friend Margret scolds her for waving flirtatiously at the Drum-Major. Marie turns her attention to the kid, whom she lulls to sleep with a song. Wozzeck arrives and unnerves Marie with talk of the visions he's just experienced in the field. He leaves Marie alone to ponder their troubled relationship.

SCENE 4 Wozzeck is in the office of a Doctor, who pays the soldier a small sum to act as a guinea pig in various scientific experiments. The soldier is going on about his hallucinations, which intrigues the medical man. He finds Wozzeck all the more interesting for his delusional tendencies.

SCENE 5 The Drum-Major, having noticed Marie's attentions, returns to her apartment. After a moment's conversation, he makes a move, which the woman rebuffs. Her resistance is weak, however. She finds him attractive and invites him in.

ACT II SCENE 1 The Drum-Major has left, and Marie is at home admiring in a broken mirror (broken mirror...bad luck...get it?) the earrings her new lover has given her. She once again sings the child to sleep. Wozzeck shows up, and she tears off the earrings, which he nonetheless notices. She indignantly claims to have found the jewels. In order to avoid a fight, Wozzeck gives Marie some money rather than confront her. This only serves to make Marie feel awful and guilty once Wozzeck has left.

SCENE 2 The Doctor and the Captain run into each other on the street and engage in an uncomfortable discussion of death. When Wozzeck ambles by, his two employers start dropping hints about Marie and the Drum-Major (news travels fast). Wozzeck, anxious and delusional, is susceptible to taunts like this and says he should probably just hang himself. He rushes off in an agitated state as the Doctor and the Captain thank their lucky stars they're not like Wozzeck.

SCENE 3 Wozzeck arrives at Marie's house and starts questioning her about the Drum-Major. She denies anything and, feeling uneasy, claims that she'd rather be stabbed to death than threatened. Wozzeck's already warped mind starts reeling.

SCENE 4 That night, Wozzeck wanders into the local bar, where he sees Marie and the Drum-Major dancing. As he approaches the illicit

A
B
C
D
E
F
G
H
I
J
K
L
M
N
O
P
Q
R
S
T
U
V
W
X
Y
Z

couple, the dance ends, and Wozzeck's friend Andres launches into a hunting song like the one he sang in the field. After the song, Andres and a disturbed Wozzeck chat briefly until an apprentice seizes everyone's attention with an intoxicated sermon on drunkenness. A mentally impaired barfly approaches Wozzeck and claims to smell blood. Thoughts of blood and death fill Wozzeck's head.

SCENE 5 Later, Wozzeck, Andres, and other soldiers are back at the officers' quarters, but Wozzeck can't sleep. The Drum-Major, stinking drunk, shows up and begins teasing Wozzeck about Marie. Wozzeck tries to remain calm, but a scuffle ensues, with the Drum-Major pushing Wozzeck to the floor in disgrace. The Drum-Major departs, leaving Wozzeck dazed and confused.

ACT III SCENE 1 Depressed and wracked with guilt, Marie sullenly reads from the Bible, while her young son frets about his mother's peculiar state. Marie scans the Good Book for passages about forgiveness and salvation.

SCENE 2 That evening, Marie and Wozzeck are strolling through the woods on the outskirts of town. They sit by a pool of water and Wozzeck bizarrely reminisces about the early days of their relationship. He leans over to kiss Marie, who nervously pushes him away, eager to get home. The rebuff sends Wozzeck over the edge: He pulls out a knife and stabs Marie in the throat. She drops dead. He flees.

SCENE 3 The murderer repairs to the tavern, where he joins in the song and revelry. He flirts with Marie's friend Margret, who spots bloodstains on Wozzeck's hands. He claims to have cut himself, but the crowd's suspicion has been raised. He races out of the bar and heads to . . .

SCENE 4 . . . the forest pond, where he finds Marie's corpse. Nearly hysterical, Wozzeck searches for the bloody knife, which he discovers shortly. He tosses the knife into the pond and begins wading into the water after it. He goes deeper and deeper until, finally, he drowns. As it happens, the Doctor and the Captain are strolling by. They make out sounds of the drowning man but cannot identify what exactly it is that they hear. Unnerved, they rush off.

SCENE 5 A famously beautiful and haunting orchestral interlude connects this scene with the one before it. Children are playing in front of Marie's house. A few other kids show up and inform Marie's son that his mother is dead. The news has little effect on the youngster, who continues to ride his hobbyhorse. After a moment, the child runs after his friends.

Lulu

Libretto by Alban Berg, based on two plays by Frank Wedekind
Premiere: Staadttheater, Zurich, 1937
Scene: Germany, late nineteenth century

PROLOGUE A circus Animal Tamer addresses the audience directly, calling on them to check out the trained animals. One of these beasts is Lulu, whom he likens to a snake.

ACT I SCENE I Lulu is posing for the Painter, who paints her portrait. Although she is married to the Doctor, Lulu has lovers, one of whom, the newspaper editor Dr. Schön, is observing the portrait session. Schön's composer son Alwa shows up and the two depart together; the Painter seizes the opportunity and begins putting the moves on his subject. After a few minutes of flirtatious cat-and-mouse, Lulu's husband arrives, breaking down the door. When he beholds his wife alone with the Painter, he drops dead on the spot. Heartless Lulu has no time for mourning: All she can do is celebrate the fortune she's just inherited.

SCENE 2 Lulu and the Painter have married and set up house. The couple is contemplating news and mail in their well-appointed living room when the doorbell rings, announcing the arrival of Schigolch, an old derelict with whom Lulu apparently has some history. He asks Lulu for money. Dr. Schön shows up just as Lulu sends Schigolch away. He casually lets it slip that the old man could be Lulu's father before speaking of his impending nuptials to a society lady. The Painter comes back in and Lulu leaves the two men alone together. Dr. Schön provides the Painter with some clues as to the nature of his relationship with Lulu. The news that Schön and Lulu are having an affair and that Schön is the source of much of Lulu's income sends the Painter into a tailspin. He locks himself in another room of the house. Lulu reenters with Alwa, with

Lulu

PHOTO BY MARTY SOHL/SAN FRANCISCO OPERA

whose help she breaks down the door to the Painter's room. He has committed suicide, a fact that fails to faze the woman.

SCENE 3 Lulu is appearing in a theatrical performance; this scene opens in her backstage dressing room. Alwa and Lulu are chatting when the Prince, from Africa, shows up seeking Lulu's hand in marriage. Lulu ignores him: Her attention is focused on Dr. Schön. Having seen the editor and his fiancée in the audience, Lulu has staged an unscripted fainting scene, after which she fled the stage, causing a stir. Alwa leaves the pair alone, and Lulu at once informs Schön that he must dump his fiancée in favor of her. At her prompting, Schön composes a letter to his betrothed announcing his intention to end the engagement. Lulu returns to the stage.

ACT II SCENE 1 Predictably, Lulu and Dr. Schön have married. And in marriage, Schön has entered a state of constant jealousy. Even the lesbian Countess Geschwitz, who visits Lulu in this scene, incites his envy. The Countess is joined at the Schön household by a number of guests, including Alwa, Schigolch, a young Schoolboy, and an Acrobat. All attention is fixed on Lulu, who withdraws to a corner to flirt with Alwa. The young man declares his passion for his vixenish stepmother. Schön has been observing the scene and becomes enraged. He produces a gun, which he hands to his wife, instructing her to kill herself. Instead, she turns the gun on Schön, shooting him in the back. As he dies, Schön warns his son to beware the wayward murderess. Alwa holds Lulu until the authorities arrive.

SCENE 2 This scene is introduced by an orchestral interlude. Lulu is in jail for killing her husband, but her motley band of admirers has hatched a plan to set her free. Schigolch and the Countess depart for the jail, leaving Alwa and the Acrobat, who plans to marry Lulu and employ her in the circus. Moments later, Schigolch reappears with Lulu, who is decked out in Countess Geschwitz's clothes (they've surreptitiously traded places to effect the jailbreak). The escapee has been afflicted with cholera; her weakened state blows any chances of her entering the circus, a fact that sends the Acrobat into a rage. He rushes off, threatening to expose the woman. Alwa, however, reiterates his love for Dad's killer.

ACT III SCENE 1 Lulu and Alwa have fled Germany, settling in Paris, where they are just now hosting a glamorous party in their fabulous apartment. The guests are celebrating the riches they've acquired by owning shares of railway stock. One of the guests, the Marquis, is aware that Lulu is on the lam, and he hatches a plan to sell her to a Cairo whorehouse.

The Acrobat also blackmails her, threatening to expose her to German authorities unless she hands over a hefty stack of cash. The revelry is interrupted by the news that the railway market has crashed. Lulu, who has run through all the money that's ever come her way, is all but ruined. The Acrobat's plot to extort money is shot to hell. Schigolch shows up and, learning of Lulu's state of affairs, offers to rub the Acrobat out of the picture. They set a plot in motion. Having angered the Acrobat, Lulu fears, rightly, that he's called the police. She changes clothes with a young male party guest and escapes with Alwa in the nick of time.

SCENE 2 The impoverished triumvirate of Lulu, Alwa, and Schigolch has made its way to London, where Lulu is turning tricks. Countess Geschwitz, unerringly devoted to Lulu, arrives with the Act I portrait of the heroine in tow. Everyone gazes at the painting and ponders the decay of Lulu's looks. Lulu and one of her johns, a Black Man, argue about her requirement of advance payment. Alwa foolishly gets into the action and is killed by the client. The unflappable Lulu runs out briefly to pick up another customer, with whom another financial dispute arises. They withdraw to her room to settle matters as the Countess at last resolves to let go of her devotion to Lulu and get her life together. Her plans are interrupted by a scream. Lulu's luck has run out: Her angry client, Jack (as in the Ripper—no joke), has killed her. On his way out of the apartment, he stabs the Countess as well. With Lulu's name on her lips, Geschwitz follows her beloved into death.

GEORGES BIZET 1838–1875

Along with Puccini's *La Bohème*, Verdi's *Aida*, and a handful of others, Bizet's *Carmen* is among the world's most popular operas (perhaps because its heroine is opera's sexiest cock-tease). Even opera novices find that they are familiar with the work's numerous tuneful passages. As a result, it's hard to fathom that at its 1875 premiere, *Carmen* was an unmitigated disaster, considered vulgar and offensive by the (who knew?) conservative Paris audiences. Up to the point of his most famous work, Bizet was known as a technically brilliant musician, whose stage works, though impressive, generally failed to thrill listeners. With *Carmen*, the composer felt that all that would change: His work was melodic, dramatically gripping, and inventive—audiences were sure to respond. And they did,

Carmen

though not with the open arms and cries of "Bravo!" that Bizet had antici-
pated. The opera's titular vixen was considered sluttish and undignified,
and her Act IV murder on stage was positively appalling. Bizet was
crushed. *Carmen*'s disastrous reception, coupled with the composer's
already poor health, probably contributed to Bizet's death three months
later at the age of thirty-six (or so melodramatic opera queens would have
you believe).

Needless to say, *Carmen* lived on long after its creator, and within a
matter of a few years was viewed to be a groundbreaking work and a forerunner of the movement known as verismo (a naturalistic approach to
opera with a focus on the passions and tendencies of realistic characters),
which would come to be the predominant operatic form of the late nineteenth and early twentieth centuries. Part of the opera's appeal lies in the
fact that Carmen is a man-eater. She can be perceived as a one-dimensional
example of female carnality, or she can be viewed as a feminist icon,
opera's first independent woman, in search of pleasure and unwilling to
submit to the force of a single man. Either way, the character is endlessly
fascinating and gets to sing some of the sexiest music ever written. Similarly, her tenor costar, Don José, lies somewhere along the continuum
between male chauvinist pig and sensitive guy driven nuts by love for his
woman. With sex as its subject matter and with a plethora of fabulous,
hummable tunes (not to mention the fact that it lacks the superschmaltzy

sentimentality of much of the standard repertory), *Carmen* is a perennial audience fave for good reason.

Carmen

Libretto by Ludovic Halévy and Henri Meilhac, based on the
   novella by Prosper Mérimée
Premiere: Opéra-Comique, Paris, 1875
Scene: Seville, around 1820–30

ACT I Soldiers are hanging out in the square in front of their guard-house. The pretty, virginal peasant girl Micaëla shows up, in search of the corporal Don José, and is immediately hit on by another corporal, Moralès. She flees, the townsfolk mill about some more, and Don José arrives to be informed that Micaëla, his foster sister and girlfriend (oddly enough), has been looking for him. Another officer, Zuniga, makes chitchat with José about the hotties who work at the cigarette factory, but José claims to be interested only in Micaëla. Shortly, the cigarette-factory girls hit the scene, on a break from work. Supersexy Carmen is immediately the center of attention. When will they get a shot to date her? the officers ask. Carmen, chronic flirt that she is, launches into an aria about love ("L'amour est un oiseau rebelle"), suggesting that the officers do have a chance with her, but that they should beware of her ferocious, insatiable nature. The only guy to ignore the gypsy during this seduction aria is Don José; as Carmen departs, she launches a flower at him flirtatiously. Micaëla returns with a message for Don José from his mother. The peasant girl lives with the old woman, who wants nothing more than for her son and her adopted daughter to marry, as she indicates in the letter. The two sing a love duet, but it's clear that Micaëla is too dull for José, who, we suspect, has a thing for Carmen. Micaëla leaves and a ruckus is immediately raised: Someone in the cigarette factory has been stabbed by Carmen. Throngs of hysterical cigarette-factory girls emerge, including Carmen, in the custody of Zuniga. Don José ties up the gypsy and tends guard while Zuniga goes off to seek help. At a slight distance from the rest of the crowd, Carmen begins another maddeningly sexy number ("Près des remparts de Séville"), which taunts the corporal for being in love with her. The song (known as the seguidilla) persuades Don José to loosen the ropes binding Carmen's hands and run away with her. Taken in by the sluttish gypsy and overcome with desire, José undoes the rope. She gives him a powerful shove and he falls to the ground (in the dubious world of opera, an ensnared gypsy girl is capable of feats of near superhuman strength). Carmen rushes off as the curtain falls.

ACT II A few months have elapsed since Carmen's escape. She's waiting for Don José to arrive and hanging out with fellow party girls Mercédès and Frasquita in the tavern of their friend Lillas Pastia. A group of bullfighting enthusiasts arrives with the matador Escamillo, who sings of his many bullring successes. There's a clear spark between him and Carmen, but the gypsy is committed to waiting for José, who has been imprisoned for letting her go. Pastia closes the tavern for the night; only Carmen, Mercédès, Frasquita, and their smuggler buddies, Dancaïre and Remendado, remain to plot their next illegal activity. Carmen protests that she cannot join them—she's waiting for José, who arrives shortly. The group invites the corporal to join their band. Carmen dances another of her sexy routines, but is interrupted by the sounds of distant bugles, the signal for José to return to the barracks. José attempts to leave but is jeered at by Carmen for his blind loyalty. Won't he join the group for a life of pleasure and freedom? José demurs when, suddenly, Zuniga hits the scene, in lascivious search of Carmen. He orders José to return to the barracks, but it's too late: José declares himself a member of the unit of thieves.

ACT III Carmen, Don José, and the smugglers are in mountainous terrain, singing about their risky but exciting lives. José can see in the distance the home of his mother, and he laments the fact that he has disappointed her. Carmen is hardly sympathetic; it becomes clear that she's fixing to dump him. She ignores her tormented paramour to read tarot cards, which suggest that both she and José are headed for destruction. The latest smuggling project must be tended to, however, and Carmen and her friends sing about how easy it is to disarm the soldiers by using their womanly charms. They leave; Micaëla improbably totters in and sings an aria conveying her desire to save her beloved José. At the conclusion of the aria (conveniently), she notices José in the distance, but hides when Escamillo enters looking for Carmen. The matador deduces that the angry man in front of him is Carmen's lover, and a knife fight erupts, from which Escamillo is saved only by the entrance of the gypsy woman. Escamillo departs, but not without challenging José to a fight (at an unspecified later date). Micaëla emerges from hiding and begs José to visit his dying mother. Carmen encourages him to get the hell out. But the corporal's departing promise is to remain faithful to the maddening gypsy.

ACT IV An excited and rowdy crowd is milling about outside the Seville bullring. Escamillo arrives and the throngs erupt in cheers. The bull-fighter spies Carmen and offers a few flirtatious words of love. Frasquita and Mercédès warn Carmen that they've seen a half-crazed Don José, who's on the lam. The fearless gypsy agrees to speak with José, but she treats him with bitchy indifference. José pleads with Carmen to leave with him, but she instead heads into the bullfighting venue to get with Escamillo. This proves to be the final straw: José snaps and stabs the woman, falling to the ground in immediate remorse. The crowds return to the horrifying spectacle of the prone crazy man clutching a dead woman. Don José surrenders to authorities, wailing about having commit-ted the savage murder.

BENJAMIN BRITTEN 1913–1976

Benjamin Britten is something of an anomaly among the titans of twentieth-century opera. While Berg, Schoenberg, and (for a time) Strauss churned out works that were self-consciously modern and dissonant, Britten wrote operas with music that most regular folks could actually enjoy. The assaultive, aggressively unpleasant sounds of, say, *Elektra* held no charms for the Suffolk native, whose reputation suffered for a time due to the rela-tive accessibility (and, as a result, presumed mediocrity) of his music.

Fortunately, however, it didn't take long for Britten to be accepted as a supreme contributor to the operatic canon, with *Peter Grimes* remaining per-haps his greatest achievement. At the work's premiere, the title role was sung by Britten's longtime companion, Peter Pears, and it's hard not to notice the impact of the composer's homosexuality on his choice of subject matter. His musical adaptation of *Death in Venice* was an openly gay piece, and *Billy Budd,* with its Adonis-like protagonist and all-male cast of sea-men . . . well, you get the picture. Debate continues to swirl around *Grimes,* however. Most audiences pick up on the character's unusual predilection for young boys (Britten himself had a lifelong fascination with boys, an impulse he never acted on), but certain interpreters do not agree (improbably) that

Grimes features a gay subtext. What everyone agrees on, though, is that the work, although easy on the ears, is modern in its own right. Grimes's downfall and death is not the result of an impossible love (as in most nineteenth-century opera) but is, rather, the result of his ostracism from society. Grimes is the quintessential twentieth-century outsider, whose downward spiral is effected by the relentless gossip of the Borough's inhabitants. Indeed, the chorus plays a principal role in the unraveling of the narrative; the work boasts some of the greatest choral music in all of opera. The orchestra has it pretty good as well, with between-scene interludes compelling enough to stand alone in a concert setting.

Peter Grimes

Libretto by Montagu Slater, based on the poem "The Borough"
   by George Crabbe
Premiere: Sadler's Wells, London, 1945
Scene: An English fishing village in the 1830s

PROLOGUE Inside Moot Hall, a group of townies has formed to witness testimony by Peter Grimes, a fisherman whose young male apprentice has mysteriously died. The lawyer Swallow questions the seaman, who claims that nasty weather kept his boat at sea for several days, during which time the boy died due to lack of nourishment. Although the town's gossips, especially Mrs. Sedley, aren't entirely sold on this story, Swallow accepts it and instructs Grimes to avoid using boys as apprentices in the future. Grimes protests that he needs help; Swallow suggests that Grimes marry in order to have a wife to look after any kids that may come into his service. Everyone departs, leaving Grimes alone with the schoolmistress Ellen Orford, the only person in the courtroom crowd to display any sympathy for the outcast.

ACT I SCENE I It's early morning in the Borough, and the townsfolk—including Auntie, the innkeeper; Captain Balstrode; and the apothecary, Ned Keene—are milling about around the harbor. Peter Grimes arrives, apprenticeless, and enlists the aid of Keene and Balstrode, the only folks willing to help the poor man. Grimes learns of a potential new apprentice, but the cart driver, Hobson, refuses to pick him up on the grounds that Grimes is not to be trusted with young boys. Ellen Orford offers to come along and care for the child. Few of the townsfolk approve, but the pair heads off anyway to fetch the boy. In the meantime, the town's resident snoop, Mrs. Sedley, a morphine addict, consults Keene about acquiring a fresh stash. The weather suddenly takes a turn for the worse: A storm is approaching. The crowd runs for shelter as Balstrode and Grimes shoot the breeze. Balstrode recommends that his friend leave town, but Grimes is insistent that he stay and clear his name. He wants to make a little money and marry Ellen in order to earn the respect of the townsfolk.

SCENE 2 Mrs. Sedley, Balstrode, and others are hanging out in Auntie's tavern, the Boar. The storm outside is out of control, prompting Auntie's frightened "nieces" (presumably prostitutes) to come downstairs. The fisherman Bob Boles flirts aggressively with the young ladies until Balstrode calms him down. Ned Keene shows up announcing that there has been a rock slide near Peter's house. Grimes himself stumbles in like a lunatic, with an existential rant that no one can understand. Balstrode has just managed to subdue Grimes when Ellen enters with the new apprentice. Grimes seizes the young boy and they exit together, to the consternation of everyone present.

ACT II SCENE 1 A few weeks later, as the rest of the town heads off to church, Ellen and the boy decide to skip services and sit outside instead. Ellen notices a bruise on the boy's neck, as well as a tear in his clothing. Grimes arrives and insists on taking the boy out fishing. Ellen objects, suggesting that the boy has been worked hard enough for one week, but Grimes will not be crossed. When Ellen laments that perhaps she should not have committed herself to the troubled man, he hits her and takes off with the boy. The principal townsfolk have all noticed the deed and sing the haunting refrain that "Grimes is at his exercise." The people are incensed and determine to go to Grimes's hut and demand an explanation. Ellen, Auntie, and the nieces are left to sing a gorgeous quartet about the nature of male-female relationships.

SCENE 2 Back at the shack, Grimes is angrily preparing the boy for an afternoon at sea. He is harsh, but his cruelty is tempered by recollections of his previous (dead) apprentice. As his neighbors approach, Grimes ushers the boy out the back door, instructing him to quickly descend the cliff to the boat. Just as his interrogators arrive, Grimes hears a scream: In his haste, the boy has fallen to his death. Grimes hurries after him, leaving an empty dwelling for the others to inspect. They admire the tidy little house and quickly depart, assuming all's well—except Balstrode, who follows through the slightly ajar back door.

ACT III SCENE 1 Moot Hall, site of Grimes's initial inquisition, is now the home of a public dance. The atmosphere is one of revelry, until gossip maven Mrs. Sedley observes that Grimes and his charge have been missing for some time. The party winds down and everyone goes home, except Mrs. Sedley, who hides when she notices Ellen and Balstrode walking by. They are discussing the fact that Grimes's boat has been spotted in the harbor but there has been no sign of the boy. Ellen admits to having discovered the kid's sweater, which she personally embroidered, down by the waterfront. Balstrode calls on Swallow and Hobson to help him search for Grimes as Mrs. Sedley eavesdrops.

SCENE 2 Late that night, Grimes has all but lost it. He stumbles through a thick fog toward his boat, the sounds of the villagers calling his name in the distance shattering his already fragile nerves. Ellen and Balstrode arrive with offerings of comfort, but it becomes clear that Grimes is crazed and past helping. They usher Grimes into his boat, which Balstrode instructs him to sink once he gets far enough out to sea. A bewildered Grimes agrees to the command and sails off. Morning breaks and the Borough residents once again engage in their daily routine. Out of sight, Grimes is apparently already out of mind.

CLAUDE DEBUSSY 1862–1918

In today's world, when opera premieres tend to produce only the slightest ripple of excitement, it's hard to fathom the profound and divisive effect the unveiling of Debussy's only complete opera had on Paris. Debussy's rabid detractors were as ferocious as his supporters, and it's said that bar brawls over the worth of *Pelléas et Mélisande* were not uncommon back in 1902. Ironically, one of Debussy's staunchest opponents was his librettist, Maurice Maeterlinck, who, incensed that the composer had cast the accomplished soprano Mary Garden as Mélisande rather than the librettist's mistress, initiated a public smear campaign urging audiences and critics to skip the opera's premiere.

Despite Maeterlinck's irrational attempts at sabotage, *Pelléas* was nevertheless quick to garner a reputation as a groundbreaking work. Like Wagner (whom he alternately idolized and dismissed), Debussy was preoccupied with eloquently fusing the various elements that go into any opera production. He felt, like Wagner, that showstopping arias would only interrupt the narrative; consequently, much of *Pelléas* sounds like one long recitative. But although Debussy sought to make the piece flow as smoothly as possible, the opera hardly had an Aristotelian unraveling of the plot. Several scenes seem to simply end without the expected resolution, and the love between the title characters seems to emerge out of thin air rather than as the result of any shared experience or set of circumstances. Gripes like this didn't bother Debussy, though. Known as an impressionist composer (who created works, like those of his painter counterparts, that aimed to evoke a feeling or mood rather than a realistic rendering of a given subject), he wanted *Pelléas* to seem more like a dream than a tightly constructed narrative. And he certainly succeeded: The opera's score has a rapturous and languid quality that seems to seep into listeners' consciousnesses. The tasteful, simple beauty of the music, combined with the relative abstraction of the setting, make *Pelléas et Mélisande* a lovely and moving experience.

Pelléas et Mélisande

Libretto by Maurice Maeterlinck
Premiere: Opéra-Comique, Paris, 1902
Scene: A mythical locale in medieval times

ACT I SCENE I Prince Golaud is wandering around a mythical forest, lost, when he encounters a young girl sitting terrified by the edge of a pool of water. As Golaud approaches, the girl warns him not to touch her, threatening to fling herself into the pond if he comes too close. The prince starts asking questions about where the girl is from and what she's doing here, but all he can get out of her is her name: Mélisande. Golaud offers to bring the fearful creature home with him (although he himself is unsure of his whereabouts); the forest is unsafe for a young girl all alone. Finally, Mélisande succumbs to his pleas and they depart together.

SCENE 2 Six months later, back at Golaud's castle, his mother, Geneviève, is reading a letter aloud to Golaud's grandfather, King Arkel. The letter was written by Golaud to his half-brother, Pelléas (Geneviève's other son), and tells of the discovery of Mélisande, whom Golaud has married. Golaud is wondering whether it's safe to come home; will his family accept his enigmatic new bride? Pelléas enters, depressed over the recent discovery that a close friend is terminally ill. Arkel, however, instructs his grandson not to visit the dying man; he must remain at the

137

castle and signal to Golaud that it's okay to return. Without having met Mélisande, the family is nonetheless pleased that the prince has remarried after the death of his previous wife, who left Golaud with the responsibility of a young son, Yniold.

SCENE 3 Golaud and Mélisande have recently arrived at the castle. While Golaud is occupied elsewhere, Geneviève gives her new daughter-in-law the grand tour. Pelléas enters, and the three watch as the ship that had delivered the newlyweds to safety sails off. Geneviève exits to tend to some domestic affairs, leaving Pelléas and Mélisande to get to know each other. Pelléas announces that he'll be leaving soon to minister to his dying friend, but despite his imminent departure it's clear that there's an immediate spark between the new in-laws.

ACT II SCENE 1 Pelléas and Mélisande are getting a little too close for comfort. This scene opens with the pair sitting together near a fountain on the castle grounds. Mélisande absentmindedly paddles the water with her hand and is horrified when the ring Golaud has given her falls off into the pool. She's panicked that they won't be able to recover it. Expected back at the castle, they have no time to search for the ring. Pelléas asserts that if Golaud asks what has happened to the gift they must tell the truth.

SCENE 2 Improbably, at the precise moment the ring fell off Mélisande's hand, her husband was flung from his horse. He now lies in bed as

Pelléas et Mélisande

his young wife tends to him. Golaud senses that the girl is bored in her new life in the castle and tries to comfort her. He becomes alarmed, however, when he notices that the ring is missing. Needless to say, Mélisande lies about what happened (for no good reason), claiming it fell off in a cave. Golaud sends the unhappy woman out with Pelléas to look for the ring.

SCENE 3 Pelléas and Mélisande know perfectly well that the ring is nowhere near the cave, but they head there anyway to keep up appearances. In the cave, they stumble on three homeless men, whose presence unnerves the already anxious girl. They head back to the castle.

ACT III SCENE 1 Rapunzel-like, Mélisande leans out a window of the castle and lets down her unbelievably long hair. Down below, Pelléas walks by, stops to chat, and starts playing with the girl's hair. Golaud approaches but Mélisande cannot withdraw because her hair is caught in the branches of a tree. Observing the childish pair, Golaud instructs them to act their age and moves on with Pelléas in tow.

SCENE 2 Golaud leads Pelléas to the castle's eerie underground vaults, where he confronts his half-brother about his blossoming relationship with Mélisande. Pelléas feels ill in the cold and damp basement. They leave.

SCENE 3 Outside, a moment later, Golaud warns Pelléas not to get too close to Mélisande. He even suggests that she may be pregnant. It would be unwise to upset the girl in her weakened condition.

SCENE 4 Golaud, increasingly annoyed by the affection shared by Pelléas and Mélisande, confronts his son, Yniold, about the nature of the in-laws' relationship: What do they talk about when Golaud's not around? The boy's replies don't indicate a whole lot. The duo generally just chats amiably. There's no evidence of any serious wrongdoing, but Golaud is not entirely convinced of the pair's innocence. His jealousy is starting to get the best of him. The window of Mélisande's room lights up. Golaud picks up his son and has him peer inside and describe what he sees. Pelléas is there, all right, but nothing's going on. Uncomfortable, the boy demands to be put down.

ACT IV SCENE 1 Pelléas informs Mélisande that he's been with his sick father (whose whereabouts are never disclosed and who is never seen in the opera); the old man has advised Pelléas to travel away from the castle. They plan to meet later that night at the fountain to discuss the matter. Arkel enters and offers some kind words to the clearly disturbed Mélisande. Golaud follows shortly after, demonstrating a considerably less embracing attitude than his grandfather's. His jealousy is quickly gathering steam. In a rage, he pushes her down and starts dragging her around the room by her copious hair. Arkel somehow manages to calm him down and he leaves the woman alone to weep.

SCENE 2 In a symbol of impending doom, Yniold, playing in a field on the castle grounds, becomes anxious when he observes a group of sheep being led to the slaughterhouse. He runs back to the castle, making room for a confused Pelléas, who is followed closely by Mélisande. Pelléas announces that he is leaving—but not before he and the girl declare their love for one another. They hear the gates to the castle crashing shut and sense that Golaud is on the warpath. Sure enough, the prince enters, breaks apart the hugging couple, and kills Pelléas with a sword.

ACT V Back at the castle, Mélisande (who was nicked by the sword in the scuffle) has fallen into a deep slumber, as Golaud reflects sorrowfully on what he's done. Arkel—the only sane one of the bunch—worries about Mélisande's health. While unconscious, she gave birth to a baby girl, and she's now showing the full effects of her condition. Golaud frets over the ailing woman until Arkel sends him away in order to let the girl die in peace. As Mélisande's life slips away, Arkel turns his attentions to Mélisande's baby daughter and contemplates her future.

GAETANO DONIZETTI 1797–1848

Like his bel canto comrade Bellini, Donizetti owes much of the revival of interest in his works to the rescue efforts of Maria Callas and Joan Sutherland. Although *L'Elisir d'Amore* and *Lucia di Lammermoor* were never significantly excluded from the repertory for particularly long stretches, it wasn't until the 1950s that many of Donizetti's sixty-plus other operas were considered seriously. Much of the neglect stemmed from the fact that the complex orchestrations and dramatic viability of operas by Wagner and Verdi, among others, made the less ambitious works of Donizetti, Bellini, and Rossini seem half-assed by comparison. This charge, however, is a little unfair with regard to Donizetti, who made concerted efforts to ensure that his operas didn't consist solely of one vocal showstopper after another, held together by the thinnest of threads.

Indeed, the comic *L'Elisir d'Amore* in particular can lay claim to a list of moving and recognizable characters. The country bumpkin and the haughty rich girl may certainly be stock theatrical types, but the combination of Felice Romani's libretto and Donizetti's tunes makes them lovable and vivid. The overwrought tragedy of *Lucia* is a little less dramatically successful (indeed, many critics who are fixated on narrative plausibility simply hate this opera), but if you're a lover of spectacular, show-off singing, you'll find much to admire.

L'Elisir d'Amore
Libretto by Felice Romani
Premiere: Teatro della Canobbiana, Milan, 1832
Scene: A Basque village in the 1830s

ACT 1 SCENE I The rich and beautiful Adina sits reading on her farm as the worker Nemorino gazes at her admiringly and sings an aria declaring how beautiful—and out of reach—she is ("Quanto è bella"). As the farm workers gather, Adina reads aloud the story of Tristan and Isolde; Nemorino and the peasant girl Giannetta are particularly intrigued by the tale's description of a powerful love potion. A group of soldiers arrives on the scene; Sergeant Belcore immediately hits on Adina, handing her a bouquet of flowers and comparing her to Helen of Troy. Nemorino is pained by the appearance of this rival, and when Belcore departs he expresses his feelings to Adina. The woman is flattered but warns the young man that, like most rich young beauties, she doesn't quite know what she wants.

SCENE 2 The country "doctor," Dulcamara, arrives in the village peddling his wares: bottles of ineffective medicines that he claims can cure all manner of illness. Poor Nemorino (not exactly a Rhodes scholar) is taken in by the quack and asks if he has any of that stuff that worked so well on Isolde. He does! Dulcamara takes the last of Nemorino's cash in exchange for the phony elixir (the bottle actually contains wine), which Dulcamara claims takes a day to kick in. Nemorino immediately pounds the liquid, and when Adina enters soon after, he behaves cockily, convinced the woman will be his within twenty-four hours. Since women are drawn to arrogant, indifferent men in the pre-Gender Studies era of the opera, Adina's interest in Nemorino is instantly piqued. Belcore enters and, as usual, is all over Adina. Hoping to provoke Nemorino's jealousy, she accepts Belcore's marriage proposal. With his platoon set to depart the

A
B
C
D
E
F
G
H
I
J
K
L
M
N
O
P
Q
R
S
T
U
V
W
X
Y
Z

next day, the sergeant suggests that they tie the knot right away. All of a sudden, Nemorino is not so confident. He begs Adina to hold off her nuptials for just one day, but she refuses, sending the boy back into a state of lovelorn depression.

ACT II SCENE 1 Back at the farm, the wedding festivities have begun, with Dulcamara and Adina providing entertainment with a rousing duet. A wedding officiator arrives to oversee the signing of the marriage license, but Adina is hesitant because Nemorino is not around for her to taunt, provoke, and humiliate. Belcore is perturbed and quickly leads his fiancée off to another room to get down to the business of signing the papers. Nemorino ambles in morosely and chats with Dulcamara, who offers him a second batch of the elixir, claiming that this new dose takes instant effect. Nemorino, however, is broke. Belcore and Adina come back; she's managed to put off the legalizing of the marriage. In a sudden flash of inspiration, the country bumpkin realizes that he can earn twenty bucks right away if he enlists in Belcore's army. He does, and, having seized the funds, races off after Dulcamara in search of the bogus potion.

SCENE 2 Friendly Giannetta opens this final scene, revealing to some friends the news that Nemorino has come into a large sum of money. He hasn't been told yet, but a rich uncle has died and left him everything. The boy wanders in, drunk on "elixir," and is surprised and gratified when the girls all flock to him. The drug really works! Adina and Dulcamara enter as Nemorino leaves amid a swarm of flirtatious ladies. The doctor explains to her that Nemorino enlisted solely to obtain the funds that would allow him to buy the elixir and thus win Adina. She is visibly moved, prompting Dulcamara to offer her some of the elixir, which, to his surprise, appears to really be working. But Adina claims she doesn't need any potion—she's sexy enough to win a man on her own. They exit, and Nemorino returns, singing the beautiful, powerhouse aria "Una furtiva lagrima," about Adina's changing attitude. When the woman comes back, Nemorino again plays it cool, but he cannot keep up the act when Adina tells him that she has bought back his independence from the service. They declare their love for each other and kiss as Belcore and the others return to the scene. Pompous Belcore is annoyed at Adina's betrayal, but declares that there are loads of women the world over who would kill to have him. Dulcamara cites Adina and Nemorino as proof that his elixir works, and throngs of villagers crowd around him to purchase some for themselves.

Lucia di Lammermoor

Libretto by Salvatore Cammarano, based on *The Bride of Lammermoor* by Sir Walter Scott

Premiere: Teatro San Carlo, Naples, 1835

Scene: Scotland in the 1600s

ACT I SCENE 1 Enrico and Normanno are on the hunt for their enemy, Edgardo. Enrico and his sister, Lucia, have taken control of Ravenswood Castle, having expelled the Ravenswood family in a political battle. But despite the family feud, Lucia is in love with Edgardo, the principal member of the Ravenswood clan. Enrico has been trying to get his sister to marry the ineffectual Arturo, over whom Enrico would be able to exert considerable influence. Normanno has learned that Lucia has been meeting with someone in regular late-night rendezvous—most likely Edgardo—a bit of news that sends Enrico into a tizzy.

SCENE 2 Lucia is waiting in the nearby Lammermoor Castle park for her secret lover, with her sidekick, Alisa, on the lookout. Right off the bat, the soprano singing Lucia has a lengthy piece of vocal showmanship to deliver: back-to-back arias that tell of the Ravenswood ghost that allegedly watches over the park and of Lucia's own lovelorn state. Edgardo finally shows up with the unfortunate news that he has to go to France on business. He declares his intention to marry Lucia (despite their families' mutual hatred), but Lucia worries about the wisdom of such a move. They sing a love duet and the curtain falls.

ACT II SCENE 1 Enrico and Normanno are discussing their plans to break up Lucia and Edgardo. Normanno has stolen all of Edgardo's letters before they could reach the poor girl, and even forged one asserting that Edgardo intends to marry someone else. Enrico, in the meantime, has arranged for Lucia to marry Arturo and has planned for the wedding to occur that very day. Lucia enters and is given the forged epistle, which sends the girl into a state of despair. Nevertheless, with the help of Raimondo, the chaplain, an unmoved Enrico guides his sister to the altar to exchange vows with a man she doesn't love.

SCENE 2 Arturo, Enrico, and the wedding guests are chilling in the wedding hall, waiting for Lucia. She finally shows up, miserable, and is compelled by her brother to sign the marriage license. Just as Lucia has finished putting pen to paper, Edgardo storms in; somehow, he's heard of Lucia's new betrothal. Edgardo and Enrico are about to come to blows

A
B
C
D
E
F
G
H
I
J
K
L
M
N
O
P
Q
R
S
T
U
V
W
X
Y
Z

when the chaplain intervenes. Edgardo declares his love for the rattled Lucia and asserts to the crowd that they are engaged. When the poor guy is presented with the signed marriage contract, he loses it, condemning Lucia and expressing his wish to die on the spot. Enrico challenges him to a fight at an unspecified later date.

ACT III SCENE 1 Edgardo sits, wretched and alone, in a tower of Ravenswood Castle. Enrico enters and the two are instantly at each other's throats. They agree to meet the next morning in the Ravenswood cemetery to duke it out.

SCENE 2 Back at the great hall, guests are still dancing the night away, celebrating the wedding, when Raimondo rushes in with a tale of horror. Lucia has lost her shit and killed her new husband, stabbing him to death just moments ago. The nutcase herself enters, covered in blood, and, in her famous mad scene, babbles on about how she's about to marry Edgardo. Enrico walks in and is embarrassed and annoyed by his sister's display until he realizes that he in fact is to blame for sending her over the edge. As Lucia's strength fades and she starts to collapse, Alisa comes to her aid.

SCENE 3 Edgardo remains unaware of his loved one's breakdown and waits in the graveyard for his enemy to show up for the big rumble. Having lost Lucia, he is prepared to die. A group of distressed mourners ambles by and informs Edgardo that Lucia is in fact on her deathbed and wants desperately to see him. He races up toward her room but is intercepted by Raimondo, who reveals that Lucia is already dead. This is too much for the unnerved nobleman. He pulls out a dagger and kills himself, to the horror of the onlookers.

GEORGE GERSHWIN 1898–1937

Critics complain that *Porgy and Bess* lacks the unified dramatic cohesiveness of the best operas: It's merely a loose arrangement of catchy tunes held together by a not particularly convincing narrative. But few would argue with the importance of the work as a landmark union of the jazz and classical vernaculars. Gershwin had been imposing classical structures on his jazzy compositions (or jazzy inflections on his classical compositions, depending on how you look at it) for some time. His quasi-concerto for piano, *Rhapsody in Blue,* had been a smash hit, and other endeavors in the realms of piano composition and the Broadway musical had also been well received. The final frontier for Gershwin—now considered by many to be the greatest and most quintessentially "American" of our native composers—was opera.

If a work like *Porgy and Bess* appeared for the first time in today's world, it would be lambasted for its unfortunate representation of blacks as killers, drug dealers, and ho's (not to mention for its objectionable and hackneyed black dialect). But at the time, Gershwin intended *Porgy* as the ultimate celebration of the black musical styles that had so influenced and inspired him. Because the piece straddled the line between opera and musical theater, presenters did not quite know what to do with it. For many years, *Porgy* was staged as a musical, with spoken dialogue used in lieu of Gershwin's recitatives. These days, however, opera houses are more and more interested in examining the opera, generally performing the score as is. Staging the piece can be tricky, though, because the composer and his librettist brother stipulated that the opera could only be performed with an all-black cast. Despite Leontyne Price's successes as Bess, many of today's top black divas have failed to show an interest in *Porgy and Bess;* and assembling an all-black cast of exceptionally trained singers, even in this millennial era, is easier said than done.

Porgy and Bess

Libretto by DuBose Heyward and Ira Gershwin
Premiere: Alvin Theater, New York, 1935
Scene: Catfish Row section of Charleston, S.C., in the late
1930s

ACT I SCENE I Outside her apartment in Charleston's black neighborhood, Catfish Row, Clara sings a jazz standard—er, lullaby—to her baby ("Summertime"). A game of craps forms on the sidewalk. Clara's husband, Jake, takes over for his wife, singing to the infant about the ways of women ("A woman is a sometime thing"). Porgy, a "cripple" (in the unenlightened parlance of the 1930s), wheels himself up on his little cart to join the game. There's talk that Porgy has a thing for Bess, girlfriend of Crown, the local tough. Porgy denies any interest in the woman, adding that it is the lot of the differently abled to be alone. Crown and Bess arrive, and the thug joins in the game, almost immediately entering into an argument with Robbins, another player who's been rolling the dice particularly successfully. Crown's temper flares and he kills his opponent with a cotton hook. He flees and the group of craps shooters breaks up. Catfish Row's resident drug dealer, Sportin' Life, offers to look after Bess, who refuses, unwilling to enter into the inevitable life of crime the man has to offer. The police are fast approaching, so Bess seeks shelter in Porgy's house.

SCENE 2 Grieving townsfolk line up in the home of Serena and Robbins to pay respects to the dead man and make contributions to finance his funeral. When Bess moves to make a donation, Serena refuses the cash, assuming that it's dirty money from Crown. Bess explains that Porgy is looking out for her these days, and Serena softens. The (white) authorities arrive on the scene and start asking questions. They quickly figure out who the murderer is and arrest one of the men, Peter, in the hope that it will hasten the search for Crown. Serena breaks down with the aria "My man's gone now." An undertaker has arrived; Serena is significantly short of the necessary burial funds. The undertaker, however, takes pity on the woman and leaves as Bess sings touchingly of the Promised Land.

ACT II SCENE 1 About a month or so later, the neighborhood fishermen are getting ready to go out for a sail. Bess has moved in with Porgy, a fact that has greatly improved the man's spirits. He sings an upbeat number ("I got plenty o' nuttin'") about the simple pleasures of his existence. Nearby, Sportin' Life has been dealing coke, inciting the ire of Maria, who fears his presence will reflect badly on her store. She pulls out a knife and instructs him to vacate the premises, when Frazier, a lawyer, shows up trying to peddle a legal divorce to Bess from Crown (not that they were ever actually married). Hard on Frazier's heels is Archdale, a white man who offers to post bail for Peter. When a buzzard flies by, Porgy takes it as a nasty omen, launching into the slightly paranoid Buzzard Song. The creature sends most of the crowd indoors, leaving Sportin' Life alone with Bess to offer more proposals of the fast life in New York City. Porgy intervenes and declares his affections (and feelings of propriety) for the woman: "Bess, you is my woman now." The crowd returns, ready to board ship for a picnic on the nearby Kittiwah Island. Porgy, handicapped as he is, can't attend, but he sends Bess to have a good time.

SCENE 2 The revelers are enjoying their island outing when Sportin' Life delivers the morally troublesome song "It ain't necessarily so." Things finally wind down, and the people get back on the boat. Crown, emerging from his island hiding spot, calls to Bess to stay behind with him. When she refuses, he violently drags her into the bushes.

SCENE 3 Later that week, a storm approaches Catfish Row as the fishermen get ready to sail. Bess has been reinstalled at Porgy's house, but her two-day stint on the island has rendered her unwell and anxious. As the locals go about their daily business, occasionally stopping in to check on the invalid, Bess gradually revives to the sight of Porgy watching over her. She expresses her fears that Crown might come back for her, but Porgy reassures her that all will turn out fine. The scene concludes with the onslaught of a major hurricane.

SCENE 4 A small group has assembled at Serena's place to wait out the storm. They are startled and alarmed when Crown busts in and seizes Bess. There is little Porgy can do to help Bess, since he is confined to his cart. Crown sneers at the circle and sings a misogynistic number about his prowess: "A red-headed woman."

ACT III SCENE 1 The violent storm has capsized Jake's boat, drowning the poor man; his wife, Clara, and other women are despondent. Sportin' Life sits around contemplating Bess's sorry state of affairs. Bess is temporarily calm as she sings the "Summertime" lullaby to Clara's now fatherless baby. Crown steals in, heading for Porgy's place and determined to reclaim Bess once and for all. But as Crown nears the doorway, Porgy leans out a window and stabs him. The villain is stunned and weakened; Porgy grabs him by the throat and chokes him to death.

SCENE 2 Once again, the authorities are back at Catfish Row to investigate a murder. Porgy is instructed to head down to HQ to identify the body. As the frightened "cripple" is led off, relentless Sportin' Life reiterates to Bess his offer of escape ("There's a boat dat's leavin' soon for New York"). Bess once again refuses, but her will is weakening and Sportin' Life knows it.

SCENE 3 Afraid of crumbling if he looked on Crown's corpse, Porgy has been held in police custody for his refusal to identify the body. Now, a week later, he's back in the 'hood, having won some cash in a jailhouse craps game. Everyone is pleased to see Porgy safely home, but Bess is nowhere to be seen. Learning that his woman has in fact gone to New York with the drug dealer, Porgy determines to follow her. The others tell him it's a lost cause, but Porgy is undeterred. The curtain falls as he prepares to depart.

PHILIP GLASS 1937–

It may seem that, having appeared in a cameo role in Peter Weir's *The Truman Show* and having been the subject of a *South Park* parody, Philip Glass has finally arrived as a cultural institution. Of course, fans of new music have been following the New York–based composer's work for about thirty years. And listeners really started to take notice in 1976, when Glass unveiled *Einstein on the Beach,* a collaboration with avant-garde director Robert Wilson. The piece immediately created a sensation at the Avignon Festival and subsequently at the Metropolitan Opera House, which was rented out for a series of performances (until recently, the stodgy old Met viewed Glass as far too progressive to actually program one of his works in the company's regular season). Considering the reverence with which *Einstein* is viewed these days, it's startling to think that at the end of the work's first run of performances, Glass had to return to driving a cab and fixing dishwashers to pay his debts.

Glass's music has been conveniently grouped under the umbrella of minimalism, although many critics agree that his work is far too rich and complex to fall easily into that designation. Having picked up a thing or two about Indian musical structures from his studies with sitarist Ravi Shankar, Glass's music is characterized by repeating patterns and overlapping meters. The Asian influence, coupled with the use of synthesizers instead of traditional orchestral instrumentation, helped Glass create a unique and original sound. It was probably inevitable that this new musical language would create a stir when married to the striking visual imagery that Robert Wilson is known for. *Einstein on the Beach* was a true collaboration between the two men, who wanted to create a plotless evocation of the life of a historical figure (Gandhi became the subject of Glass's subsequent opera, *Satyagraha*). The work is more than four hours long and is performed without intermission. But because *Einstein* has no linear narrative to keep up with, audience members are encouraged to wander in and out of the auditorium as they please. Because the piece is like a series of tableaux, concocting a synopsis isn't easy. As a result, my description of the action below should be taken with a grain of salt. If you're lucky enough to attend a performance of Glass and Wilson's musically gorgeous and conceptually stunning "opera," it may end up unfolding quite differently from what you read here. (For the record, I used Glass's excellent book *Music by Philip Glass,* which has a lengthy section about *Einstein on the Beach,* to help me re-create the scene-by-scene synopsis.)

148

Einstein on the Beach

Libretto by Lucinda Childs, Samuel M. Johnson, and Christopher Knowles

Premiere: Avignon Festival, 1976

Scene: Somewhere in the twentieth century

KNEE PLAY 1 A simple theme, played on an electronic keyboard, is already heard in repetition as the audience enters the theater. Two women begin counting as the chorus enters. The ensemble joins in the counting for a while and the lights go down.

ACT I SCENE 1 The true start of the opera is signaled by the entrance of a young boy, who is situated on top of a tower. A woman (dressed, like everyone in the cast, in an Einsteinesque outfit of slacks, a white button-down short-sleeve shirt, suspenders, and sneakers) arrives on the scene to perform a solo dance, during which she holds a pipe. A man pretends to write on a blackboard, as an actual-size train begins moving across the stage. Various dancers enter. The train exits and the stage goes to black.

SCENE 2 The "trial scene" opens with the appearance of the chorus, which sits in a jury box. Einstein, in a corner of the stage, plays violin, while a young woman, positioned as if under cross-examination, reads an abstract speech. At the back of the stage is an enormous clock, which becomes obscured, in a solar eclipse reference. An elderly man delivers a speech about a pair of lovers in Paris, the city of lights.

KNEE PLAY 2 As Einstein continues to play violin, the two women from the first Knee Play recite a strange, semi-sensical text.

ACT II SCENE 1 A spaceship hovers overhead, while the dancer from Act I performs another piece.

SCENE 2 The moon lights up a train, which is positioned in the middle of a field. A couple, decked out in nineteenth-century garb, appears at the caboose and soundlessly acts out a duet, as the chorus is engaged in chanting. The moon becomes obscured (remember the solar eclipse of Act I?), and the couple moves to reenter the train. The woman whips out a gun and points it at her man. He puts his arms above his head and the train continues on.

KNEE PLAY 3   The two women are now in front of some sort of control panel. The chorus, as is its custom, chants for a while before pulling out toothbrushes and pretending to brush their teeth.

ACT III   Scene 1   Act III proper opens with a similar trial scene, although this time part of the stage is outfitted to look like a jailhouse. The "defendant" moves from her position on the witness stand to a bed, where she lies in apparent distress. She delivers a speech about being confined in a heavily air-conditioned supermarket. Throughout the speech, she picks up various props and items of clothing that eventually have her costumed like a mid-bank robbery Patty Hearst.

   Scene 2   A dancer performs in the field of Act II, with the spaceship once again looming.

KNEE PLAY 4   The women lie on glass tables while the chorus chants.

ACT IV   Scene 1   Onlookers stare at Einstein through the window of a building as he furiously writes out equations.

   Scene 2   The bed from Act III slowly levitates as a soprano sings a textless aria.

   Scene 3   We are now inside the spaceship, which is divided into cubes, like the set of *Hollywood Squares*. A glass elevator moves up and down. One by one, the company enters, climbing ladders and assuming positions in the various squares. Lights are flashing like crazy. At the foot of the stage, two pods begin smoking; an astronaut emerges from each of the pods and falls to the ground. The curtain comes down; on it is written $E=MC^2$.

CHARLES GOUNOD   1818–1893

As far as operatic retellings of Goethe's *Faust* story go, I'd put my money on Boito's *Mefistofele* any day. That being said, Gounod's *Faust* is one of the most popular works in the repertory, and you're far more likely to encounter it in your local opera house than you are a production of the Boito piece. People (although not critics, who, frankly, aren't really people anyway) are nuts for this opera, and while I don't really share in the enthusiasm, *Faust*'s nonstop assault of ear-pleasing melody has made it a staple of houses all over the world.

In its initial incarnation, *Faust* was an opéra comique, which is to say the work's numerous tunes were connected by dialogue rather than by recitative. The Parisian Gounod spent several years composing music for this dialogue, eventually turning *Faust* into the quintessential nineteenth-century grand-opera experience. In all, Gounod produced about a dozen operas, with *Roméo et Juliette* trailing *Faust* as the most popular. I'd argue that few of the world's innovative opera directors would show much interest in working with *Faust*. It's really become sort of a museum piece that, owing to its musical charm, manages to regularly pack 'em in. A performance of the Gounod favorite is not likely to have you on the edge of your seat, biting your fingernails, but it will certainly accommodate you if you want to sit back and soak in waves of beautiful sound. And it definitely attracts top singers: Everyone wants to sink their teeth into the vocally lush principal triumvirate of Faust, Marguerite, and Méphistophélès.

Faust
Libretto by Jules Barbier and Michel Carré, based on Goethe's
   play
Premiere: Théâtre-Lyrique, Paris, 1859
Scene: Sixteenth-century Germany

ACT I Dejected Dr. Faust is having a late-night existential dilemma and resolves to kill himself. But joyful singing heard from outside interrupts the old man just as he's about to ingest poison. Faust follows the song's advice to engage in prayer, but quickly becomes disillusioned and angry, invoking the devil rather than God. Who should magically appear but Méphistophélès himself, in the guise of a gentleman and offering Faust whatever he wants. When the doctor confides that he'd like to reclaim his youth, the devil says no problem, just sign on the dotted line. Faust is initially uncertain, but when Méphistophélès presents the man with an image of the young and beautiful Marguerite, he falls instantly in love and agrees to sell his soul. He drinks a potion administered by Méphistophélès, and is transformed into a young man.

ACT II A chorus of students, soldiers, and young women is getting drunk and rowdy at a village fair. Valentin is becoming depressed over the fact that he must depart shortly to go to war, leaving behind his sister,

A
B
C
D
E
F
G
H
I
J
K
L
M
N
O
P
Q
R
S
T
U
V
W
X
Y
Z

Marguerite. Siébel, who has romantic designs on the girl, promises to look out for her. Wagner, one of the students, launches into a drinking song but is quickly halted by the appearance of Méphistophélès, who intends to sing his own number. He delivers a song about the Golden Calf, and engages in some eagerly attended fortune-telling. His dismal predictions for Wagner, Siébel, and Valentin irritate the young men, who become alarmed when Méphistophélès uses his powers to make wine flow out of the tavern's sign. Sensing that they are in the presence of the devil, the men make the sign of the cross and quickly exit. Faust walks in, and his new mentor magically summons Marguerite, who enters with a group of revelers. Faust moves to the young woman and starts paying her amorous attentions. She lightly shuns him, but Méphistophélès encourages him to keep after her.

ACT III Siébel is alone in the garden outside Marguerite's house. He picks a flower for the girl, but it instantly withers in his hand (thanks to Méphistophélès's Act II prophecy). The problem, however, is evidently solved by Siébel's dipping his hand in holy water prior to plucking the flower out of the ground. He leaves a bouquet for his beloved and exits. Faust and Méphistophélès enter and determine that they, too, need to present Marguerite with a gift. Méphistophélès exits to find something appropriate, and Faust sings a declaration of love. The devil returns, bearing a box full of jewels. They drop the box and go into hiding as Marguerite emerges from the house, singing alternately about the legend of the king of Thule (who worshiped his woman even long after she died) and about Faust, who apparently made quite an impression earlier that day at the fair. She notices the jewel box, opens it, and tries on some of the baubles, singing the famous Jewel Song. Her neighbor, Marthe, shows up and marvels at the jewels. Méphistophélès appears and distracts the old woman (pretending to woo her) in order to leave Marguerite alone with Faust. The two chat, and it becomes clear that there exists a strong mutual attraction. They express their love for each other, but Marguerite insists that Faust must go. He moves to depart, but Méphistophélès casts a spell on the scene, sending his protégé through the open window to Marguerite's bedroom, where they promptly engage in God knows what.

ACT IV Scene i Almost a year later, Marguerite is miserable. She has had Faust's baby, but the man (compelled by Satan) has deserted her. Siébel enters and offers words of comfort.

SCENE 2 Marguerite, in church, prays for salvation. Méphistophélès appears, however, informing the poor woman that her soul is doomed.

SCENE 3 Out in the street, Valentin and the rest of the soldiers return to town, singing triumphantly. Siébel pulls his friend aside and drops hints about what has happened to Marguerite. Valentin enters the house in search of his sister. Méphistophélès and Faust walk in. Faust is depressed, desiring to see Marguerite, whom Méphistophélès has placed off-limits. The devil sings another of his scornful, immoral jams, at which point Valentin races out of the house in a fury. He and Faust engage in a sword fight, but Valentin is no match for a man with Satan on his side. He is mortally wounded and dies cursing Marguerite.

ACT 5 SCENE 1 Méphistophélès brings his charge to the Harz Mountains for a supernatural gathering of ghosts and spirits. Faust has a hard time getting into the party spirit, and becomes unnerved when he has a vision of Marguerite with a slit throat. He demands to see her again.

SCENE 2 Méphistophélès and Faust arrive at a prison, where Marguerite has been incarcerated for the murder of her baby daughter. Once they're alone, the pair sings fondly of the love they once shared. Méphistophélès reappears and the two try to persuade the semi-deranged girl to flee with them. She refuses and, finally grasping the particulars of Faust and Méphistophélès's relationship, curses and repels the father of her child. Méphistophélès is preparing to return to the underworld with both Faust and Marguerite, when a chorus of angels intervenes, whisking off poor Marguerite to heaven in the nick of time.

GEORGE FRIDERIC HANDEL   1685–1759

In an effort to be somewhat comprehensive and to have a representative of Baroque opera seria, I've included Handel's *Giulio Cesare* in this roundup of fifty operas. But, frankly, I wouldn't recommend the opera to someone who wasn't already familiar with the opera seria format: historical subject matter; long, repetitive arias strung together by recitatives; little in the way of dramatic movement. It's not the kind of stuff contemporary audiences unaccustomed to florid Baroque vocalism really get into, although *Giulio Cesare* is undeniably a masterpiece of its genre.

Handel is best known for the inevitable Christmastime chestnut *Messiah* (I defy anyone to claim not to know the "Hallelujah" chorus). But despite the ubiquity of that oratorio, Handel was chiefly an opera composer, having written more than forty over the course of his life. The whole point of opera seria was vocal showmanship; indeed, at the time, operatic scores seemed virtually extraneous, the mere basis for a singer's riffing, and so very few operas of the period actually survive. It's fortunate that many of Handel's works still exist, because whereas many opera serias were true drivel unless sung by master vocalists, the German expatriate (who ultimately chose London as his base of operations) managed to highlight the emotional state of his characters by means of ornamentation, rather than by creating embellishment for mere embellishment's sake. Handel composed his vocally oriented music at a time when castrati dominated the stage. As a result, it's impossible today to experience *Giulio Cesare* as it was intended to be performed, although the recent influx of extremely capable countertenors has brought us a little closer to the original sound of Baroque vocalism.

Giulio Cesare

Libretto by Nicola Haym
Premiere: King's Theatre, Haymarket, London, 1724
Scene: Egypt, 48 B.C.

ACT I SCENE 1 Julius Caesar arrives in Alexandria, via the Nile, having just defeated Pompey, whose wife, Cornelia, and son, Sesto, beg the victor for leniency. Caesar indicates that he plans to be merciful, when Achilla—henchman of Tolomeo (Ptolemy), who rules Egypt with his sister, Cleopatra—struts in bearing a box that contains Pompey's disembodied head. The "gift" is intended to ingratiate Tolomeo to Caesar, but the Roman is not pleased. Cornelia becomes hysterical; the kind words of Curio (who's in love with her) do little to calm her down. Sesto vows to avenge the horrific treatment of his father.

SCENE 2 Cleopatra has learned of her brother's barbarism and decides to try and align herself with Caesar against him. Hot mama that she is, she thinks she'll have no problem winning over the lusty Roman. Achilla informs Tolomeo of Caesar's displeasure about the head in the box. Achilla says that he'll get rid of Caesar in exchange for permission to marry Cornelia. Tolomeo agrees.

SCENE 3 Caesar pays tribute to his dead rival, Pompey, at a memorial service. Cleopatra enters in disguise as Lidia (one of her maids), and bitches to Caesar about how awful Tolomeo is. Caesar is immediately turned on by the sexy woman and agrees to help. Cleopatra hides when Cornelia and Sesto enter. The mother and son are planning their revenge. Overhearing their discussion, Cleopatra emerges and offers to help.

SCENE 4 Tolomeo and Caesar have agreed to a summit, but each is wary of the other. Cornelia and Sesto enter, and Tolomeo finds that he, too (like Achilla), is attracted to Cornelia. Sesto rashly challenges Tolomeo to a fight. The Egyptian calmly responds by placing the young man under arrest. Mother and son bid each other farewell and the curtain falls.

ACT II SCENE 1 Cleopatra, in disguise as Lidia, summons Caesar, and in the aria "V'adoro pupille" furthers her seduction.

SCENE 2 Achilla continues his unsuccessful attempts to win over reluctant Cornelia. He leaves, dejected, and Tolomeo enters to pick up where Achilla has left off. Cornelia rejects Tolomeo even more forcefully. Sesto enters and the two continue to plot revenge.

SCENE 3 "Lidia" and Caesar are chilling in the queen's bedroom when Curio arrives to warn the pair that Tolomeo's lackeys are on the warpath. Cleopatra comes clean about her identity and encourages her new lover to escape. He bravely insists on fighting.

SCENE 4 Tolomeo is informed by Achilla that Caesar, in an attempt to escape, has jumped out of a window into the ocean to his (presumed) death. Having effected the Roman's destruction, Achilla once again asks for permission to marry Cornelia. Naturally, Tolomeo refuses. Sesto is becoming despondent, but his mother reminds him that they must tend to their unfinished business with Tolomeo.

ACT III SCENE 1 Tolomeo has placed Cleopatra under arrest, his forces having defeated hers in battle. Things aren't looking particularly good when, all of a sudden, Caesar enters: His leap through the window apparently did him no harm, and he was able to swim to shore. He heads off in search of Cleopatra, and Sesto enters with the queen's emissary, Nireno. He stumbles onto Achilla, at death's door due to a battle wound, who bestows on the young man a seal that gives him control over much of Tolomeo's army. It seems that Achilla is sufficiently pissed over the whole Cornelia debacle to betray his evil king. Caesar reenters as life slips out of Achilla, and instructs Sesto that he, Julius Caesar, will take over from here to ensure the safe recapture of Cornelia and Cleopatra.

SCENE 2 Cleopatra, in chains, is despondent. She is stunned and thrilled, however, when none other than Caesar walks in and releases her.

SCENE 3 In another room of the palace, Tolomeo is once again trying to kick it with Cornelia. Sesto rushes in and, to Cornelia's delight, kills him.

SCENE 4 Order has been restored in Alexandria. The entire cast takes the stage to watch as Caesar declares Cleopatra not only the woman of his dreams but the queen of Egypt.

LEOŠ JANÁČEK 1854–1928

Czech operas generally don't dominate the repertory of most opera houses (except perhaps those in the Czech Republic). If you look at a list of the twenty most frequently produced operas, you'll find nary a one from a Czech composer. Fortunately, however, the last twenty-five years or so have seen a revival of interest in Czech operas, particularly those of Janáček, who, believe it or not, didn't compose his first opera until he was in his sixties. That first foray produced *Jenůfa,* which remains the most frequently performed (and perhaps most highly regarded) of Janáček's works. *The Makropoulos Case* has also found its way into certain houses. But my favorite is *Kát'a Kabanová,* a dramatic and musically fascinating work that's not too long and not overly pretty. What could be better?

To my mind, *Kát'a Kabanová* is an excellent example of an opera whose music and drama serve each other equally. Listening to the opera, you never feel as if the tunes are overwhelming the plot; neither do you sense that the action makes the music irrelevant. The opera is a stream-lined work that unfolds from start to finish with perfect pacing. The creation of indelible characters like *Kát'a*'s Kabanicha, Jenůfa, and Emilia Marty (of *The Makropoulos Case*) is all the more impressive when you consider the suddenness of their appearance on the operatic scene. Janáček had spent most of his life teaching and playing the organ in Brno when suddenly, at the age of sixty-two, he started churning out operatic master-pieces. Janáček's operas will surely never achieve the ubiquity of the old reliable Italian repertory staples, but works like *Kát'a* are devastating pieces nonetheless and exerted an important influence over mid-twentieth-century composers like Berg.

Kát'a Kabanová

Libretto by Leoš Janáček based on *The Storm* by Aleksandr
  Ostrovsky, translated by Vincere Červinka
Premiere: National Theater, Brno, 1921
Scene: Kalinov, Russia, in the 1860s

ACT I SCENE I Kudrjáš stares out at the Volga River and shoots the
breeze with Glaša, the Kabanov family's maid. The merchant Dikoj and his
nephew Boris amble by, in the middle of an ongoing argument. Dikoj keeps
moving, while Boris stays behind to explain to Kudrjáš the strange nature of
his relationship with his uncle, who oversees an inheritance the young man
is entitled to after the death of his parents. If he wants to see that cash, he
has to submit to Dikoj's whims. Church has just let out, and folks have
begun to walk past. Boris spies Kát'a, who lives with her husband, Tichon,
and his mother, Kabanicha. Boris admits to Kudrjáš that he's in love with
young Kát'a, who doesn't seem particularly happy in her marriage. Old
Kabanicha is a real ball-buster; she demands constant attention from her
son and daughter-in-law, who try to persuade her that she is beloved and
important in their lives. Kabanicha bitchily offers her son some unsolicited
business advice, and they enter the house. The young woman Varvara, who
lives with the family as a sort of foster child, expresses her sympathy for
Kát'a, who's got the mother-in-law from hell on her hands.

WINNIE KLOTZ/METROPOLITAN OPERA

Kát'a Kabanová

SCENE 2 Kát'a and Varvara are chilling in the house, the former recalling her lost freedom and happiness. She even lets on that she's been having fantasies about a man other than her husband. At Kabanicha's command, Tichon has committed to a business trip to the city of Kazan. Kát'a is disturbed over the idea of being left behind; she's afraid of what she might do and asks to come along. Her request is refused, and she bizarrely asks that her husband at least promise not to speak with any strangers while he's away. Kabanicha sweeps in to send Tichon on his way, insisting that he lay down the law to Kát'a before he goes. He asks his wife to defer to his mother in all things, an instruction that makes poor Kát'a feel like a child. Tichon kisses his wife (to his mother's repulsion) and leaves as the curtain falls.

ACT II SCENE 1 The three women of the Kabanov household are sitting together working on embroidery when Kabanicha excoriates Kát'a for not being visibly distressed over her husband's absence. She leaves, and Varvara confides in Kát'a that she has obtained a key to the gated garden, where she plans to meet a certain special someone later that night. She gives Kát'a a copy of the key and suggests that she meet Boris in the same spot. Kát'a refuses at first, but her desire to see the man is strong and her will quickly frays. Dikoj enters, stinking drunk, with Kabanicha, to whom he bemoans the various trials of being Dikoj. No-nonsense Kabanicha has no time for this sort of maudlin self-pity.

SCENE 2 Kudrjáš is waiting in the garden for Varvara when Boris enters, having been invited himself to the garden at this particular hour. Varvara shows up; she and Kudrjáš take a stroll. Kát'a enters, and Boris is all over her. Her intention is just to talk, but it doesn't take long for Kát'a herself to get all horned up. She and Boris head off in search of a secluded spot as the other pair of lovers returns. Varvara and Kudrjáš sing a folk song that somehow returns Kát'a to her senses. She and Boris return, and all four decide to head home.

ACT III SCENE 1 Several days later, a tremendous thunderstorm blows into town. Kudrjáš and his friend Kuligin seek shelter in an abandoned building near the river, along with other passersby. Dikoj enters the building in his usual state of irritation; he becomes incensed when Kudrjáš gets all scientific on him, talking about electricity. Boris shows up, followed by Varvara, who pulls him aside to inform him that the return of Tichon has made Kát'a crazed with guilt. The heroine herself arrives shortly with her husband and Kabanicha. All eyes are on the near-hysterical Kát'a. When she sees Boris hiding in a corner of the shelter, she loses it and confesses to all present that she cheated while her husband was away. The onlookers appear stunned and horrified as demented Kát'a races out into the storm.

SCENE 2 The storm has subsided and a search party, led by Boris, is on the hunt for Kát'a. Varvara and Kudrjáš help with the search, but the whole fiasco has unnerved them and they decide to flee to Moscow. Kát'a enters in a state, crying that she must see Boris before she dies. Her lover enters, similarly dazed, and they kiss. Boris announces that his uncle has banished him from town. He says good-bye and exits. Completely destroyed, Kát'a runs toward the Volga and flings herself into the treacherous river. Kuligin has witnessed the rash act and summons the others. Mama's boy Tichon finally turns on Kabanicha, accusing her of having killed Kát'a. The unflappable matriarch prevents her son from going in after his wife, whose body is dragged out of the river by the search party and presented to the family. Tichon wails hysterically, while his steely mother merely thanks the townsfolk for all their help.

RUGGIERO LEONCAVALLO 1857–1919

The teary clown in the tentlike white outfit and pom-pom–topped dunce cap has become the quintessential opera icon to people who have never even set foot in an opera house. With his troubled *pagliaccio,* Canio, Leoncavallo created one of the most recognizable characters in opera. It was a feat the composer would never repeat: Although he's responsible for a fairly well known opera based on the same story as Puccini's vastly more successful *La Bohème,* Leoncavallo is pretty much remembered today as a one-hit wonder, albeit one with a monumental single triumph.

Pagliacci stands as one of the foremost representatives of verismo opera, the movement that sought to direct opera's plots to the passions and problems of ordinary people in extraordinary circumstances. Historical and mythological subject matter and lofty themes were abandoned in favor of more immediate slice-of-life (and death) pieces, which stunned early audiences with their sometimes shocking representations of down-home folk. *Pagliacci* is a short opera that's usually paired in performance

A
B
C
D
E
F
G
H
I
J
K
L
M
N
O
P
Q
R
S
T
U
V
W
X
Y
Z

with Mascagni's *Cavalleria Rusticana,* another symbol of verismo and an important work in its own right. Indeed, I've chosen to focus on *Pag* rather than *Cav* simply because the clown symbol is so familiar to most of humanity. Neither of these composers took verismo to the heights achieved by Puccini, but they share that composer's way with melody and a certain schmaltzy sensationalism that drives some people nuts but that can nevertheless be quite moving if you're in the right frame of mind. As with soap operas on TV, these operas hardly exist at the highest level of artistic achievement, but at the right time they can certainly sustain your interest and even get you a little choked up.

Pagliacci

Libretto by Ruggiero Leoncavallo
Premiere: Teatro dal Verme, Milan, 1892
Scene: Calabria, Italy, in the late 1860s

PROLOGUE Tonio, dressed as a clown, emerges from behind the curtain to introduce himself and the opera directly to the audience. He explains that, yes, the play within a play they are about to witness is indeed fictional. But the characters are nevertheless very real.

ACT I The traveling theater company presided over by Canio rolls into town, to the apparent pleasure of the villagers. Canio announces that there will be a performance that evening. Nedda, his wife, is getting out of her wagon when Tonio (who's a hunchback) comes over to help her. Canio is annoyed and pushes Tonio aside, instructing him to keep his hands off his woman. Tonio heads off, incensed, and the others tease Canio about his new rival. He replies that the stage is the stage and real life is real life: You can only flirt with Nedda if it's part of the performance. Canio and the rest of the troupe leave to get drinks, and Nedda sits alone, contemplating her marriage, which is not going quite as well in her mind as it is in Canio's. Just then, Tonio enters, expresses his love for Nedda, and goes in for a kiss. She cruelly beats him off and asserts that he's got no chance with her. He vows to avenge his ongoing humiliation at the hands of this particular husband-and-wife team and leaves. Nedda's not interested in Tonio, but she's not totally opposed to an extramarital fling. Her lover, Silvio, enters and they rhapsodize about their affection and bemoan the circumstances of their separation. The pair promises to run away together after the show that night. Tonio has sneaked back in and is eavesdropping on the conversation. He dashes off to get Canio, who arrives just after Silvio has fled but who still has a clear picture of what's going on. He screams at Nedda to reveal the identity of her lover and pulls out a knife. Canio's actor friend Beppe intervenes to restore some peace and tells Canio to get ready for the performance. Everyone leaves, and Canio laments his sorry state of affairs in the showstopping aria "Vesti la giubba."

ACT II The play is about to get started and folks are hurriedly finding seats in the audience. Silvio sneaks in and confers surreptitiously with Nedda about their post-show flight. She runs backstage to get into place and the curtain rises. The play within a play opens with the clown Harlequin (played by Beppe) singing a ditty to Colombine (played by Nedda). In an ironic stroke of life imitating art (or art imitating art), Colombine rebuffs Harlequin because she's secretly seeing Taddeo (Tonio), even though she's married to Pagliaccio (Canio). Taddeo enters with a picnic basket and declares his love for Colombine. Harlequin intercedes and kicks Taddeo out, retaining the feast for Colombine and himself. The pair sits happily eating and singing songs of love to each other when Pagliaccio enters, overhearing the lovers' plans to run away together. Canio loses it, forgets he's in charac-ter, and once again shrieks at Nedda to tell him who she's seeing. Consum-mate theater professional that she is, Nedda somehow steers her husband back to the action of the play. They keep going for a few moments, but Canio once again forgets himself and resumes his interrogation. The audi-ence, meanwhile, has no clue what's going on and thinks they are witness-ing a really terrific play. Nedda can't keep it up any longer and falls out of character, admitting that, yes, she's in love with someone else. Canio once again whips out his knife, and Silvio rushes the stage to help Nedda. It's too late, however: Canio stabs and kills his wife, then directs his rage toward Sil-vio, who quickly becomes corpse number two. Finally, the audience gets it. A few people manage to grab hold of the murderer. Tonio turns to the audi-ence and remarks, deadpan, "La commedia è finita."

JULES MASSENET 1842–1912

More famous than Massenet's *Werther* is the composer's *Manon*, which is often described with words like "confection," "sensuous," and "superficial."

Werther is not exactly Schoenberg, but it's certainly weightier than Massenet's other famous opera, and a lot more gratifying as a result. For *Werther,* Massenet seized on the enormous and ongoing popularity of Goethe's *The Sorrows of Young Werther,* the story of a young man who kills himself in order to avoid the despair of an unrequited passion. The title character of both the novel and the opera is the quintessential moody artist; indeed, it's a relief that Massenet's creation has a lot of beautiful music to sing, because he'd otherwise be a truly irritating figure.

Charlotte, on the other hand, the object of Werther's affection, is a woman who's got her act together. A far cry from the petulant, pleasure-seeking Manon, the religiously inclined Charlotte grounds the action of the opera and serves as the stable antidote to Werther's self-indulgent sentimentality. It is this balance of youthful passion and moral obligation that makes *Werther* superior, in my opinion, to the relative cream-puffery of *Manon.* Massenet was a master of the long, arching romantic musical phrase, and in *Werther* his lush, stirring orchestrations don't disappoint. But they also don't take over the action, fortunately. For the operagoer who can't quite stomach the atonality of some of the most purely dramatic works but who also has no interest in a strictly vocal display, *Werther* offers a happy middle ground where story and music meet, neither one overwhelming the other.

Werther

Libretto by Edouard Blau, Paul Milliet, and Georges Hartmann, based on Johann Wolfgang von Goethe's *The Sorrows of Young Werther*
Premiere: Imperial Opera, Vienna, 1892
Scene: Wetzlar, Germany, in the 1780s

ACT I The Magistrate is a widower who has numerous children, with whom he is just now practicing Christmas carols—even though it's July—in the garden outside their house. Johann and Schmidt, friends of the Magistrate, swing by for a bit of chitchat with the man and his second daughter, Sophie, as the Magistrate's oldest girl, Charlotte, gets ready for a dance later that evening. It seems that in the absence of Charlotte's fiancé, Albert, the young woman is to be accompanied to the ball by Werther, a spacey artist type who nonetheless appears to have a promising future as a poet. Johann and Schmidt depart and the others go inside just as Werther arrives on the scene, singing about how beautiful the Magistrate's garden

162

is. Just inside the house, Charlotte is serving dinner to her young siblings. The Magistrate spies Werther and introduces him to his daughter, as well as to Brühlmann and Kätchen, a couple from next door who are also going to the party. Everyone leaves, including the Magistrate, whom Sophie has sent out to the local bar while she takes care of the kids. Once everyone has left for the evening, who should stumble in but Albert, Charlotte's betrothed, who has been away for several months. He and Sophie chat briefly, and the man leaves, promising to return the next morning to see his beloved Charlotte. Werther and Charlotte hit it off at the party, and as they arrive back at the house, the young poet declares his love. Charlotte feels the same, but she asserts that she has to focus on being a parent to her siblings now that their mother is dead. Still, the connection between the two is undeniable. The Magistrate has returned and been told by Sophie of Albert's return. He calls Charlotte into the house with the news. Poor Werther is left alone in the garden to bitch and moan.

ACT II A few months later, Johann and Schmidt are chilling in town when Albert and Charlotte—now married—pass by en route to church. They are assuring each other of their nuptial happiness. Just out of sight, Werther observes the couple, and once again despairs over his unrequited passion for Charlotte. Brühlmann enters, having broken up with Kätchen, and is consoled by Johann and Schmidt. Albert spies Werther and approaches the poor wreck, telling him that he understands and is cool with the fact that he was after his woman. Werther assures him that he's over Charlotte. Sophie enters, carrying a bouquet of flowers. She and Albert exit together, leaving Werther to scold himself for his continued desire for Charlotte. The latter, of course, arrives on the scene and tells Werther he must leave so that she can work on her marriage. She nonetheless invites him to return for Christmas. She leaves. Werther is contemplating suicide, when Sophie reappears, asking him to dance at nearby church festivities. He declines and leaves. Charlotte and Albert reenter to console Sophie, a sensitive girl who has started to cry. Albert is aware that Werther is not over Charlotte.

ACT III A few months have rolled by and Christmas Eve has arrived. Inside her and Albert's house, Charlotte sits alone reading letters that Werther has sent her. Sophie enters, notices that her sister is out of sorts, and tries to cheer her up. She leaves and Charlotte becomes agitated and depressed, her condition heightened by the arrival of Werther. The poet

A)
B)
C)
D)
E)
F)
G)
H)
I)
J)
K)
L)
M)
N)
O)
P)
Q)
R)
S)
T)
U)
V)
W)
X)
Y)
Z)

asserts that he had many times contemplated suicide, but he could not stand the idea of not accepting Charlotte's Christmas invitation. They chat about poetry, and Werther launches into a musical version of an Ossian verse (Werther's big aria, "Pourquoi me réveiller?"). Werther implores Charlotte to admit that she loves him, too, but she jets out of the room. Werther leaves. Albert returns home, having heard that Werther's back. He's annoyed, and concerned about his wife's state of mind. A servant enters with a letter from Werther requesting that Albert lend him two pistols for a journey he is planning to take. Albert sends the servant off with the guns. Fully aware of Werther's intent, Charlotte races out to look for him and prevent the potential suicide.

ACT IV Later that night, Charlotte bursts into Werther's house, where he lies dying from a self-inflicted gunshot wound. Seeing that there's no hope for his survival, Charlotte admits her love for the young man and kisses him. In the distance, the sound of the kids' caroling can be heard, which Werther takes as a sign of his imminent salvation. Charlotte is overcome as she watches Werther die. The caroling increases in volume, accompanied by laughter and sounds of revelry just outside.

CLAUDIO MONTEVERDI 1567–1643

Up to now, I've been making a lot of noise about two camps of opera composers: those whose works feature melodic numbers designed to captivate and thrill an audience and those who favor dramatic plausibility over vocal display. Well, Monteverdi could be said to fall into neither category. Opera's first true genius, who worked in early seventeenth century, Monteverdi was focused on the initial concern of early opera composers: marrying text and music. Consequently, his *Orfeo* is basically one long start-to-finish recitative. There are no jaw-dropping coloratura fireworks, and there is also no inevitable unraveling of plot. Furthermore, the orchestrations are fairly simple (although constructed with almost mathematical precision). So why have I chosen to include *Orfeo* in this roundup of operas appropriate for newcomers?

First off, it's short. The opera comprises five acts, but they manage to go by swiftly. Second, the subject matter—the myth of Orpheus and his beloved Eurydice, whom he attempts to rescue from Hades, failing miserably—is one of the most often used stories in opera. Gluck's take on the tale is perhaps equally important in operatic history, but since Monteverdi came first, and since his *Orfeo* is regarded as opera's first masterpiece, I've decided to go with the man from Mantua. These days, opera producers are more and more interested in Baroque and other early repertory. And so Monteverdi's *Orfeo* is making the rounds of the world's opera houses with increasing frequency. The somewhat static narrative and the dearth of hit tunes can in fact sometimes work to the piece's advantage, as directors feel compelled to jazz things up with arresting visual imagery and novel interpretations.

Orfeo

Libretto by Alessandro Striggio
Premiere: Palazzo Ducale, Mantua, 1607
Scene: A mythical place

PROLOGUE A woman embodying the character of Music sings of music's inescapable power. She introduces the audience to the story of Orfeo, whose singing held sway even over the denizens of Hades.

ACT I Orfeo and Euridice have been married, a fact that is celebrated by a chorus of shepherds and nymphs. Orfeo sings a song of joy, to the delight of the crowd. He asserts that it was the power and beauty of his voice that won over his blushing new bride. The ensemble implores the heavens to watch over the couple.

ACT II It's a hot day, and Orfeo and his shepherd friends are sitting in the shade. The singer recalls former days of despair, before he had won his lady, who has bestowed total happiness on him. Just then, a messenger friend of Euridice's rushes in to announce that the woman is dead, having been bitten by a snake while picking flowers. Orfeo is devastated and says he wishes he were dead. The crowd marvels at how quickly good fortune can turn sour.

ACT III Orfeo is determined to follow Euridice into the underworld and bring her home. The goddess Speranza guides the man to the River Styx, the first stop on his route down under. The ferryman warns Orfeo not to cross the river: Only the dead can do that. But Orfeo is insistent and craftily sings the boatman to sleep. He boards the boat and paddles it toward his dead wife across the water.

ACT IV Plutone and Proserpina, the king and queen of the underworld, are debating Orfeo's request to bring Euridice back to life. Enchanted by the man's singing (and weary of his wife's demands for compassion) Plutone finally agrees, but on one condition: As he leads Euridice back to earth, Orfeo is forbidden to look back at her. He can only gaze on her once they are safely back home. Orfeo thinks this will be a cinch and is overjoyed. He begins leading Euridice back, but temptation quickly gets the best of him. He can't help but sneak a peek, ensuring his wife's speedy return to Hades. Orfeo is out of his head with grief.

ACT V Orfeo has returned to earth, where he wanders aimlessly, beating himself up over his foolishness. His father, Apollo, hears the man's laments and descends from the heavens to offer condolences. Orfeo must steel himself to this grief, he asserts. He explains that in heaven, Orfeo will be able to look on the image of Euridice perpetually. He transports his son heavenward as the shepherds and nymphs sing in praise of Orfeo's imminent salvation.

WOLFGANG AMADEUS MOZART 1756–1791

It's hard to know where to begin when discussing Mozart, perhaps the most famous and (I think) the greatest composer ever. Pretty much everyone is familiar with the movie *Amadeus,* so much of the lore surrounding the Salzburg native is familiar: child prodigy, iconoclast, bawd, genius. It's all, for the most part, accurate. Perhaps the most impressive factor of Mozart's short but prolific career is the man's mastery of all types of composition: No one so dominant in the field of symphonic music was also able to completely master (and revolutionize) opera. Okay, Beethoven also worked in both genres, but he only wrote one opera, so he doesn't really count. As an opera composer, Mozart wrote what's probably the best opera seria ever composed, *Idomeneo,* as well as the style's swan song (mercifully), *La Clemenza di Tito.* I'd be hard-pressed to name a better opera buffa than *Le Nozze di Figaro* (or, frankly, a better opera, period).

And as far as dramatic operas go, no one would deny the power and beauty of *Don Giovanni* (also technically an opera buffa despite the somewhat sinister subject matter). Essentially, Mozart could do anything, and as an opera innovator he has no peer, except, perhaps, Wagner.

Le Nozze di Figaro marks the first installment of Mozart's hugely successful triple collaboration with librettist Lorenzo Da Ponte. He'd written other operas before (starting at the age of eleven), but *Figaro* is the supreme example of Mozart's ability to create real people with conflicted feelings, something the earlier operas of Handel (Mozart's great forerunner) generally failed to achieve. It seems like every few minutes or so the opera offers up another unforgettable moment or powerhouse aria; I think the Countess's last-act acceptance of the Count's apology is one of the most moving moments in all of opera. *Figaro* is my personal favorite, but most people would probably cite *Don Giovanni* as Mozart's greatest triumph. Underappreciated in his native Austria, Mozart unveiled *Don Giovanni* in Prague, where the opera's reception was incredible. The last Mozart–Da Ponte work, *Così fan tutte,* is a little more problematic because of its ambiguous ending. The wayward couples of that opera end up back together in the end (it's a comedy, after all), but there's little assurance that all's well that ends well. *Così* feels like something of an experiment the collaborators were trying, but it's a masterpiece nonetheless. With *Die Zauberflöte,* Mozart switched librettists (turning to Emanuel Schikaneder, who was also the first Papageno) and genres, trying his hand at singspiel, a form that included spoken dialogue. The work was meant as pure popular entertainment, and as a result contains comedy that I find a bit hokey and dated. But musically, needless to say, the opera is out of this world.

Le Nozze di Figaro

Libretto by Lorenzo Da Ponte, based on *Le Mariage de Figaro* by Beaumarchais
Premiere: Burgtheater, Vienna, 1786
Scene: Seville in the late eighteenth century

ACT I Figaro and Susanna, servants to the Count and Countess Almaviva, respectively, are preparing for their impending nuptials by measuring a space for the matrimonial bed in their new room of the household. Figaro notes how convenient their new quarters are, being so close to the Count and Countess's rooms. A little too close for comfort, according to Susanna, who mentions that the Count has been chasing her with not exactly the most honorable intentions. It seems that the outlawed concept of droit du seigneur (which provides that male heads of households are entitled to a little sex from their unmarried female servants) is alive and well in the Almaviva homestead. Figaro angrily asserts that the Count better watch his ass if he intends to toy with Susanna. He exits, and Dr. Bartolo and Marcellina enter in the throes of a scheme to prevent the marriage of Figaro and Susanna. Bartolo has a long-standing beef with Figaro; Marcellina, desiring Figaro for herself, hates Susanna. Bartolo vows to stop the wedding, and Marcellina and Susanna engage in a bit of bitchy mock-politesse. The older pair exits as Cherubino, the horny teenage page boy, rushes in to consult with Susanna. It seems that Cherubino has the hots for the Countess; realizing she's probably not going to return his affection, he's been keeping himself occupied with the gardener's daughter Barbarina. He sings an aria ("Non so più") bemoaning the anxiety that accompanies his raging hormones. Count Almaviva, who intends to get rid of Cherubino because of his exploits with Barbarina, walks in, driving the young boy to hide behind a chair. The lascivious Count is trying to persuade Susanna to meet with him later that night, when the Almavivas' music teacher, Don Basilio, shuffles in. Cherubino adjusts his hiding place so that he is sitting *on* the chair, hidden under a sheet; the Count assumes the kid's previous post behind the recliner. Gossipy Basilio suggests to Susanna that a little dalliance with the attractive and powerful Count could be fun, and mentions Cherubino's relentless though fruitless pursuit of the Countess. Hearing this, the Count emerges from behind the chair and starts fuming, bitching about how he had discovered Cherubino in hiding earlier that day. Re-creating that scene, he pulls aside the sheet to reveal the absurd boy. The Count is forced to keep his rage under control when Figaro enters with a group of locals who are celebrating the upcoming wedding. Figaro asks the Count's permission to marry; the Count testily agrees, determined to get a piece of Susanna before it's too late. He instructs Cherubino to pack his bags: The boy is being sent into Seville proper to get a little experience in the military. As Count Almaviva exits, Figaro warns the young flirt of the hardships of military life ("Non più andrai"), scaring the poor kid witless.

ACT II The Countess, alone in her bedroom, sings a lament over her husband's growing lack of interest in her (the sublime "Porgi amor"). Susanna enters and asserts that, yes, the Count is after her, and the two hatch a scheme to frustrate his plans. Figaro walks in to inform the women that the Count and Marcellina are working together to prevent the marriage. The three decide to forge a letter (which they'll allow to fall into the Count's hands) that indicates that the Countess is meeting with an unidentified suitor. In the meantime, Cherubino will meet with the Count that evening in drag as Susanna. Figaro exits. Young Cherubino is game with the plan, and sings a love song to the Countess ("Voi che sapete") before they deck him out in women's clothes. Suddenly, the Count knocks at the door. Cherubino hides in a closet, Susanna hides in a corner of the chamber, and the Countess lets her husband in. The Count has stumbled on Figaro's phony letter and has come to confront his wife. Having overheard the ruckus caused by Cherubino's haste to hide in the closet, the Count is convinced that the Countess is concealing a lover. The closet is locked, so the Count whisks his wife away to help him find tools to break down the door. Luckily, Susanna has been privy to these events, and while the couple is away, she unlocks the closet door and takes Cherubino's place. The kid, meanwhile, jumps out the window as the Count and Countess return. Unaware of the switch, the nerve-wracked Countess is as surprised as her husband when the door is opened and Susanna appears. She manages to cover, claiming it was all a plan to shame her husband into recognizing how he's been ignoring her. It looks as if it's all going to work out for the schemers when the gardener, Antonio, enters to complain that someone has jumped out the window onto his flowerbeds. Figaro, pretending to limp, enters and assumes responsibility, but the discovery of Cherubino's letter of military service (which apparently fell out of his pocket) sets off the Count. Bartolo enters with Marcellina, who claims that Figaro must marry her to cover a debt he has not yet paid. This sits well with the Count, who is now more determined than ever to prevent the Figaro-Susanna union.

ACT III The curtain rises on the Count, who tries to straighten out in his mind the various passageways of the intrigue. Susanna enters and the two have a tête-à-tête, agreeing to meet later that night. The Count is pleased about the rendezvous but nonetheless suspicious that Susanna may have some new plan he should be wary of. Indeed, he overhears Susanna and Figaro plotting just outside and his ire is once again raised. He exits. Figaro enters with Bartolo, Marcellina, and Don Curzio, a lawyer, who declares that Figaro must in fact marry Marcellina if he can't otherwise pay off the financial debt he owes her. Figaro insists that he cannot marry without the permission of his parents; although he's now a manservant, it seems he is actually of noble birth, having been abandoned by his parents as an infant. He displays an identifying mark on his arm, which, to the Oedipal astonishment of all, proves him to be the long-lost son of Bartolo and Marcellina themselves! Marcellina hugs her son as Susanna enters, understandably annoyed by the spectacle. Everything is explained; Marcellina and Bartolo joyously give their consent to their son's marriage. The Count stews. Everyone exits, clearing the stage for the Countess, whose marital unhappiness increases. She sings another sad song, which nonetheless strengthens her resolve to make things work. She calls on Susanna to once again write a note to the Count requesting a meeting. A group of local girls enters, among them Barbarina and Cherubino in drag. Antonio, the gardener, has observed the costuming of the young man and brings in the Count to unmask the fellow. The Count is incensed and ready to punish Cherubino, but Barbarina (who's been secretly seeing the Count on occasion) intervenes and Almaviva simmers quietly. Figaro arrives with news that all is set for the wedding. The Count (pissed off) and Countess (sad but hopeful) observe the proceedings. At one point, Susanna surreptitiously hands the Count the note she's written to set up a rendezvous. It looks like he's going to have his way with the girl after all.

ACT IV Susanna's note to the Count was sealed with a hat pin. Barbarina has been commissioned by the Count to return that item to Susanna as an indication that he will meet her at the prescribed time. Figaro and Marcellina walk in and chance upon the young girl, who is frantically looking for the pin, which she has dropped somewhere. The plan is for the Countess to meet with her husband in disguise as Susanna, but Figaro is unaware of this. Convinced that his new bride is already set to stray, he presents Barbarina with a different pin to deliver and storms off in a rage. Barbarina goes off to give Susanna the pin, while Marcellina sings an aria expressing her hope that everything turns out all right. Barbarina returns and hides, lying in wait for Cherubino. Figaro enters with Bartolo and Basilio, and implores them to observe as the Count puts the moves on Susanna. Once they've gone, he sings an aria despairing over womanly duplicitousness. He hides as the Countess (decked out as Susanna) enters with Susanna (decked out as the Countess). Aware that her husband is eavesdropping, Susanna sings an aria ("Deh vieni non tardar") about an unnamed lover, whom Figaro rashly assumes is the Count. Cherubino stumbles in, thinking the Countess is Susanna, and starts chatting. The Countess, trying to trick her husband, has no time for this, and manages to get rid of the boy as her husband enters. The Count has spied a male form, which he assumes is Cherubino; when Figaro wanders in, the Count mistakes him for the boy and slaps him in the head. The Count starts wooing "Susanna" (who is actually the Countess), while Figaro confronts "the Countess" (who is actually Susanna). Recognizing his new wife's voice, Figaro finally understands the plot. Without revealing that he knows who she really is, Figaro suggests to "the Countess" that they get back at their spouses by jumping into bed together. Susanna drops the act and, irate, starts hitting Figaro. He laughs, explains that he knew it was her all along, and they dissolve into an embrace. The Count, of course, witnesses this outpouring of affection and thinks that his servant is doing his wife. He calls in everyone to witness as he hypocritically condemns his wife for her alleged infidelity. The real Countess reappears and removes her "Susanna" costume. When he realizes the profundity of his error and the humiliation to which he has exposed his wife, the Count makes a grand public apology, which his wife magnanimously accepts. Finally, order is restored and the group rushes off, at long last, to enjoy the wedding festivities.

Don Giovanni

Libretto by Lorenzo Da Ponte
Premiere: Gräflich Nostitzsches Nationaltheater, Prague, 1787
Scene: Seville in the eighteenth century

ACT I SCENE 1 Leporello, servant to Don Giovanni, stands guard outside the house of Donna Anna and her father, the Commendatore, as his master seduces the young woman inside. Habitually reduced to this watchman position while Don Giovanni gets all the action, Leporello bitches about his state of affairs. Don Giovanni, his face concealed by a mask, emerges from the house with Donna Anna on his coattails. She's determined to identify the masked seducer, and she screams to her father to help in the pursuit. The Commendatore arrives on the scene and demands a fight. Don Giovanni swiftly kills the old man, leaving him to die in the arms of Donna Anna and her husband-to-be, Don Ottavio. The couple vows to avenge the poor old man's murder.

SCENE 2 Don Giovanni is strolling through town with Leporello, who expresses his disapproval of his employer's immoral ways with women. Don Giovanni essentially tells him to shut up and focus on his

A
B
C
D
E
F
G
H
I
J
K
L
M
N
O
P
Q
R
S
T
U
V
W
X
Y
Z

task of keeping track of all of Don Giovanni's conquests. Another young beauty, Donna Elvira, enters, singing a lament over having been deserted by a lover. She's singing, of course, about Don Giovanni, but the man does not yet recognize her. Instead, he follows her, preparing to pounce. He approaches Donna Elvira, who, after a moment of mutual recognition, launches into a verbal attack on the man who mistreated her. Don Giovanni exits hastily, leaving Leporello to clean up the mess. The servant explains to the stunned woman that she is but one of thousands of women Don Giovanni has loved and left. Donna Elvira makes the now-familiar vow of vengeance and leaves.

Scene 3 This scene opens in a country village on the outskirts of Seville. Zerlina and Masetto, a young peasant couple, are getting ready for their imminent wedding. Predictably, Don Giovanni and Leporello walk by; Don Giovanni is taken with Zerlina; Leporello is commissioned to get rid of Masetto. It takes about ten seconds for Don Giovanni to persuade the country girl Zerlina to go to bed with him. Luckily, Donna Elvira enters in the nick of time and whisks the young girl away. Donna Anna and Don Ottavio arrive on the scene and, ironically, implore Don Giovanni to help them find Donna Anna's masked seducer. Donna Elvira returns and warns the couple to stay away from Giovanni. They argue, Don Giovanni leaves, and Donna Anna suddenly recognizes Giovanni's voice as that of the virtual rapist from the other day. She instructs Ottavio to defend her honor and storms off, leaving her fiancé to steel himself for the upcoming act of revenge.

Scene 4 In Don Giovanni's castle, Leporello and his master prepare for a party. Having been quite taken with Zerlina and her rustic ways, Giovanni has decided to invite over a bevy of country folk from whom he intends to choose a new lover or two.

Scene 5 Masetto is annoyed with Zerlina for her easy acquiescence to Don Giovanni's wishes. But she easily uses her flirtatious feminine wiles to calm him down. Don Giovanni approaches. Zerlina moves to hide, but the seducer has spotted her. Masetto makes his presence known and they all three head into the house for the party. Donna Elvira, Donna Anna, and Don Ottavio, all wearing masks, enter and swear an oath before entering the castle to exact revenge.

Scene 6 The party is in full swing, and Don Giovanni cannot keep his eyes off Zerlina, much to Masetto's dismay. The three masked vengeance seekers enter warily. Leporello welcomes them before turning his attention to distracting Masetto so that Don Giovanni might make a move on Zerlina. The revelry comes to a screeching halt when Zerlina is heard screaming. She reenters with Don Giovanni hard on her heels; he insists it was Leporello who tried to rape her. Anna, Elvira, and Ottavio are having none of it. They pull off their masks and confront the Don, who angrily storms off as the curtain falls.

ACT II SCENE 1 Don Giovanni and Leporello are at their exercise of strolling through the streets of Seville looking for booty. Giovanni has decided he'd like to have a go at Donna Elvira's maid, so he and his servant swap coats and hats in order to perpetrate one of their deceptions. As Leporello keeps Elvira tied up with assurances that he (meaning Giovanni) truly cares for her, the actual Giovanni (in disguise as Leporello) serenades the woman's maid, accompanying himself on a mandolin. Before he can move in for the kill, however, Masetto appears (accompanied by other peasant henchmen) with the intention of finding and killing Giovanni. "Leporello" persuades Masetto to send off his men and remain behind. Giovanni proceeds to beat up the poor man, leaving him to the ministrations of Zerlina, who arrives momentarily.

SCENE 2 Leporello, as Giovanni, is doing his damnedest to keep Elvira occupied and in the dark. Donna Anna, Ottavio, Masetto, and Zerlina enter in succession, and, assuming him to be Giovanni, pounce on Leporello, who is shielded by a softening Elvira. He cannot keep up the deceit, however, and shortly doffs his Giovanni disguise. The group is pissed, but Leporello manages to escape. Ottavio sings an aria declaring his commitment to achieving revenge on behalf of his betrothed. Elvira follows his number with one of her own, expressing her conflicted feelings about the treacherous but attractive seducer.

SCENE 3 Don Giovanni and Leporello are hiding out in a cemetery, where they spy a statue of the dead Commendatore. Leporello becomes alarmed when the thing begins to speak, but Giovanni manages to keep his cool, even though the Commendatore warns the lecher of impending doom. His brazenness apparently knowing no bounds, Giovanni invites the statue over for dinner, an invitation the dead creature bizarrely accepts.

SCENE 4 Don Giovanni may still be at large, but Don Ottavio promises his fiancée that he will eventually pay for what he's done. Donna Anna replies that their wedding must nonetheless be postponed while she gets over her father's murder.

SCENE 5 Don Giovanni is back home in his castle, where he prepares for dinner and enjoys the music being played by his own private band. Donna Elvira enters, once again exhorting the man to repent. Giovanni

A B C D E F G H I J K L M N O P Q R S T U V W X Y Z

is unfazed. Elvira is on her way out when she screams in terror at the sight of the statue just outside. Giovanni lets the undead being into the house, whereupon he is called upon to repent or die. Giovanni laughs this off and is instantly struck dead by some invisible force. An unseen chorus of (ostensible) demons magically whisks him off to hell amid stage effects of smoke and fire.

SCENE 6 A shaken Leporello runs into Donna Anna, Don Ottavio, Masetto, and Zerlina and breaks the news of Giovanni's demise. Elvira enters and fills in the particulars of the story of the homicidal statue. The group announces its plans for the future: Elvira swears off men for good and decides to enter a convent; Donna Anna and Ottavio will mourn for a year before marrying; Masetto and Zerlina are going to catch a bite to eat; Leporello will seek new employment. The quintet ultimately addresses the audience directly with a word of warning to avoid a life of treachery and deceit.

Così Fan Tutte

Libretto by Lorenzo Da Ponte
Premiere: Burgtheater, Vienna, 1790
Scene: Naples in the late eighteenth century

ACT I SCENE 1 Inseparable pals Ferrando and Guglielmo are sitting at a cafe with their friend Don Alfonso, chatting about—what else?—chicks. Ferrando says that he's confident his girlfriend, Dorabella, would never stray. Guglielmo feels similarly about his woman, Fiordiligi, Dorabella's sister. Alfonso is a little older and a bit more jaded: He claims that women—even Fiordiligi and Dorabella—are not to be trusted. They all agree to a friendly wager, and Alfonso insists he can prove the ladies' untrustworthiness.

SCENE 2 The sisters Fiordiligi and Dorabella gaze lovingly on pocket-size portraits of their respective men. Alfonso arrives with the disappointing news that the girls' officer boyfriends have been called away on duty. Ferrando and Guglielmo enter in full military gear to trade adieus and assurances of fidelity with their women. The girls make their men promise to write every day, and the lads board a boat, which promptly sails off. Everyone exits except Alfonso, who foresees that his plan will work out splendidly.

SCENE 3 The sisters' maid, Despina, is home cooking dinner (and bitching about it) when the girls enter in a state of despair. Dorabella goes so far as to sing an aria in which she wishes she could be put to death in order to escape her misery at being left alone. No-nonsense Despina tells the girls to calm down, and informs them that they're nuts if they think those two men are going to remain faithful while away. She suggests they let loose while they've got a little freedom, and all three exit. Don Alfonso enters, concerned that Despina might screw up his plan. When she reenters, he gives her a little cash and enlists her help. Ferrando and Guglielmo arrive, heavily disguised, with the intention of wooing the girls to see how they react. Fiordiligi and Dorabella claim to be scandalized by the presence of the two "Albanian noblemen," but it becomes clear that they're somewhat intrigued. Nevertheless, Fiordiligi launches into an aria ("Come scoglio") asserting her steadfastness, to which Guglielmo responds with his own number detailing his and his friend's attractive and desirable qualities. The serenade misses its mark, however, and the girls exit, to the delight of the real Ferrando and Guglielmo, who believe that they're en route to winning the bet. Alfonso is undeterred.

SCENE 4 Fiordiligi and Dorabella have retreated to their garden, where they once again despair over their boyfriends' absence. The disguised twosome shows up, threatening suicide over their lack of success with the lovely ladies. They pretend to drink poison and drop dead on the spot. In-on-it Despina runs off for help with Alfonso, while the girls marvel at the instant and fatal devotion they have inspired. Alfonso leads Despina back onstage; she's disguised as a doctor and performs some absurd quackery, which (of course) miraculously revives the prostrate fellows. The girls (not exactly the sharpest tools in the shed) are astonished, but maintain their composure sufficiently to instruct the Albanians to leave.

ACT II SCENE 1 Despina thinks her mistresses are ridiculous. Flirt a little, for God's sake! The girls are hesitant but also a little restless, and they agree to give it a shot.

SCENE 2 Fiordiligi and Dorabella head out into the garden, where their disguised lovers (at Alfonso's prompting) renew their attempts at flirtation. Despina gives the girls a last-minute pep talk and exits with Alfonso. The foursome quickly pairs off: Ferrando with Fiordiligi (not his usual woman) and Guglielmo with Dorabella. Guglielmo gives Dorabella a locket to replace the miniature portrait of Ferrando that she usually wears. She accepts the gift and the pair withdraws. Ferrando returns with Fiordiligi, who's proving to be a bit more obstinate than her sister. He leaves the woman alone, and she sings an aria in which she expresses that she wants desperately to remain true to Guglielmo but that she is indeed interested in the newcomer. Ferrando and Guglielmo reconvene, the former with the happy news that Fiordiligi is steadfast, the latter with his not-so-hot news. Guglielmo, trying to be sympathetic, launches into an antiwoman tirade. Ferrando, however, responds sadly that he still loves his Dorabella. Alfonso is halfway to winning the bet.

SCENE 3 Fiordiligi is more determined than ever to avoid the advances of her new admirer. She decides that she and her sister must head out to military headquarters to visit their men. As they're readying to leave, however, a still-disguised Ferrando enters and reiterates his offer of love. When he demands that she either acquiesce or kill him (since there's no point to a life without her), Fiordiligi finally gives in.

SCENE 4 Now both Ferrando and Guglielmo are irate. Along with Alfonso, they sing angrily that, sure enough, "Così fan tutte" (women are all like that). Despina enters with the news that her mistresses want to be made honest women and to get married to their new Albanian sweethearts.

SCENE 5 Guests are assembled for the double wedding. The four principals exchange a few words of affection. A mistress of disguise, Despina enters decked out as some sort of wedding officiator, brandishing a bogus marriage contract. Everyone is poised to sign on the dotted line when the soldiers' march is heard in the distance, ostensibly announcing the return of the real Ferrando and Guglielmo. The girls are bugging out; their "fiancés" rush off, pretending to hide. The two friends enter, at last without their disguises, and demand to know what's going on. The girls despondently admit to their infidelity. Alfonso is gleeful as the men reveal the elaborate intrigue they have created. The girls are embarrassed and mortified but, above all, relieved. The couples pair off appropriately as the curtain drops on a joyous reunion with somewhat disturbing and ambiguous undertones.

Die Zauberflöte

Libretto by Emanuel Schikaneder
Premiere: Freihaustheater auf der Wieden, Vienna, 1791
Scene: Ancient Egypt

ACT I SCENE I Prince Tamino, while wandering through a forest, is chased, caught, and knocked unconscious by an enormous serpent. In the nick of time, Three Ladies enter with spears, with which they kill the snakelike beast. All three are immediately hot for handsome Tamino; someone has to report the incident to their mistress, the Queen of the Night, but no one wants to leave the young stud. They decide at length to head off together. Tamino promptly awakens and meets the bizarre, feather-covered birdcatcher Papageno, who takes credit for killing the serpent. The Three Ladies, on their way back, overhear Papageno's lies and padlock his mouth shut. One of the ladies withdraws a miniature portrait of Pamina, the Queen of the Night's daughter, and presents it to Tamino, who falls instantly in love. Suddenly, the Queen herself shows up and implores the prince to save her daughter, who, she says, is being held captive by evil Sarastro. She leaves. The ladies remove Papageno's padlock and give him a magic glockenspiel; to Tamino they give a magic flute. The instruments will protect the men during their potentially dangerous journey. They are warned to avoid the influence of anyone they meet except the Three Boys, who will provide periodic guidance.

SCENE 2 Pamina is imprisoned in a chamber in Sarastro's palace. The Moor Monostatos, one of Sarastro's henchmen, is guarding the girl and is itching to act on his lustful feelings for the princess. She is begging him to just kill her when Papageno bursts in (having been inexplicably separated from Tamino for the time being). Papageno and Monostatos are scared witless of each other; the latter rushes offstage. Papageno tells Pamina not to worry: She'll be rescued soon by a man who's already in love with her. The pair sings a friendly duet to end the scene.

SCENE 3 The Three Boys appear to Tamino and inform him that he's on the right track. Left alone, Tamino continues wandering and stumbles on three temples lined up next to each other. Voices emanating from two of the temples warn Tamino to stay away. At the third temple, the prince is greeted by a priest, who suggests that Sarastro is not the evil figure the Queen of the Night has made him out to be. Tamino keeps moving and begins playing his magic flute. In the distance, Papageno responds on his pipe. But before the instruments can guide the friends to each other, Monostatos enters with his lackeys and attempts to seize Papageno and Pamina. The birdcatcher pulls out the magic glockenspiel, the sounds of which miraculously manage to subdue the Moor and his men. Sarastro himself enters and Pamina apologizes for having run away. Sarastro says it's not a problem, but that the girl needs to free herself from the influence of her mother, who's up to no good. Monostatos reenters with Tamino (who for some reason forgot to ward off the dangerous man by means of the flute). Face to face for the first time, Tamino and Pamina notice the palpable electricity between them. Before they can get too close, however, a priest blindfolds Tamino and his bird-man pal and takes them away.

ACT II   SCENE 1   Sarastro confers with his platoon of priests, informing them that he's decided Tamino should be tested in the areas of wisdom and bravery before he marries Pamina. He invokes the Egyptian gods Isis and Osiris to watch over Tamino and his feathery sidekick.

SCENE 2   Outside the temple, a Speaker and a Priest consult with Tamino and Papageno, who are instructed that the first phase of their trial requires that they not speak to any woman. The Speaker and the Priest leave, and the Three Ladies promptly waltz in. They try to engage the two men, but Tamino glares at Papageno and the two manage to keep silent. The ladies, annoyed, leave, and the Speaker and Priest return to lead the twosome on to step two.

SCENE 3   Pamina is sleeping under the stars when Monostatos enters, intending to rape the vulnerable girl. He's scared off, however, when the Queen of the Night arrives bearing a dagger. The Queen gives the dagger to her daughter and orders her to kill Sarastro with it. When the Queen has gone, Monostatos returns to pick up where he left off, but Sarastro interferes. Pamina recognizes that her mother is a horrendous bitch, but she implores Sarastro to nonetheless be merciful with her. Sarastro tells her not to worry.

SCENE 4   Tamino and Papageno are sitting in a room of the temple waiting for further instructions. Ornery Papageno is hungry and tired. An ancient Old Woman enters and flirts with Papageno, claiming weirdly that she's only eighteen years old. She disappears when the Three Boys arrive with the magic flute and glockenspiel. Pamina walks in and joyously approaches Tamino, who is not allowed to speak. Pamina thinks she's being dissed and is despondent. Sarastro enters to commend Tamino on a job well done. He brings Pamina back in to say goodbye to her man, who must head off for the next stage of his test. Papageno laments the fact that he has no ladyfriend, at which point the Old Woman reappears. She tells Papageno that if he wants a woman, his only choice is to accept her as his bride. He finally agrees and the Old Woman is transformed into a young bird-girl hottie, Papagena. A priest tells excited Papageno to hold his horses and leads the creature off for further testing.

The Magic Flute

SCENE 5 The Three Boys are admiring the sunrise when Pamina enters, half crazed and determined to kill herself with her mother's dagger. The boys seize the knife before Pamina can go through with the act and tell her to relax: Tamino still loves her and everything will turn out fine.

SCENE 6 Two men inform Tamino that the final phase of his bizarre initiation rite involves trials of fire and water. Pamina is brought on to accompany the prince as he enters dangerous caves of fire and water. He plays the flute as they walk through; the instrument protects the lovers and they emerge unscathed. They're elated.

SCENE 7 Papageno is despondent over the absence of his new girlfriend. The Three Boys enter and instruct him to play the magic glockenspiel. He does, and, sure enough, Papagena returns. The two sing a duet expressing their joy and good fortune.

SCENE 8 The Queen is plotting a last-ditch effort to overthrow Sarastro, with the help of Monostatos and the Three Ladies. It's too late, however. A supernatural blast destroys the group.

SCENE 9 Tamino and Pamina exchange vows in front of Sarastro and a temple full of onlookers. Everyone sings in praise of Isis and Osiris as the curtain falls.

MODEST MUSSORGSKY 1839–1881

One of the most appealing things about Modest Mussorgsky is that, to a certain degree, he didn't know what he was doing. He was perpetually calling on other composers, like his friend and, posthumously, musical editor, Nikolai Rimsky-Korsakov, to help him with orchestration and to clean up the loose ends of his work. Mussorgsky, who traded a life as an army officer for a career in music, was able to use his limited resources to write two terrific operas (*Boris Godunov* and the less popular but perhaps equally powerful *Khovanshchina*). He also essentially created the distinctly Russian sound and vibe that seems to characterize the work of all his countrymen. It's hard to imagine how the alcoholic Mussorgsky managed to achieve this, considering he was wasted most of the time.

What makes *Boris Godunov* so successful to my mind is its careful balance of intimacy and grandeur. The opera conducts focused character studies of its handful of protagonists at the same time that it explores lofty historical themes. This mix of the general and the particular is reflected in the music, which often uses simple folk tunes most Russian audiences would be familiar with, sung by huge choruses in fiercely dramatic situations. I, for one, would sooner die than go to a choral concert (they bore me to tears), but choral moments in opera can be tremendously stirring. And *Boris* offers some of the best. Indeed, the opera's chorus is almost as important a character as the czar himself, who does not dominate the proceedings quite so completely as the title characters of many other operas. Still, no one who saw legendary Russian bass Fyodor Chaliapin's portrayal of the part could ever forget it; these days, Samuel Ramey pretty much owns the role. *Boris Godunov* is long, complex, and political, but I would still recommend it as a starting point for a newcomer to opera. The historical subject matter is gripping, the music attractive, though difficult, and the title character dies in the end. What more could you want?

Boris Godunov

Libretto by Modest Mussorgsky, based on the play by Aleksandr Pushkin

Premiere: Mariinsky Theatre, Saint Petersburg, 1874

Scene: Russia, around 1600

PROLOGUE SCENE 1 A crowd of Muscovites mills about outside a monastery. Inside, a group of nobles tries to persuade Boris Godunov to assume the currently unfilled position of czar of Russia, but the man is uneasy about accepting the job. The government official Shchelkalov (he's secretary of the Duma, or council) emerges from the monastery to report Boris's reluctance to the agitated crowd. A group of pilgrims arrives, adding to the general chaos of the moment.

SCENE 2 A day later, outside the Kremlin, the crowd is pleased to learn that Boris has finally agreed to become the new czar. Prince Shuisky (a boyar, or nobleman) introduces the man himself, who makes a brief speech that illustrates his concerns about the state of Russia and about his doubts regarding his new position as czar. The audience nonetheless goes crazy.

ACT I SCENE 1 Inside a country monastery, old Pimen toils away at the massive history of Russia that he's writing. It has been five years since Boris Godunov assumed the throne. Young Grigori, a monk under the tutelage of Pimen, suddenly awakens from a dream he's had before, in which Moscow residents point and jeer at him. Pimen reminisces, recalling the time, years ago, when Boris ordered the murder of young Prince Dimitri, son of then-czar Fyodor, whose power Boris sought to upend. Pimen mentions that Dimitri, had he lived, would now be Grigori's age, a fact that gives the young man a shudder—and an idea.

SCENE 2 Not far away, the wayward monks Varlaam and Missail enter the inn of a happy-go-lucky woman, who serves them wine. Grigori, disguised as a peasant, follows the two men into the inn and listens as Varlaam launches into a rousing and bawdy drinking song. Grigori has hatched a plan to cross the border into Poland, where he plans to establish himself as the pretender Dimitri and plot to seize the Russian throne. Policemen enter the inn with a warrant for Grigori's arrest. Fortunately for the young man, the officers can't read; Grigori himself reads aloud the description of the wanted man, extemporaneously substituting Varlaam's physical characteristics for his own. Varlaam grabs the paper and begins reading it himself, a bit drunkenly, but accurately, nonetheless. Before the old man can finish, Grigori jumps out the window and races toward the border.

ACT II The fiancé of Boris's daughter, Xenia, has died, and the girl is in tears. Xenia's brother, Fyodor, and their nurse try to distract the girl by singing nonsense songs. Boris enters, and Fyodor proudly points out on a globe the expanse of the Russian empire. Boris is pleased with his son's interest and intelligence, but he's nonetheless fundamentally troubled. Left alone, he contemplates the state of the nation and copes with the personal demons that haunt him perpetually for the murder of young Dimitri. Prince Shuisky is ushered in for a meeting with Boris, who is displeased by reports of uprisings that Shuisky has allegedly orchestrated. Shuisky asserts, however, that Boris's real problems lie in the hands of Dimitri of Poland (Grigori's new alias), who is plotting an overthrow. Boris is freaked out by the idea of a young rival Dimitri and presses Shuisky for confirmation that the czar-to-be was definitely killed twelve years before. Shuisky leaves, and Boris is once again consumed with guilt. A clock strikes, setting off a hallucination that convinces Boris that the dead child is in the room.

ACT III SCENE 1 The ambitious Polish princess Marina Mniszek has fallen in love with Grigori, whom she hopes will marry her so that they can together summon Poland's resources and attempt to usurp the throne of Russia. Inside her castle, Marina shuns the shallow attentions of her ladies-in-waiting, preferring to think aloud about politics and the future. Rangoni, a monk who wishes to impose Roman Catholic authority on Russia, enters and encourages Marina in her attempts to ensnare Dimitri.

SCENE 2 Grigori and Marina have planned a late-night rendezvous on castle grounds. But before Marina arrives, Grigori is greeted by Rangoni, who offers his services to the young politico and pulls him aside for a tête-à-tête. Music is heard, and Marina enters with a group of guests, who toast to all things Polish. Grigori reenters and expresses his love for Marina. The princess assures Grigori that she loves him, too, but she's more interested in how they can help each other seize power in Russia. Rangoni's plan to create the ultimate Slavic power couple is working.

ACT IV SCENE 1 Shchelkalov presides over a meeting of the Duma, at which the council members agree that Dimitri poses a serious threat and should be assassinated as soon as possible. The duplicitous Shuisky enters and tells the group how, unseen, he witnessed Boris's freak-out, and describes the scene of the czar's vision of dead Dimitri. Boris himself enters, still half crazed and raving. He manages to pull it together as Shuisky escorts in old Pimen, who tells a peculiar tale of blindness being miraculously cured by a visit to the grave of little Dimitri. This pretty much sends Boris over the edge; he kicks everyone out and sends for his son, whom he warns to steer clear of the boyars' dubious influence. Then he drops dead.

SCENE 2 In a forest, an angry crowd of peasants has tied up the boyar Khrushchov; they taunt and jeer at the poor man. A Simpleton enters and sings bizarre religious nonsense. The monks Varlaam and Missail arrive, encouraging the crowd to support the upstart Dimitri. A pair of Jesuit priests is dragged in and prepared to be hanged. Suddenly, Grigori himself rides in on horseback to rally the crowd. He leads them all off toward Moscow to stage an insurrection, leaving the Simpleton alone on stage to bemoan Russia's ongoing troubles.

JACQUES OFFENBACH 1819–1880

Offenbach came to Paris from Germany as a young man, and stayed the rest of his life, writing more than one hundred operettas and just a single opera: *Les Contes d'Hoffmann*. It was the final work of his life (he died during the rehearsal period of the premiere production), and it had been undertaken to acquire for the composer some degree of serious musical credibility, as well as a nice chunk of change for his descendants. Having become a strong musician as a young man in the orchestra of the Opéra-Comique, Offenbach turned to composition, cranking out short comedic pieces throughout the 1860s and 1870s that were hugely popular. It's odd to think that a man who built his reputation writing satirical romps and who composed his only opera essentially on his deathbed would have been able to produce such a weird, mystical, and enduring work.

The opera is based on the writings of E. T. A. Hoffmann, a late-eighteenth-century renaissance man who enjoyed a certain cultural currency for a while but whose legacy now seems to consist mainly of Offenbach's opera. One school of commentary cites the choice of Hoffmann's dreary, supernatural literature as an indication that, in the final stretch of his life, Offenbach was revealing a dark nature that he'd studiously kept hidden for years. But, if anything, Offenbach managed to lighten Hoffmann by means of the opera: There may be some evil characters and some scary circumstances, but *Les Contes d'Hoffmann* isn't exactly *Wozzeck*. Indeed, one can surely attribute the opera's continuing popularity not so much to its plot as to its abundance of catchy tunes. When Offenbach succumbed to illness in 1880, *Hoffmann* remained unfinished. As a result, opera companies have presented the piece in drastically varying ways throughout the years, shifting the order of scenes, beefing up or cutting back certain roles, and adding and subtracting various pieces of music. The synopsis I've provided below depicts the opera as it's most often (though not always) staged.

Les Contes d'Hoffmann

Libretto by Jules Barbier, based on the play by Jules Barbier
    and Michel Carré, after the stories of E. T. A. Hoffmann
Premiere: Opéra-Comique, Paris, 1881
Scene: Nuremberg, Paris, Munich, and Venice in the nineteenth
    century

PROLOGUE The curtain rises on a Nuremberg tavern, where voices are heard extolling the virtues of beer and wine (good start, huh?). At the opera house next door to the tavern, the well-known soprano Stella is singing in *Don Giovanni*. Lindorf, a city official, has the hots for the singer; he enters the tavern, approaches Stella's sidekick, Andrès, and demands that the man hand over a letter Stella has written to her lover, Hoffmann. The letter indicates the time and place for an amorous rendezvous, which Lindorf plans to attend himself. The opera is at intermission, so a group of students from the audience rushes in to catch a quick drink before the next act. Hoffmann arrives momentarily with his friend Nicklausse. For some reason, Hoffmann is not his usual jovial self this evening, but he manages to rouse himself by singing a comic song about a dwarf named Kleinzach. He spots his rival, Lindorf, and it looks like the two are about to throw down when the students start talking about girls. Hoffmann is always ready for this subject, and he enters into a flashback narrative about the three loves of his life.

ACT I Spalanzani, an inventor who lives in Paris, has created a daughter for himself, the life-size windup doll Olympia. Hoffmann has become a student of Spalanzani's, and when he arrives and lays eyes on Olympia he falls instantly in love. Nicklausse teases his friend, but Hoffmann takes no notice. Another inventor, Coppélius (who, having created Olympia's eyes, is sort of a stepfather to the "girl"), enters and encourages Hoffmann to try on a very special pair of eyeglasses he has made. Through the specs,

Olympia becomes still more vivid and lifelike. Spalanzani and Coppélius have invited some folks over to get a gander at the doll, and they argue about how to split the proceeds from her display; the former appeases the latter by writing him a bogus check. The guests arrive, and Spalanzani reveals his new creation, who sings a spectacular coloratura ditty, to the astonishment of everyone present. Every once in a while, the doll loses steam and needs to be wound up again, but no one seems to care. The crowd disperses to get some dinner, and Hoffmann is left alone with the doll, who is awkward and mechanical whenever her admirer touches her. Olympia rushes off stage, and Nicklausse tries to explain to Hoffmann (to no avail) that he's in love with a piece of machinery. Dinner over, the guests return with Olympia in tow. Music plays and everyone dances— Hoffmann with the object of his affection. The jig gets faster and faster and soon the pair is out of control. Hoffmann is on the floor, his glasses shattered; Spalanzani takes the doll out of the room to give her some rest. Moments later, the sound of crashing and of machinery being broken is heard. Coppélius, in a fit of pique, has destroyed the doll. Hoffmann comes to his senses and realizes that Olympia is not real.

ACT II In Munich, Hoffmann has fallen for Antonia, daughter of Crespel. Antonia's mother, a singer, has died of tuberculosis, a condition to which the girl herself is prone. She's promised her father never to sing, because the activity renders her ill. She manages to eke out a quick number before her father scolds her and she exits. Hoffmann arrives and is unaccountably let in by a servant, Frantz, who has been instructed to deny Hoffmann entry since he apparently exacerbates Antonia's health problems. Antonia greets her man, they kiss, and he persuades her to sing a duet. The song knocks the wind out of the girl, and when her father is overheard approaching, she rushes out of the room and Hoffmann hides. Crespel enters, followed by Dr. Miracle, who claims he can cure Antonia even though her mother died under his care. Crespel is eager to get rid of the strange medic, who calls out to Antonia to sing. Her voice is heard from another room of the house. Crespel kicks the doctor out, but he *miraculously* returns, not through the door but by walking through a wall. Crespel keeps up the pressure and the doctor finally departs. Antonia reenters and Hoffmann emerges from his hiding place. They decide to run away together the following day, and Hoffmann exits. But that night, Antonia has visions of Dr. Miracle, who urges the girl to enjoy her talent and keep singing. In a moment, the portrait of her mother, which hangs on a wall of the room, comes to life and insists that the near-hysterical girl sing, sing, sing! Suddenly, the painting becomes a painting again and the Miracle apparition fades. Antonia has collapsed and is near death when her father rushes to her side; when Hoffmann walks in, Crespel blames him for his daughter's demise. Nicklausse is dispatched to find help. He returns in a flash with Dr. Miracle, who says that Antonia is dead.

ACT III Hoffmann's latest love is the courtesan (read: hooker) Giulietta, who sings a duet with Nicklausse from inside her Venice palace on the banks of the Grand Canal. But Hoffmann is not alone in his affection for the woman; she's already got a boyfriend: Schlemil. Flirty Giulietta introduces the two men, who, needless to say, hate each other from the get-go. Left alone with Nicklausse, Hoffmann makes it clear that his feelings for Giulietta are more lustful than loving. Suddenly, the evil (and vaguely supernatural) Dapertutto, the requisite villain of Act III, appears, bearing diamonds that serve as payment to Giulietta in exchange for ensnaring his enemies. Dapertutto has decided that Hoffmann must go down; he presents Giulietta with the diamond and orders her to lure the hero in front of a mirror, through which Dapertutto will be able to seize his soul. When Hoffmann reenters the room, Giulietta is all over him. She offers words of love and leads him toward a mirror. An instant is all it takes. When Schlemil and Dapertutto reenter together, they carry a mirror and tell Hoffmann to look into it. He's lost his reflection! Hoffmann is horrified at having been deceived by Giulietta but is even more determined to have his way with her. When Schlemil refuses to hand over the key to the woman's room, Hoffmann seizes Dapertutto's sword and kills his rival. He heads for Giulietta's room, but it's too late. She's already outside in a gondola, cavorting with a new lover.

EPILOGUE Hoffmann has told the tale of his three great loves, and the scene returns to the tavern. Cries of "Bravo!" are heard from the opera house next door, where Stella's performance is being celebrated. Nicklausse is the only one hip to the fact that Stella embodies all the characteristics of Hoffmann's three women. His audience of students departs, leaving Hoffmann alone with Nicklausse, stinking drunk. Stella enters with Lindorf (he of the stolen letter of the Prologue). When she sees Hoffmann's condition, she decides to head off with the other guy.

GIACOMO PUCCINI 1858–1924

Puccini gets something of a bad rap these days. His operas are among the most popular in the repertory, but the composer is viewed by many classical-music professionals as an inferior artist because he wrote only for the musical theater stage, never endeavoring to make forays into orchestral or chamber music. In a sense, the Lucca-born composer is not unlike the Celine Dion of his day: hugely popular and with undeniably hooky music but lacking a certain degree of credibility. In Puccini's case, this is hardly fair. While it's true that the composer's extremely accessible operas (and their high schmaltz factor) can become wearying after repeated listenings, Puccini's devotion to and championship of the verismo style has produced works whose characters are vivid and for whom audiences feel an instant and lasting sympathy. And say what you will about treacly sentimentality, I defy anyone not to tear up when Mimì and Rodolfo separate in Act III of *La Bohème* (Cher sure did in *Moonstruck*).

Bohème is perhaps Puccini's best-loved opera and was a success right from the start. I find *Tosca*, the follow-up to *Bohème*, a little less appealing, but it's certainly a perfect place to start if you're just getting into opera. It's intensely dramatic (indeed, *melo*dramatic) and contains all the themes and incidents expected of old-school Italian opera: love, jealousy, murder, revenge, suicide—all packed into an easy-to-endure three hours. While I'll defend Puccini's work any day, I must say that I can't stand *Madama Butterfly* (although the masses will disagree with me). The work can be read as an indictment of American imperialist arrogance (which is a good thing), but it's hard to stomach the orientalist representation of the teenage geisha girl just sitting around waiting patiently for her insensitive brute of a husband to pay attention to her. Still, I suppose thousands of adoring fans of the opera can't be all wrong. If *Bohème* is an exercise in intimacy, Puccini's final opera, *Turandot* (left unfinished at the composer's death), is the ultimate in over-the-top spectacle. Set designers have a field day with the legendary Chinese setting. It's seems a shame that the title character (a teenage Asian hottie) has such difficult and heavy vocal music; the part can usually be portrayed only by enormous women of Wagnerian persuasion, which requires monumental suspension of disbelief on the part of the audience.

La Bohème

Libretto by Giuseppe Giacosa and Luigi Illica
Premiere: Teatro Regio, Turin, 1896
Scene: Paris, around 1830

ACT I It's Christmas Eve in Paris, and Marcello and Rodolfo (a painter and a writer, respectively) are freezing in their unheated garret. The fire is fading fast; what can they use to feed it? Rodolfo magnanimously offers the manuscript of a play he's working on. They throw in the first few pages as their friend and roommate Colline arrives, complaining of how broke he is. The three are watching the fire die when the fourth bohemian, Schaunard (a musician), bursts in, carrying food and firewood, which he managed to pay for by giving a few music lessons to an Englishman. The group is preparing to go out for the evening when their landlord, Benoit, shows up to excoriate them for being months behind on rent. They manage to distract and get rid of the old fellow and head out for Café Momus, their local hangout. Only Rodolfo remains behind to get a little work done. He sits down at the desk, puts pen to paper, and hears a knock at the door. Mimì, an upstairs neighbor, enters and asks that Rodolfo light her candle, which has blown out on the trek up to her apartment. The girl is clearly unwell, so Rodolfo invites her in, settles her in a chair, and brings her a glass of Schaunard's wine. She feels a little better and is about to leave when she realizes that she can't find her key. Together, the pair searches for it; Rodolfo discovers the thing momentarily but hides it in his pocket in order to keep young Mimì by his side a little longer. He touches her hand, which is stone cold, and tells his new friend a little bit about what he does ("Che gelida manina"). She replies with her own biographical aria ("Mi chiamano Mimì"), detailing her love of flowers and embroidery. Marcello, Colline, and Schaunard are heard calling for their buddy from outside. Rodolfo and Mimì have fallen madly, instantly in love, and after the de rigueur love duet, they head down together to join the poet's friends.

ACT II Throngs of people crowd the square outside the Café Momus. The scene is chaotic: Children run around, street vendors advertise their goods, and partyers drink and whoop it up. Marcello, Colline, and the others are involved in the activity; they finally find a table at the café, where Rodolfo and Mimì promptly reconnoiter with the group. Musetta, the quintessential flirt (and a former girlfriend of Marcello), comes in with

Alcindoro, an older man who's currently providing her with the various comforts she requires. The woman tries to attract Marcello's attention, but he resolutely ignores her. Finally, all activity seemingly comes to a standstill as Musetta launches into a provocative aria about her power over men. Marcello can't help but focus on the siren, who dispatches her older companion to find her a new pair of shoes (the ones she's got on are too tight). Left alone, she turns her attention to her former flame, Marcello, with whom she engages in a passionate reconciliation. The local regiment of soldiers is heard approaching in the distance, which adds to the general frenzy of the scene. Alcindoro returns, and, amid the confusion, is stuck with the bill for dinner as the group races off.

ACT III A few months later, Marcello and Musetta have moved just outside Paris, where they operate a local inn. Outside, street sweepers clean up and working-class folks amble by with goods for sale. Musetta is heard singing from inside the inn. Mimì enters, knocks on the door to the inn, and asks for Marcello, who is shocked to see the now seriously tubercular girl coughing on his doorstep. Mimì sadly complains that she's having difficulty coming to terms with Rodolfo's outrageous jealousy. Marcello suggests that perhaps they should break up and Mimì agrees that it would probably be for the best. The girl hides when Rodolfo appears, confiding in his friend that his girlfriend's openness with other men is getting to be a problem. Marcello has a hard time buying that consumptive Mimì would even have the strength to flirt with another man, and Rodolfo comes clean: In truth, he's worried that a life of squalor, which at this point is all he can offer her, will lead to Mimì's untimely demise. Having heard everything, Mimì bursts into tears and rushes to her man. Marcello leaves them alone to sadly say good-bye, after which he and Musetta launch into one of their habitual arguments.

ACT IV A few more months pass, and Rodolfo and Marcello find themselves both single and, once again, sharing the garret. They reminisce about the good times with Mimì and Musetta, and are cheered when Schaunard and Colline enter in high spirits. The revelry is interrupted, however, by the appearance of an uncharacteristically somber Musetta, who's got Mimì in tow. The poor girl is at death's door and has requested to be near Rodolfo, the man she loves, during her final hours. They make the girl comfortable and offer up personal belongings to pawn in exchange for her medical care. Marcello rushes off for help, while Musetta prays for a miracle. Schaunard looks over and notices that Mimì has expired; he indicates the news to Marcello, who has returned, and Musetta. They look miserably at Rodolfo, who seizes Mimì's lifeless body and cries out in agony.

Tosca

Libretto by Giuseppe Giacosa and Luigi Illica
Premiere: Teatro Costanzi, Rome, 1900
Scene: Rome, 1800

ACT I Cesare Angelotti, an escaped political prisoner, rushes into the Church of Sant'Andrea della Valle and hides from the authorities in the private chapel of his sister, the Marchesa Attavanti. The church Sacristan enters, carrying paintbrushes for Mario Cavaradossi, who follows him in momentarily to continue work on a painting of Mary Magdalene. The painter is using for the Magdalene's likeness the face of the Marchesa since she shows up every day to pray. The Sacristan finds the resemblance of the religious figure to an ordinary woman somewhat questionable. Cavaradossi merely notes the difference in appearance of the blond model and his dark-haired girlfriend, the famous opera singer Floria Tosca. The Sacristan leaves and Angelotti emerges from his hiding place, unaware that Cavaradossi remains. Fortunately, the two men are on the same political team, and Cavaradossi assures his friend that he will keep the secret of his presence in the chapel. Tosca is heard approaching, so Angelotti dashes back to his hiding place, locking the door of the sanctuary behind him. Tosca, having heard the slight commotion, is immediately suspicious and demands to know if the painter is hiding another woman. Cavaradossi manages to change the subject, and the lovers plan a rendezvous for later that night. On her way out, Tosca notices the Magdalene portrait—and its resemblance to the Marchesa—and flies into a rage. Once again, Cavaradossi tells her to chill and sends her out. Angelotti again comes out of hiding, explaining that he is on the lam from the villainous police chief, Baron Scarpia. Mario feels similarly about Scarpia and offers to hide Angelotti in his own house. Angelotti appreciates the gesture, and when a cannon is heard in the distance (the signal that there's been a jailhouse breakout), they rush off, emptying the church for the arrival of an influx of priests, worshipers, and altar boys. Scarpia himself enters, looking for Angelotti, and notices that the Marchesa's chapel has been recently occupied. He's also immediately aware that she's the

Tosca

inspiration for the Magdalene portrait. When Tosca arrives, he takes advantage of her ridiculous diva jealousy, sending her off to Cavaradossi's place in a fit of pique. He has her trailed, determined to see both Angelotti and Cavaradossi dead and to have his way with Tosca.

ACT II Back at the Palazzo Farnese, his grand residence, Scarpia dines alone. He's convinced (rightly) that Angelotti is hiding out at Cavaradossi's place. He assumes Tosca will lead his men directly to his two enemies and has sent his henchman, Spoletta, to follow the woman to Cavaradossi's villa. Spoletta returns posthaste: There were no signs of Angelotti, but he's brought in the painter, as well as Tosca herself. Cavaradossi is presented, handcuffed, and Scarpia administers the third degree—to no avail. Tosca enters, appalled at the treatment of her lover. Cavaradossi is sent to the dungeon to endure some sort of torture. The sound of her lover's screams of agony in the distance sends the woman into a tizzy, and she regretfully reveals Angelotti's whereabouts. The guards bring back a traumatized Cavaradossi, who rages at Tosca when he learns of her betrayal of the escapee. Cavaradossi is taken away, and Scarpia is left alone with the object of his lust. She asks how much money it will cost for Cavaradossi to be let go. Scarpia replies that it's not money he wants but booty. Horrified, Tosca sings an aria (the famous "Vissi d'arte") wondering how a woman such as she, who has devoted her whole life to art and music, could have sunk so low. Nevertheless, she agrees to the police chief's demands. Scarpia conveys to Tosca a plan for a mock execution: To keep up appearances, Cavaradossi will be shot by a firing squad—but with blanks. Out of Tosca's earshot, he tells Spoletta to actually go ahead with the assassination. Tosca insists that Scarpia fill out the necessary paperwork to allow her and Cavaradossi to flee when the smoke clears. The moment Scarpia has signed the document, Tosca seizes his dinner knife from the table and stabs the villain to death. A religious girl, she lays a cross on the dead man's chest before hastening from the palazzo.

ACT III From offstage, a young shepherd sings a lament. Cavaradossi is being prepared for his execution on the roof of the Castel Sant'Angelo, site of the prison. He declines the offer of a meeting with a priest, requesting instead that someone deliver one final love note to Tosca. He reminisces about the good times they've shared, and suddenly the woman herself appears. Mario is predictably stunned by the news of Scarpia's murder. Tosca explains everything, including the bit about the phony firing squad. Professional actress that she is, Tosca provides a few tips for dying realistically when the blanks are shot. A group of men with rifles enters and prepares for the execution as Tosca observes from the sidelines. Shots are fired, Mario collapses, and Tosca waits a few beats until the crowd has dispersed before running over to her lover's prostrate body. The coast is clear, honey! Get up! Sure enough, the bullets were real and Cavaradossi is dead. In the meantime, Spoletta has learned of Scarpia's murder and rushes in to capture the opera singer. Overcome, Tosca jumps off the roof to her death.

Madama Butterfly
Libretto by Giuseppe Giacosa and Luigi Illica, based on the
   play by David Belasco
Premiere: La Scala, Milan, 1904
Scene: Nagasaki in the early twentieth century

ACT I The American navy lieutenant Pinkerton has decided to settle in Japan and take a local girl for his wife. The curtain rises on Pinkerton and the marriage broker Goro, who gives the lieutenant a tour of his new house. He meets Suzuki, his bride-to-be's maid, and everyone settles in to wait for the woman of the hour, Cio-Cio-San (known as Butterfly), to show up with her family and get the wedding under way. Sharpless, an American officer, is the first of the wedding guests to arrive; he and Pinkerton immediately start shooting the breeze. It seems that Pinkerton, imperialist Yankee scumbag that he is, has rigged it so that he gets to marry the young Japanese girl but can cancel their vows at a moment's notice if he so pleases. He even goes so far as to suggest that someday, in the not-too-distant future, he plans to get himself a bona fide American girl to marry. This doesn't sit particularly well with Sharpless, who possesses less of the brazen sense of entitlement that characterizes Pinkerton; he already feels sorry for young Butterfly. Finally, the girl arrives with her entourage and starts providing the Americans with her personal information: She's a geisha, her father is dead, and she's only fifteen years old. All the guests chat it up, guardedly trying to get to know one another. Butterfly's kimono is weighted down by some personal items, including a knife (left to her by her dead father), which she keeps in the sleeve of the garment. She mentions that she has already converted to Christianity as the first step toward becoming a Yankee wife. Goro pulls out the marriage contract, which the principals sign, and the toasting begins. Suddenly, Butterfly's uncle (a Buddhist monk, known as the Bonze) bursts in, horrified by his niece's conversion. It seems that none of her family members had been told. Marrying an American is bad enough, but renouncing their religion is more than they can stand. With harsh words for Cio-Cio-San, they hurry off. Suzuki drags out Butterfly's intimate bridal wear; Pinkerton comforts the girl with assurances of his affection. Left alone, they sing a love duet and the curtain falls.

ACT II Three years have elapsed since the wedding, and Butterfly has been alone for most of that time. Pinkerton was called back to the States shortly after his marriage to Butterfly, who has heard neither hide nor hair of him since. Suzuki suggests that he's probably not coming back, but Butterfly is convinced her husband will one day return to reclaim her. She's played out the whole reunion scenario in her head; she describes the events she envisions in the famous aria "Un bel dì." Goro enters with sympathetic Sharpless, who has not seen Butterfly since the wedding but who has just received word for her from Pinkerton. Butterfly is overjoyed and starts chattering about how she's patiently shunned all the potential new husbands Goro has sent her way. Prince Yamadori, one of Butterfly's admirers, enters to reiterate his offer of marriage, but the geisha once again claims to already have a husband. Left alone with the girl, Sharpless starts reading aloud the letter from Pinkerton. But he can't quite bring himself to inform Butterfly that, although Pinkerton is on his way back to Nagasaki, he doesn't want any contact with his Japanese wife. Instead, he tries to feel out how she would react if she learned of Pinkerton's lack of interest. She says she'd rather die than endure her husband's abandonment. She introduces Sharpless to her son with Pinkerton, Trouble (or "Dolore" in Italian). Pinkerton doesn't know about the child. Sharpless is horrified by the injustice that has been perpetrated on the unsuspecting teenager, and leaves. The sound of a cannon shot in the distance indicates that a ship is pulling in to port. Butterfly is bugging: Her husband has finally returned! She slips into her wedding-night outfit and waits. And waits. And waits.

ACT III Butterfly has pulled an all-nighter and, sure enough, no sign of Pinkerton. Suzuki manages to persuade her to get some sleep; if her husband shows up, she'll wake her. She agrees. Momentarily, Sharpless arrives with Pinkerton, but they instruct Suzuki not to wake her mistress. Outside, Pinkerton's "real" American wife waits patiently. Sharpless has told the couple about Trouble. The Pinkertons want to take the kid home with them. Back in the house, Pinkerton finally starts to feel a little remorse. His wife, Kate, speaks with Suzuki and promises that she would be a good mother to Trouble. Pinkerton goes out (for a little air or something); Butterfly enters the room and sees Sharpless, Kate, and Suzuki. She knows something is up, and Suzuki breaks the news to her. Butterfly agrees to give up her son on the condition that Pinkerton himself come to pick the kid up a half hour later. They agree, and everyone exits. Butterfly takes out the knife her father left her (and with which he himself committed suicide). She's getting ready to turn the dagger on herself when Trouble runs in. The loving mother hugs the boy and blindfolds him. Then she stabs herself. The two American officers arrive on the scene to witness the dying woman give her son one last kiss.

Turandot

Libretto by Giuseppe Adami and Renato Simoni
Premiere: La Scala, Milan, 1926
Scene: Ancient Peking

ACT I A huge crowd has gathered to hear a Mandarin read the terms under which the icy bitch Princess Turandot will agree to marry. A man of royal birth must correctly answer three riddles of Turandot's design to win the princess's hand. If he responds incorrectly to any of the three questions, he'll be beheaded. So far, Turandot has enjoyed an uninterrupted string of decapitations. The Prince of Persia is the latest failure, and the crazed crowd anxiously awaits his public execution. An old blind man is pushed to the ground in the excitement; his slave girl, Liù, rushes to his aid and calls for help. Who should come to the old man's assistance but an Unknown Prince, who, in a strain on the story's credibility, is the old man's long-lost son. The old man is called Timur, and was at one time heir to the throne, which was snatched away by a usurper. As a result, he and his son, Calaf, generally keep their identities secret. Timur introduces Calaf to Liù, but the pair has actually met before; in fact, Liù claims that the only reason she was compelled to stay with old Timur is because his son once smiled at her. Suddenly, the Prince of Persia is brought in. When the crowd sees how young and fresh the poor prince is, they change their tack and beg Turandot to be merciful. She faces her people from a balcony of her palace, but wordlessly denies the request for leniency. Off with his head! She may be a bitch, but she's undeniably hot; Calaf wants her something awful. He decides on the spot to accept the challenge of the riddles, but the princess's minions (Ping, Pang, and Pong) warn him that he shouldn't be so foolish. Timur and Liù (as well as visions of dead admirers) add their voices to the argument that Calaf should avoid Turandot at all costs. But no one can dissuade the prince from the task at hand. He strikes the ceremonial gong three times, crying out Turandot's name with each blow—the signal of entry into the contest for the princess's hand.

ACT II SCENE 1 Ping, Pang, and Pong prepare to make arrangements for either a wedding or a funeral (most likely the latter). They yearn for the good old days, before Turandot became such a homicidal bitch. The three men reminisce about their earlier (more peaceful) lives prior to coming into the employ of the princess. But their reverie is cut short by the news that Turandot is just about ready to deliver her riddles.

SCENE 2 In front of the palace, old Emperor Altoum greets the crowd and implores Calaf to back off from this virtual suicide. The prince refuses to retreat. Turandot enters, decked out splendidly, and launches into her ferocious, showstopping aria ("In questa reggia"), which details the origins of her hatred for men. Several hundred years before, Turandot's ancestor, Princess Lou-ling, was cruelly raped by a foreign invader. In a show of solidarity, Turandot has decided to refuse the attentions of any man unless he can answer the three riddles. She begins. Riddle number 1: What is born in the heart of all humans every night only to die the following morning? Calaf's answer: "Hope." Correct! Number 2: What burns like fire but is not fire? "Blood." Two for two. Finally, Turandot poses her last riddle: What kind of ice inflames the prince? Calaf hesitates for a moment before answering, "You, Turandot!" The crowd goes wild; Turandot is incensed, having met her match; and the Emperor insists that she go through with the wedding. Observing the woman's reluctance, the Unknown Prince gives her an out. If Turandot can figure out his name by the time the sun rises, she not only doesn't have to accept him as her husband, she can have his head.

ACT III Scene 1 It's nighttime, and Turandot has commissioned everyone in the kingdom to work on figuring out the prince's name. Calaf sings about the fact that no one is sleeping that night—the aria "Nessun dorma," perhaps the most famous aria in all of opera. Ping, Pang, and Pong consult with Calaf, begging him to take money, women, anything but Turandot. The whole affair is turning the city upside down. But nothing will change his mind. A group of soldiers brings in Timur and Liù for questioning. The slave girl admits that she knows the prince's name but refuses to give it up. She is threatened with torture, but Turandot enters, asking why the girl is so fearless in the face of such danger. Liù replies that her love for the prince is strong enough for her to withstand anything. She sings an aria explaining her feelings, and even goes so far as to suggest that Turandot will eventually succumb to the prince's charms. At the conclusion of the song, she grabs a knife and stabs herself. The onlookers are appalled and pray for the girl's salvation. Turandot and the prince are left alone. The woman resists as Calaf removes her veil, pulling her near and planting a kiss on her lips. She begins to cry and admits that he is the first man to ever cause her to do so. She acknowledges his victory over her, but begs that he nonetheless leave her in peace. Instead, he tells her his name, essentially putting his life in her hands.

SCENE 2 Back in front of the palace, another huge gathering has convened. Turandot leads in Calaf. No one knows who has won. Turandot announces that she knows the prince's name: It is Love. She's finally softened. The crowd goes nuts.

GIOACCHINO ROSSINI 1792–1868

Over the first thirty-five or so years of his life, Rossini composed operas at a frenetic pace. But with *Guillaume Tell* in 1829, his tally of operas had reached more than thirty, and he quit composing, preferring instead to become the life of the party. He spent his remaining years coasting on his considerable reputation and enjoying the wealth that had come from his numerous stage successes. Instead of competing with the young guns of the opera world, he enjoyed life as a gourmand and socialite. Everyone loved the gregarious man from Pesaro, and his frothy operatic comedies had made him an Italian national hero. Part of the monumental bel canto threesome that also included Bellini and Donizetti, Rossini remains the best loved of these composers. He also wrote perhaps the most challenging vocal music of the three: His extravagant arias require virtuosic technique to handle their tricky coloratura runs. His operas are also funnier by far than those of his compatriots.

Of course, humor in opera is not exactly like a Chris Rock special or a *Friends* episode. *Il Barbiere di Siviglia* needs a clever director or it can become hokey and irritating. Indeed, many people can't stand Rossini, finding him simply too cutesy for words. Nevertheless, *Barbiere* has had a firm place in the repertory since its 1816 premiere, and with good reason. Even if you've never been to an opera, there are a handful of numbers in this piece that I guarantee you're already familiar with. *La Cenerentola*, on the other hand, is not so well known; indeed, among Rossini's works, *L'Italiana in Algeri* probably gets more play. But thanks to the interest of superstar mezzo-soprano Cecilia Bartoli, who has made the title character her signature role, Rossini's take on the Cinderella story is making the rounds of the world's opera houses with increasing frequency. These operas straddle a middle ground between fairy tale and sitcom, and as a result are easy for just about anyone to follow.

Il Barbiere di Siviglia

Libretto by Cesare Sterbini, based on *Le Barbier de Séville*
   by Beaumarchais
Premiere: Teatro Argentina, Rome, 1816
Scene: Seville in the eighteenth century

ACT I SCENE I Dawn is approaching, and Count Almaviva has come to Rosina's window to serenade the girl with a song. Apparently, Rosina is a

A
B
C
D
E
F
G
H
I
J
K
L
M
N
O
P
Q
R
S
T
U
V
W
X
Y
Z

sound sleeper, because she doesn't appear at her balcony. Figaro enters, singing the rousing (and superfamiliar) aria "Largo al factotum." Almaviva enlists Figaro, the town barber and yenta, to help him win the girl, whose name he doesn't know. Figaro knows Rosina well: She's the ward of Dr. Bartolo, whose hair Figaro cuts regularly. Finally, Rosina steps onto the balcony, having heard the serenade and written a letter to her admirer. She drops the letter from the balcony, and instructs doddering Bartolo to fetch it in order to keep the old man occupied. The letter lands safely in the hands of Almaviva, who reads the girl's tale of woe. She's a virtual prisoner in Bartolo's household and fears that her warden may force her to marry him. Poor Almaviva doesn't know what to do. He sings another song (in which he claims to be called Lindoro), but Rosina is summoned indoors. Almaviva offers Figaro money for his help; once he's on the payroll, Figaro's bright ideas start flowing. Why don't we deck you out as a soldier? he suggests. That oughta get you inside the Bartolo household. The two men head off to Figaro's barbershop to concoct a disguise.

SCENE 2 The scene changes to the inside of the house, where Rosina sings about her determination to get the guy she wants, regardless of Bartolo's designs ("Una voce poco fa"). Figaro enters, hoping to confer with Rosina, but is sent away by Bartolo. Don Basilio, the household's music instructor, walks in and informs his aging employer of Almaviva's interest in the girl. Basilio suggests that spreading nasty rumors about the count might help get him off their hands. Bartolo decides instead, however, that he should just marry Rosina himself ASAP. They exit and Figaro returns, calling for Rosina. He explains that "Lindoro" is his cousin. If she wants to write the man a letter, Figaro could deliver it for her. Rosina is on top of the situation; she's already composed a letter, which she promptly hands over to the barber to messenger to Almaviva. Bartolo enters and threatens Rosina, but she ignores him, sufficiently sure of her own finesse to be confident she'll get what she wants. Almaviva bursts in, decked out as a soldier, pretending to be drunk, and demanding accommodation for the night. Bartolo insists that he's been exempted from the then-customary practice of lodging the military and rushes off to get the paperwork to prove it. Rosina, figuring out who the drunken soldier is right off the bat, accepts a note from the man, but not before Bartolo has returned in time to see the handoff. Everyone jostles for the letter; hilarity ensues. Soon, the cops show up to shut down the party; this soldier is making too much noise. When Bartolo momentarily turns away, Almaviva identifies himself to the police, who immediately release him with words of apology, much to Bartolo's confusion.

ACT II Almaviva returns to Dr. Bartolo's house, again disguised, this time claiming to be one Don Alonso, a music teacher subbing in for Basilio. Bartolo is convinced (improbably) that Alonso is on the up-and-up when the "music teacher" hands him a letter from Rosina to Almaviva, which he alleges he discovered at Almaviva's house, where he's also the music man. Rosina enters, delighted that it's time for her music lesson, and sings an aria whose message of love is pointedly directed at "Alonso." Of course, Rosina doesn't know that Alonso is in fact Almaviva; she thinks he's the fictional "Lindoro." Bartolo gets in on the action, singing a decidedly less alluring number, which is interrupted by the arrival of Figaro, all set to administer the old man's shave. Things get a bit bumpy when Basilio arrives (he's supposed to be sick, remember); while Figaro distracts Bartolo, Almaviva hands the real music teacher a stack of cash, which he happily accepts and walks right back out the door. Figaro keeps Bartolo occupied, covering him with hot towels and shaving cream, while Almaviva and Rosina plan their elopement for later that night. Bartolo's maid, Berta, comments on the insanity of the proceedings. Once Figaro has finished shaving him, Bartolo resumes the task at hand: keeping Rosina and Almaviva as far apart as possible. He shatters his young ward by suggesting that Alonso/Lindoro is just a pawn in some master plan of Count Almaviva's to obtain the girl. He shows her the letter as proof. Count who? Feeling duped and used, Rosina resigns herself to marrying Bartolo and reveals the particulars of her plan for escape with Almaviva/Lindoro/Alonso. They both exit as a tremendous thunderstorm arrives, stalling Almaviva and Figaro, who are on their way back to usher Rosina out of the house. When she sees the pair, she's livid, but they quickly explain everything: Almaviva and Lindoro are one and the same, and whatever you call him, he's in love with her. A wedding officiator arrives with the intention of marrying Rosina and Bartolo. Instead, he confusedly presides over the union of Rosina and Almaviva. Bartolo enters a second too late and rages at the pair. But when he learns Almaviva's true, noble identity, he softens and gives the young lovers his consent.

La Cenerentola

Libretto by Jacopo Ferretti
Premiere: Teatro Valle, Rome, 1817
Scene: The house of Don Magnifico in the late eighteenth
  century

La Cenerentola

ACT I Scene i Clorinda and Tisbe, daughters of Don Magnifico, are involved in a (hopeless) self-grooming session, while their stepsister, Angelina (known as Cenerentola, i.e., Cinderella), cleans the house. She pauses for a moment to sing a depressing lament about people from different socioeconomic strata uniting in marriage. A homeless man knocks on the door, begging for a handout. Clorinda and Tisbe are disgusted, but good-hearted Cenerentola gives the guy a cup of coffee. A pair of messengers enters to announce that Prince Ramiro is on his way into town and he's looking to hook up. The hottest girl in town gets to be his wife. Clorinda and Tisbe are bugging and start screaming at Cenerentola to fetch their gowns and jewelry. Don Magnifico walks into the room and recounts a dream he just had about a flying donkey. Improbably, he sees the dream as an omen that one of his girls is sure to captivate Ramiro. Everyone exits to get ready for the prince's arrival except Cenerentola, who continues to clean up around the house. It seems that this Prince Ramiro is a clever sort: He enters the house dressed as his own valet in order to get a sense of the family minus their inevitable obsequiousness. Cenerentola and the "valet" chat, and the girl reveals that when her mother died, she was essentially relegated to the role of household help. Magnifico enters with Clorinda and Tisbe, who are all over the entering Prince Ramiro (actually his servant, Dandini, in disguise). A ball is about to get under way and everyone is invited. But Don Magnifico forbids Cenerentola to attend. Ramiro, disgusted with Magnifico's treatment of the girl, leaves with Dandini. The beggar momentarily returns, this time claiming to be a census-taker. He asks where Magnifico's third daughter is. "Dead," Magnifico replies. Everyone leaves for the ball except Cenerentola and the beggar, who all of a sudden removes his beggar garb and reveals himself as Alidoro, Cenerentola's guardian angel. Get dressed, sister! You're going to that ball!

SCENE 2 At Ramiro's palace, Dandini, still pretending to be the prince, can't get a moment's peace with the sisters and Magnifico following him around. He takes them to the wine cellar as a distraction, and assures the sisters that they've got a shot with him.

SCENE 3 Dandini has a tête-à-tête with his boss, Ramiro. Clorinda and Tisbe are making him crazy. The real prince *has* to take one of them off his hands. The girls enter, and Dandini offers his "valet" as an escort for one of them, but neither is about to slum it with a servant. Alidoro enters with Cenerentola, who's wearing a veil; he says she's an unknown woman newly come to town. She removes her veil, and while everyone senses a resemblance to Cenerentola, no one actually thinks it's her. The entire cast joins in the Act I finale, which conveys a growing sense of confusion.

ACT II SCENE 1 Magnifico is pissed about the new obstacle to his daughters' capture of the prince. The three argue and exit. Dandini, still in costume as the prince, is way into Cenerentola. Forgetting the purpose of the whole trading of places, he proposes, but Cenerentola says she's actually into (who she thinks is) his servant. Ramiro, having eavesdropped on this exchange, now appears. Cenerentola gives him a bracelet and retains a matching one. If he wants to know her true identity, he must find her and bring the pair of bracelets together again (the whole Cinderella's slipper thing has been slightly modified). She rushes out, and Ramiro immediately puts together a search party.

SCENE 2 Dandini has now changed back into his usual valet gear. Magnifico enters and is confused. You're the prince, right? Well, which daughter do you want? Dandini infuriates the mercenary Magnifico when he comes clean and asserts that he's just a servant.

SCENE 3 Magnifico, Clorinda, and Tisbe return home, irritated by their lack of success with Ramiro. Cenerentola has beaten them home and is back at her housework when they walk in the door. The sounds of a thunderstorm are heard from outside. Dandini enters, requesting help; the prince's coach is stuck in the mud. The prince himself walks in, and Cenerentola instantly recognizes him as the valet she fell for; he, too, perceives the woman he loves. Clorinda and Tisbe, needless to say, pounce, but Ramiro is having none of it. The sisters and their father are made insane when it becomes apparent that Cenerentola is the girl the prince desires.

SCENE 4 The scene shifts back to Ramiro's palace, where Magnifico and the girls have arrived in shame to witness the wedding. Infinitely patient, Cenerentola excuses their prior cruelty and launches into a mind-bogglingly difficult aria ("Nacqui all'affanno ... Non più mesta") in which she rejoices in her newfound happiness.

CAMILLE SAINT-SAËNS 1835–1921

Opera was never really Saint-Saëns's thing. And even *Samson et Dalila*, the composer's one big success in the operatic arena, doesn't really work as well as it could. Having gotten off to that terrific start, I should backpedal a bit and mention that the Frenchman was a fabulous musician, a piano prodigy as a child, and, as an adult, a superb composer of concertos for that instrument as well as for violin and cello. Indeed, you're more likely to encounter his work in the concert hall than in the opera house. But *Samson* does have its loyal devotees, and with its sexy biblical subject matter, it's not a bad place to start.

Samson et Dalila was originally intended as an oratorio, and it shows. Dramatically, the opera has the requisite narrative arc, but not much of what happens between point A and point B is all that compelling. Fortunately, the opera offers some lovely, passionate music to enjoy: Dalila's sexy come-on of an aria, "Mon coeur s'ouvre à ta voix," when sung by a talented mezzo, is worth the price of admission alone. And the orchestrations come from a man who knew how to put together a rich wall of sound; if he lived today, Saint-Saëns would make a kick-ass record producer. One reason the opera manages to enjoy fairly frequent appearances with major companies is that singers simply love to sink their teeth into the two meaty title roles. And one reason audiences keep coming back is the hot Philistine orgy in the last act.

Samson et Dalila

Libretto by Ferdinand Lemaire
Premiere: Grossherzogliches Theater, Weimar, 1877
Scene: Gaza in biblical times

ACT I Outside the Philistine temple of Dagon, a crowd of Hebrews bemoans the sad fact that they're under Philistine rule. Samson, the Fabio-like Jewish leader, speaks to the people and asserts that God has spoken to him. Just sit tight; they will all be made free soon. The Philistine official Abimelech arrives and pisses everyone off by saying they'll never be free. Spurred on by his people, Samson kills Abimelech with the Philistine's own sword. A Philistine High Priest enters and tries to calm the situation, but to no avail. Gaza has been plunged into chaos and confusion. The Priest turns angry and launches epithets at the Jews, who are fortunate to have Samson—and his superhuman strength—on their side. The Hebrews' spirits are raised, and, led by an Old Hebrew, they sing praise to God. Sultry Dalila, a Philistine vixen, enters and approaches Samson. The Old Hebrew warns Samson to stay away, but Dalila's aria of seduction ("Printemps qui commence") proves extremely arousing. It looks like the Philistine woman has the leader of the Jews wrapped around her finger.

ACT II Dalila is toying with Samson. A proud Philistine, she's determined to conquer her Jewish enemy by using her considerable sex appeal. She's tried before to convince him to reveal the source of his strength, but was unsuccessful. The High Priest arrives at her house to give her a pep talk for that night's attempt at getting the secret. The Priest leaves and Samson shows up, determined to break things off. Dalila changes his mind, however, with the fiercely sexy aria "Mon coeur s'ouvre à ta voix." "What's the secret of your strength?" she asks. But Samson demurs. Dalila heads inside, confident that the man will follow. Sure enough, he does. A few moments go by, and Dalila leans out her window to inform the Philistine soldiers hiding outside of the big secret. Samson's strength comes from his superlong hair.

ACT III SCENE I Samson has been arrested, bound, and blinded. The Philistines have also cut off all his hair. He's been sentenced to hard labor, and is currently engaged in operating a wheat mill. A group of Jews enters, incensed that Samson's lust has led to his capture.

SCENE 2 Inside the Dagon temple, the High Priest and Dalila lead a huge crowd of Philistines in a celebratory bacchanal. Blind Samson is brought in by a small child, as the group jeers raucously. The High Priest and Dalila laugh at the emasculated Samson, who prays for a miracle. The child is instructed to lead Samson to the altar. Positioned between two of the temple's supporting pillars, Samson once again begs God to return his strength, if only momentarily. Sure enough, his power returns, and he pulls down the pillars. The temple comes crashing down, burying Samson and the Philistines alive.

ARNOLD SCHOENBERG   1874–1951

I can't think of another composer who elicits such a wide range of reactions as Arnold Schoenberg. Brilliant modernist innovator! Tone-deaf serialist! Take your pick. Schoenberg's legacy seems indeed to be the creation of the twelve-tone system of composition, which cast to the winds traditional notions of key and melody. It was a movement of tremendous power and influence; indeed, it's really only fairly recently that a composer willing to embrace melody and old-school notions of musical beauty wouldn't be derided as backward and anti-intellectual. Schoenberg's image, even fifty years after his death, is still that of the archetypal musical elitist, who respected only the most rigorous and challenging musical works.

In fact, considering Schoenberg's focus on complex formal issues, it's almost a surprise that he deigned to write operas at all, since they are often considered to be inferior to symphonic works. And yet, for all its difficulty and dearth of easily identifiable melody, *Moses und Aron* offers a truly fabulous dramatic experience. There are no displays of vocal showmanship, but Schoenberg's wide tonal palette offers insight into his characters by means of sound. Moses, in fact, doesn't really sing, but rather employs a technique called *sprechstimme*, which is sort of a middle ground between singing and speaking. The opera is based on the biblical story of the prophet Moses and his quest to free the Israelites. The story must have been particularly affecting to Schoenberg, an Austrian Jew who fled Nazi Europe, relocating to Los Angeles, of all places (it's funny to see home movies of the intense master on the tennis court under the southern California sun). Unfortunately, Schoenberg died before he had the chance to compose the music for the opera's third and final act, although he had written its libretto. Opera companies generally stage the first two acts and provide program notes about Schoenberg's intentions for the final scene, in which Moses has his brother arrested for misrepresenting his ideas. He later allows Aron to be released, but the man dies soon after regaining his freedom. Needless to say, it's fascinating to think what the opera would have been like had it been completed, but, finished or not, *Moses* stands as perhaps the most impressive and progressive musical-dramatic work of the last hundred years.

Moses und Aron

Libretto by Arnold Schoenberg
Premiere: Stadttheater, Zurich, 1957
Scene: Egypt in biblical times

ACT I Moses is chatting with the Voices from the Burning Bush, who inform him that he's the guy to free the enslaved Jews in Egypt. He'll let his brother, Aron, do the talking as they engage in this endeavor. The brothers pray together and discuss how to galvanize their people, who have been beaten down by their enslavement. A group of Israelites discusses the wisdom of letting Moses be their guide. They muse on the nature of God and pray that the brothers will deliver them from this sorry state of affairs. Moses and Aron address the crowd, Aron interpreting his brother's words. The crowd has a hard time grasping what he's saying, which causes the brothers to argue. Finally, in an attempt to convince the people that the time is ripe for an uprising, Aron grabs his brother's walking stick and hurls it to the ground; the thing miraculously transforms into a snake. The Jews start to think that maybe they should listen to Moses and Aron. They are further convinced when the pair manages to turn water into blood, interpreting the transformation as a sign of impending freedom. Go on, Moses and Aron. Do your thing. We're behind you all the way.

ENTR'ACTE It's been forty days since Moses went off in search of the word of the Lord. The people are getting antsy and wonder where he is.

ACT II When the curtain rises, the Jews are pissed about Moses having been gone so long. Aron tries to calm the group, claiming it's not easy to force God to speak if He's not in the mood. Privately, however, he, too, is unsure of what could have happened to his brother. The chaos builds until Aron finally oversees the construction of a Golden Calf for the Israelites to focus their anxiety on. The people truly start to go nuts, drinking, dancing, sacrificing virgins, and, yes, engaging in an orgy. As things start to wind down, Moses at last returns, shocked and disgusted by the wanton display. He gets rid of the Golden Calf and lays into his brother, who was supposed to keep things orderly while he was on leave. Aron is defensive, and the brothers argue. In a fit of anger, Moses smashes to pieces the tablets he retrieved from the mountaintop. The Jews return to the stage, having finally calmed down and presumably achieved a certain necessary release. They are ready to proceed, with Aron among their number, to a new home-land. Moses is devastated by the group's focus on Aron's words rather than on the spiritual meanings Moses perceives behind the words.

RICHARD STRAUSS 1864–1949

Conductor and music scholar Leon Botstein once told me that Strauss, like Mozart and Haydn, seldom if ever made a musical misstep. Essentially, every note he put down on paper turned out great. Well, I'm sure many would argue that pieces like *Die Ägyptische Helena* or *Daphne* are not exactly high points in Strauss's career, but for the most part I would agree that the composer possessed an almost unerring taste and ability. Even less exciting works like *Capriccio*, a ponderous statement on the essence of opera, contain moments of extreme musical beauty.

Beauty, however, wasn't always the point in Strauss's operas. Indeed, the Bavarian composer's first big success was *Salome*, an adaptation of Oscar Wilde's play, which used a German translation of the source material for a libretto. The opera premiered in 1905, at a time when Strauss was finding his voice as a modernist composer; he sought to evoke, through music, the violence and primitivism of the historical era of his subject, as well as a sense of unbridled teenage female sexuality. As a result, the sounds of *Salome* are not pretty. *Salome* was a success right from the start, but the opera was nevertheless viewed as scandalous and ugly, although not as ugly as its follow-up, *Elektra*. I had a tough time deciding which of these two operas to include here (there wasn't room for both), and chose the first solely because it proved to be Strauss's big breakthrough. Both, however, are powerful, violent, one-act dramas that gave Strauss a reputation as a ferocious proponent of dissonance. *Elektra* was the first product of Strauss's legendary collaboration with librettist Hugo von Hofmannsthal, with whom he had a vexed but fruitful relationship (von Hofmannsthal felt that Strauss was his intellectual and artistic inferior, and he wasn't shy about saying so). The pair's next project, *Der Rosenkavalier*, proved to be their most successful and popular opera; it's truly one of the greatest romantic operas ever written and a complete about-face from the modernism of their earlier work. Strauss worshiped Mozart, and *Rosenkavalier* works as Strauss's version of *Le Nozze di Figaro*, with the Marschallin and Octavian characters doubling for (and perhaps even improving on) the Countess and Cherubino, respectively. *Der Rosenkavalier*'s last-act love trio for three female voices is the ultimate outpouring of lush vocal extravagance. Strauss and von Hofmannsthal next produced *Ariadne auf Naxos*, which, though not as well loved as *Rosenkavalier* or as important as *Salome*, is nevertheless staged all the time, thanks in large part to sopranos' attraction to the vocal and dramatic grandeur of the title role and to the compelling spitfire Zerbinetta character.

Salome

Libretto by Hedwig Lachmann, based on the play by Oscar Wilde
Premiere: Hofoper, Dresden, 1905
Scene: Biblical Galilee

ACT I Outside Herod's palace, the guardsman Narraboth is chatting with a page about the sexy princess Salome. The page tells him to pipe down; it's not a good idea to get involved with the girl. The pair is guarding a cistern that contains Jokanaan (or John the Baptist), who has been captured and imprisoned by Herod. Jokanaan's voice is heard emanating from the tank; he declares the imminent arrival of a new leader to follow in his footsteps. A Cappadocian man wanders by, his curiosity piqued by the strange intonation, and chats with a soldier. Salome soon comes out to escape the lustful attentions of her stepfather, Herod. She knows that Jokanaan has been imprisoned because of his objection to Herod's marriage to Herodias (Salome's mother). Hearing his muffled voice, she decides she wants to get a gander at the fellow. Narraboth is under strict orders to bar anyone from visiting with the young prophet, but Salome manages to persuade him to let the man out for just a moment. Jokanaan takes the stage and immediately expresses his disgust at Herod and Herodias. Salome is not offended; she's turned on. The girl finds something about Jokanaan fiercely sexy and she

A
B
C
D
E
F
G
H
I
J
K
L
M
N
O
P
Q
R
S
T
U
V
W
X
Y
Z

sets about trying to seduce him, expressing her desire to kiss him. Jokanaan wants nothing to do with the nymphet, but she is persistent. The scene becomes increasingly alarming to Narraboth, who will be in serious trouble if the prisoner is not returned to his jail posthaste. In a fit of anxiety, Narraboth pulls out a knife and kills himself. Jokanaan is appalled by the scene and heads back into the cistern of his own volition. Herod and Herodias arrive, and Herod instantly leers at his stepdaughter. Herodias is irritated, but the focus shifts temporarily to dead Narraboth lying at their feet. The body is removed and Herod resumes his attentions to Salome, to whom he offers wine, fruit, and love. Salome, however, is not interested. Suddenly, Jokanaan speaks again from the cistern, annoying Herodias. But Herod is aware of the man's power as a prophet and opts to let him be. There are several Jews on the premises, and they presently start arguing about Jokanaan's prophetic gifts. Jokanaan then offers harsh words for an unnamed "daughter of Babylon." Herodias assumes he's talking about her and starts pitching a fit. Herod is less interested in his wife's woes than in sexy Salome, whom he asks to dance for him. She doesn't want to but is persuaded by Herod's promise that she can claim a prize of her choosing once she's finished. The girl performs the infamous and maddeningly seductive Dance of the Seven Veils. It's like a scene from a strip club and Herod loves it. When she's done with the dance, Salome requests Jokanaan's head on a silver tray. Spiteful Herodias loves this, but her husband is reluctant. Isn't there anything else that would satisfy Salome? No. She wants the head. Herod gives the order and an executioner makes his way down into the cistern. The deed is done quickly and quietly. After a few moments, the executioner emerges, bearing the tray with Jokanaan's head. Nutty Salome is out of her mind. She rolls around with the head, kissing and speaking to it. Herod cannot believe what he's seeing. He and Herodias hurry inside, but not before he gives the command to have his demented stepdaughter killed. Soldiers use their shields to crush the girl to death.

Der Rosenkavalier

Libretto by Hugo von Hofmannsthal
Premiere: Hofoper, Dresden, 1911
Scene: Vienna in the mid eighteenth century

ACT I The Marschallin (or Princess Werdenberg) is in her bedroom with the young count Octavian (sung by a mezzo-soprano to convey the character's youthfulness). The couple has been up half the night having sex, and as the morning sun fills the room, they pour out words of affection. Octavian is considerably younger than his lover, who, furthermore, happens to be married. When they hear the Marschallin's little black page boy arriving with the breakfast tray, Octavian hides. When the boy has gone, the couple resume their pillow talk, but they're interrupted again momentarily by the sound of another man approaching. Octavian hides in a closet, as Baron Ochs auf Lerchenau (not the Marschallin's husband) walks in to discuss with the woman his impending marriage to little Sophie von Faninal. In mid-eighteenth century Viennese culture, it is customary for a man to send an emissary bearing a silver rose to his beloved to confirm the engagement. Who should he get to be his *rosenkavalier?* Octavian emerges from his hiding place, decked out in drag as a maid. Ochs may be there to discuss his fiancée, but he nonetheless eyes "Mariandel" lasciviously, which garners the Marschallin's reproach. She suggests her friend Octavian as a suitable rose messenger, and shows Ochs a portrait of the young man. "How strange!" says the baron. This Octavian looks just like Mariandel! A servant arrives to inform the Marschallin that she has company. The woman dresses and receives visitors: a poor woman asking for money, a gossipmonger and his wife (Valzacchi and Annina), a flutist, and a singer—all come to curry favor with the princess. Finally, everyone leaves, including Ochs, who has left his silver rose for the Marschallin to hand off to Octavian. Left alone, the woman laments the swift passing of the years. She's not as young as she once was and realizes that her relationship with the younger man can only go so far. Octavian, having doffed the Mariandel costume, returns and assures his lover that he would never leave her for a younger woman. The Marschallin sends him away, but suddenly feels bad that she acted so curtly. She sends a servant to fetch Octavian, but he has already left the premises. The Marschallin wistfully plays with the silver rose for a moment and calls on a servant to deliver it to her young friend.

ACT II The arrangements for Octavian to deliver the silver rose to Sophie are all set up. As the curtain rises, the girl's father, Herr von Faninal, is walking out the door; he's not supposed to be present for the bizarre floral ritual. Marianne, Sophie's nurse, is chaperoning the proceedings. Faninal is off to fetch Baron Ochs, whom Sophie is eager to meet, considering they're engaged. Octavian arrives, decked out magnificently in silver and white and carrying the rose. He solemnly presents Sophie with the flower, singing the gorgeous set piece "Mir ist die Ehre widerfahren." The two young people have a hard time focusing on the ritual, since they're instantly attracted to each other. Finally, the rose is handed over to Sophie, and the pair begins to chitchat. Faninal returns with Baron Ochs, who immediately tries to plant a kiss on Sophie. He sings a naughty, innuendo-filled waltz that furthers the girl's disgust. Soon, he and Faninal retire to another room to write out a marriage contract. Sophie is distraught; can't Octavian do something to save her from this repulsive fiancé? The pair sings a love duet that cements their feelings for each other. When Ochs returns, Octavian tells him to get lost. Sophie doesn't want to marry him. They argue and ultimately pull out their swords. A brief sword fight ensues, in which Ochs is nicked on the arm. Faninal is furious and screams that he doesn't care who this Octavian person is; Sophie *will* marry Ochs. Octavian is kicked out, Sophie rushes to her room with Marianne, and Faninal exits. Ochs is left alone to contemplate the events, when Annina arrives with a note from Octavian-as-Mariandel requesting a meeting the next night. His engagement not exactly going smoothly, Ochs is pleased to at least have a date set up to keep him occupied.

ACT III Octavian has carefully planned a date for "Mariandel" and Ochs that should expose the baron for the lecher that he is. Annina and Valzacchi are in on the plot and prepare themselves behind the scenes of a seedy inn to execute Ochs's humiliation. Disguised as Mariandel, Octavian sits with Ochs at one of the inn's tables. The baron offers her wine, but, affecting a nasal, lower-class accent, she refuses. He tries to kiss her, but when he gets close, Mariandel's resemblance to Octavian stops him in his tracks. The whole setup has him a little anxious: the overattentive waiter (actually Valzacchi in disguise), the odd placement of a bed near the table, the emergence of a head through a trapdoor in the floor. Ochs starts to think he's going bananas. He tries to keep it together and resumes his attentions to Mariandel. Suddenly, a disguised Annina bursts in with a group of children; she loudly claims to have been abandoned by Ochs, who's left her with a slew of kids. The children crowd around the man and repeatedly shriek "Papa! Papa!"—which further unsettles Ochs. The cops all of a sudden arrive and demand to know what's going on. Trying to cover, Ochs claims that he's merely dining with his fiancée, Sophie. Octavian has arranged for Faninal to be summoned at the precise moment of Ochs's lie. Mariandel is clearly not Sophie, and Faninal is livid. Sophie enters as things are coming to a head. Octavian slips out and changes out of the Mariandel costume, reappearing a moment later. The children are still screeching, Ochs's wig has fallen off at some point in the hilarity, and everyone is confused except Octavian. The Marschallin suddenly arrives on the scene, the only one with her head screwed on properly. It only takes her a minute to figure out that a deception has been perpetrated. And she can see from the nervous energy between Sophie and Octavian that the youngsters are in love. She tells Ochs to go home and forget about the wedding; it'll never work out. She tells the police that it was all just a joke and that she can restore order herself if they just go. Ultimately, only the Marschallin, Octavian, and Sophie are left, and together they sing the opera's famous and beautiful trio, in which the Marschallin magnanimously decides to give up Octavian and in which Sophie and Octavian express their love for each other. It's a moment of deep humanity after the hysteria of the Mariandel farce, and one of the most poignant and stunning moments in all of opera. As the young lovebirds gaze into each other's eyes, the Marschallin discreetly exits. Sophie and Octavian commit themselves to each other and leave the stage. It seems, though, that Sophie has left her handkerchief behind. The Marschallin's little black page boy dashes back out to fetch it.

Ariadne auf Naxos

Libretto by Hugo von Hofmannsthal
Premiere: Hofoper, Vienna, 1916
Scene: Vienna in the eighteenth century

PROLOGUE A rich Viennese gentleman is having a party and has commissioned for his guests' entertainment both an opera and a commedia dell'arte. Why he's slated both for the same night is something of a mystery, but there you have it. A Music Master (the Composer's teacher) finds out from the Major-domo that the opera has to share the limelight with a frothy comedy, but temporarily keeps the news from his young student. The Composer, meanwhile, is desperate to get in a little last-minute rehearsal, but the Prima Donna who stars in his opera won't answer her dressing-room door when he knocks. The Composer is distraught over what he perceives to be the imminent disaster of his creation's debut. One by one, the players in the various productions emerge from their dressing rooms: first a Tenor, irritated by the look of his wig; then Zerbinetta, a firecracker comic actress from the comedy troupe; then the Dancing Master; followed by the Prima Donna herself. The Music Master pulls the

Ariadne auf Naxos

Composer aside and heightens his anxiety with the news that he's going to have to cut some of the opera, since the host plans to show both productions that same night. Zerbinetta chats with the Dancing Master, assuring him that her performance will lighten the mood after that boring old opera. Similarly, the Prima Donna expresses her confidence that her performance will mark the artistic highlight of the evening. The Majordomo reenters with the latest news: Not only will the two shows be performed on the same night, they must somehow be combined to run simultaneously. Everyone (the Composer in particular) is mortified, but they set about figuring some sort of compromise. Zerbinetta enlists the Dancing Master to give her the plot of the opera. He explains that the lead character, Ariadne, has been left by her man, and she wants to die. Why doesn't she just get a new boyfriend? wonders Zerbinetta aloud. That's not the way it works in opera, he says. The Composer takes over trying to teach her the plot. She seems game with the idea of throwing herself into a new show, an attitude not shared by the Prima Donna, who's pissed at the turn of events.

THE OPERA The curtain rises on the opera within the opera. Ariadne (the Prima Donna) is asleep on the island of Naxos, where she has been abandoned. Three nymphs—Naiad, Dryad, and Echo—sing about the woman's pathetic state of affairs. Ariadne wakes up and sings a lament over the loss of her man, Theseus. The comedy players, in the meantime, line the wings of the stage and periodically jump in to offer their suggestions of how to increase Ariadne's happiness. Harlequin sings an upbeat aria of hope, but Ariadne doesn't respond, preferring to mope about the stage. Everyone dances in an attempt to cheer her up, but the woman continues to wallow in her grief. Zerbinetta has had about as much negativity as she can take. She kicks the others out and sings to Ariadne directly, trying to engage her in a little girl talk. Zerbinetta offers up tidbits about her own love life; she, too, has been dumped, but she got over it. Ariadne walks off silently, and Harlequin returns to hit on Zerbinetta. She's not into it, but she flirts a little nonetheless; the duo exits. The three nymphs dash back on, having heard the sound of the god Bacchus approaching. Ariadne comes back out, thinking the man is Death himself. Bacchus and Ariadne start chatting, but the god is confused by the woman's apparent death wish. She, in turn, thinks he's got an awfully roundabout way of taking her to the afterlife. Amid the confusion, however, they begin to feel stirrings of attraction for each other. Finally, they kiss, and Ariadne realizes happily that she's not going to die after all. They go off together, presumably to get busy in a deserted spot on the island. Zerbinetta reenters to claim that she knew it all along: Ariadne didn't need to die; she just needed a new man.

IGOR STRAVINSKY 1882–1971

Stravinsky was born in Russia, lived in Paris and Switzerland, and ultimately settled in the United States. Just as he moved around a lot in life, his music, too, covered a lot of disparate ground. It wasn't so much that he composed in a multitude of genres (including ballet, oratorio, mass, orchestral music, and opera), but that he seemed to call on different styles and eras as inspiration. In the 1950s, Stravinsky was generally considered a serialist composer in the tradition of Arnold Schoenberg and Anton von Webern. Just before his move into that avant-garde arena, the composer was in the thick of what's known as his neoclassical phase. It was during this period of focus on Mozartean practices that Stravinsky wrote his one true opera, the spectacular *The Rake's Progress*.

Because the opera employs harpsichord-accompanied recitatives and character-revealing arias of simplicity and beauty, *The Rake's Progress* falls under the neoclassical rubric. But, in fact, Stravinsky called on a variety of different operatic styles to put together a work that's often criticized for being a pastiche (essentially, a mishmash of disparate elements fused together). I find (and I'm not alone) that the mix of elements doesn't make *The Rake's Progress* derivative (as some charge) but, rather, original. The opera sounds like no other, and it takes a moment or two to get accustomed to its jumpy melodies and peculiar voice. I think it's safe to say that *The Rake's Progress* can claim the best English-language libretto ever written, thanks to the genius of W. H. Auden, who, with Chester Kallman, turned Hogarth's series of prints of the same title (which Stravinsky had encountered at the Art Institute of Chicago) into a narrative of poetry and power. The early-eighteenth-century source, the multiplicity of musical influences, and Stravinsky's standing as a forward-thinking twentieth-century composer combine to give *The Rake's Progress* a certain timelessness and make it one of opera's most compelling morality tales.

The Rake's Progress

Libretto by W. H. Auden and Chester Kallman
Premiere: Teatro La Fenice, Venice, 1951
Scene: England in the eighteenth century

ACT I SCENE 1 Tom Rakewell and Anne Trulove are flirting in the garden of Anne's father's house. Trulove himself comes out and asks to have a word in private with Tom. He informs the young man that he's found him a job in London, but Tom doesn't want to get caught up in a nine-to-five grind. Trulove is concerned about his daughter marrying a man without a steady paycheck, but there's not much he can do. He goes back in the house, leaving Tom to rhapsodize about a life of fun and adventure. Tom does acknowledge, though, that "I wish I had money." At this, Nick Shadow all of a sudden materializes. The man has come bearing the unlikely news that Tom has been left a small fortune by a distant uncle, who's recently died. Anne and Trulove reenter and are stunned by Tom's good fortune. Nick will take him to London to take care of the necessary paperwork. Tom tells Anne he'll call her when he gets there, and leaves with his new friend, who asserts out of hearing that "the progress of a rake begins!"

SCENE 2 Shadow's first stop in London with Tom is a whorehouse, presided over by a woman called Mother Goose. Everyone is in a hard-

WINNIE KLOTZ/METROPOLITAN OPERA

The Rake's Progress

core party mood. Tom sings distractedly about Anne, but Mother Goose knows how to take his mind off the girl. She leads the young man off to show him what she can do.

SCENE 3 Anne has heard neither hide nor hair from Tom. She decides to go to London and track him down.

ACT II SCENE I When the curtain opens, Anne is just a distant memory to Tom, who has bought a house and who's already bored with the city. Ubiquitous Nick Shadow emerges from the—um—shadows, with an idea to spice things up in Tom's life. He shows the rake a picture of Baba the Turk, a bearded lady. Since Tom couldn't possibly be attracted to such a creature, he should marry her. A marriage without lust is a marriage without headaches. Tom's into the idea and they set off to find the woman.

SCENE 2 Anne has somehow found Tom's London abode, and anxiously steels herself for the inevitable confrontation. Servants are going in and out of the house carrying packages. Tom appears and, embarrassed, tells his former flame that she should leave. A carriage shows up bearing Baba, who demands help getting out of the vehicle. Anne is shocked that Tom would marry this woman and hurries off. Baba, meanwhile, pauses to let passersby stare for a moment before going into the house.

SCENE 3 Tom and Baba are having breakfast in their house. The bearded lady is driving her husband crazy with her nonstop chitchat. He in turn angers her for his lack of interest in her. She complains vociferously and Tom replies by covering her entire head with a wig. Baba pulls the silent treatment, and Tom takes a nap. Shadow enters with a strange machine. You put a stone in on one side and bread comes out the other. Tom wakes up and announces that by some fluke he's just had a dream about such a machine! Tom's idealistic streak comes out, and he says he'd like to feed the hungry. Shadow thinks this is a terrific idea, but that they should consult with some potential rich backers of the project.

ACT III SCENE 1 Baba hasn't moved an inch since her argument with Tom in the last act, but considerable time has elapsed. Tom made a go of his stone-to-bread money-for-charity scheme, but it ended up causing him to lose everything. An auctioneer arrives at the house to sell off everything he owns. Anne has heard of Tom's misfortune; she shows up to lend her support. Customers, including Baba, bid on every item in the room. Baba, who has seen fit to start speaking again, addresses Anne, telling the girl that Tom is still in love with her. Find him and save him! she exhorts. Anne rushes off in search of the man she still loves.

SCENE 2 In a graveyard, Tom finally learns that Nick Shadow is the devil. Shadow had promised to help Tom for a year and a day, after which he would demand payment. Well, the time has come and he wants the man's soul. Nick is feeling lucky: Why don't they determine Tom's fate by means of a game of cards? With thoughts of Anne filling his head during the game, Tom miraculously defeats his opponent. Shadow accepts that he won't have Tom's soul, but in a last-ditch act of cruelty, consigns the poor rake to a life of insanity. Tom loses his mind on the spot, convincing himself all of a sudden that he is Adonis.

SCENE 3 Tom is in an insane asylum (called Bedlam), where he still imagines himself to be Adonis, awaiting the arrival of his beloved Venus. Infinitely patient and understanding, Anne enters to comfort Tom, who takes her for Venus. Anne sings the madman to sleep and leaves. When he wakes up to find that "Venus" has left him, "Adonis" drops dead on the spot.

EPILOGUE The company takes the stage to address the audience directly with the moral of the story. Together, they sing, "For idle hands/And hearts and minds/The devil finds/A work to do."

PIOTR ILYICH TCHAIKOVSKY 1840–1893

Tchaikovsky reminds me of Madame Bovary: They're both quintessential nineteenth-century romantics, desperate to find love and sex but trapped in confining circumstances. The composer is said to have identified heavily with Tatyana, the heroine of his most successful opera, *Eugene Onegin;* the character, like Emma Bovary, extracted her ideas about love and romance from the novels she was constantly reading. Tchaikovsky spent his entire life trying to acquire a measure of happiness, an endeavor that was thwarted by his inability to deal with his homosexuality. Just as the two above-mentioned heroines had difficulty establishing a sexual identity, so Tchaikovsky allegedly poured his secret heart and soul into his hyperromantic and passionate music. Debates about "gay music" (whether a composer's sexual orientation can somehow inform his work) are all the rage these days, but I'll skip the tedious and not very helpful (or well-grounded) analysis of that subject and head straight to the opera.

Tchaikovsky was a Romantic composer with a capital *R*, and *Eugene Onegin* possesses the grand, throbbing music that characterized his nonoperatic works, with which the Saint Petersburg resident had more success. Pushkin's poem of the same name provided source material for the opera, and although Tchaikovsky's adaptation is considerably more sentimental than his countryman would have liked, the piece is, thankfully, restrained by the balance of the composer's romanticism and the poet's straightforwardness. Tchaikovsky returned to Pushkin about ten years after *Onegin* with a setting of *The Queen of Spades,* a work that has not enjoyed the same degree of popularity as its predecessor. Neither opera comes close to achieving the recognition factor of *The Nutcracker,* Tchaikovsky's most famous work. Indeed, the Sugarplum Fairy is best remembered as a composer of ballets and symphonies rather than of operas. Still, *Eugene Onegin* is musically stirring and dramatically plausible. It's perhaps not the obvious choice that, say, *La Bohème* would be for a first-timer, but it is nonetheless an easy-to-stomach and rewarding opera.

Eugene Onegin
Libretto by Piotr Ilyich Tchaikovsky and Konstantin
     Shilovsky, based on the poem by Aleksandr Pushkin
Premiere: Moscow Conservatory Theater, 1879
Scene: Russia in the early nineteenth century

ACT I Scene 1 Madame Larina and her servant, Filippyevna, are making jam. From inside the house, they hear Larina's daughters, Tatyana and Olga, singing a song about love and romance. Larina recalls the old days, when she was a silly, romantic girl. An arranged marriage and a life of stability have changed all that. Her reverie is interrupted by the arrival of a group of farm workers, who arrive with a gift from the wheat harvest for Madame Larina. How thoughtful! Larina offers the group a drink as Tatyana and Olga emerge from the house. Everyone remarks that Tatyana looks like hell; she claims the novel she's reading is really getting to her. Olga's fiancé, Lensky, walks in with a friend, Eugene Onegin, whom the girls have never met before. Tatyana and Onegin are attracted to each other, but she's feeling it a little more than he is. The two young people are left alone to get to know each other. They chat for a while, until Larina calls for everyone to come in for dinner. Filippyevna, more than anyone else, notices Tatyana's instant infatuation with their new neighbor.

Scene 2 It's bedtime, but Tatyana can't sleep. She needs girl talk, and enlists Filippyevna to chat for a bit about love and marriage. After some talk about boys, Filippyevna exits, leaving Tatyana to write an awkward love letter to Onegin. Morning soon rears its head, and Tatyana hands off the letter to Filippyevna to deliver to the man.

Scene 3 Tatyana walks into the garden, causing a group of young girls picking berries to disperse. Onegin is on his way over and Tatyana is a nervous wreck. When the man arrives, he thanks Tatyana for the letter, but admits that he doesn't think marriage is in the cards for him. He leaves; Tatyana is out of her head, and the peasant girls resume their exercise of berry-picking.

ACT II Scene 1 A few months have elapsed, and Larina is hosting a party at the house in honor of Tatyana's name day. Lensky has brought Onegin, who dances with Tatyana but soon turns his attention to Olga. He didn't want to come to the stupid party anyway, so to get back at Lensky for dragging him along, he asks Olga to dance. They quickly become the talk of the party, and Lensky, predictably, is annoyed. Olga and Onegin tell him to chill; what's the harm in a little dance? The French tutor Triquet enters and sings to Tatyana, the semi-ignored woman of the hour. Olga and Onegin start dancing again, and Lensky, out of his head with jealousy, challenges his buddy to a duel. Larina manages to usher them out of the house. Everyone is surprised that the two friends would fall to such a ridiculous level, but neither can contain his anger and they agree to duke it out the following day.

SCENE 2 Lensky shows up at the allotted time with his homey, Zaretsky. Lensky is ready to fight, but nonetheless voices his regret over the collapse of his friendship and expresses his continued love for Olga. Onegin walks in with his servant, Guillot, and gets ready for the duel. Aside, both Onegin and Lensky sing about the absurdity of this argument, but neither has the balls to call it quits. The two men pull out their pistols, and do the back-to-back, pace-and-turn routine. At a cue from Zaretsky, they turn and shoot. Lensky is killed. Onegin is beside himself.

ACT III Scene 1 Years have passed, and Onegin has spent his time traveling the world, trying to rid himself of memories of Lensky's killing. He's at a party in Saint Petersburg, where everyone is dancing. Onegin, however, ruminates on how pathetic his life has become. The host of the party is one Prince Gremin, who enters with his wife, who turns out to be none other than Tatyana. Gremin introduces Onegin to his wife, whom, the prince says, he just adores. Tatyana explains to her husband that she and Onegin knew each other back in the old days, and hastily makes an exit. It is only now, of course, that Onegin realizes how attractive his former admirer is. He wants her.

SCENE 2 This time, Onegin has written a letter to Tatyana, who sits alone in her house reading the epistle. She's barely finished reading when Onegin enters and kneels, seizing her hand and avowing his love. Tatyana tries to keep it together, but can't help admitting that she loves him, too. He begs her to leave Gremin and accept him as her husband. Tatyana, however, has resigned herself to the life of stability her mother has enjoyed. Emotionally, she declines the offer and instructs Onegin to go. Devastated, he runs out.

GIUSEPPE VERDI 1813–1901

Every few years or so, someone proclaims a new Golden Age of Opera. But the mid-nineteenth century truly was the greatest era in the form's history, and it was dominated by two men: Richard Wagner and Giuseppe Verdi. If Wagner was the intellectually rigorous innovator who challenged his audiences, Verdi was the guy you turned to for beautiful melodies and memorable tunes—which, however, is not to denigrate his artistic achievement. For much of his career, Verdi was considered a tunesmith more than a purveyor of integrated musical dramas. *Il Trovatore*, for example, boasts one powerhouse number after the next, though its narrative could scarcely be dumber. But in his later years, Verdi proved himself to be Wagner's equal (this is, of course, debatable) in terms of through-composed marriages of music and drama in which neither stepped on the other's toes (see p. 232). The man from Parma's mid-career blockbusters were like extremely accomplished bel canto exercises, but as an old man, coming out of retirement, he took on Shakespeare, and, miraculously, heightened the experience of the bard's plays. Verdi was a productive artist for a huge chunk of the nineteenth century, and for most of that period he was also an Italian national hero, a genius who had come from poverty and managed to create an international reputation.

In choosing which Verdi operas to focus on, I've skipped his early years, during which he produced operas like *Nabucco, Ernani, Macbeth,* and others—all of which are still performed regularly today. These works are strong (for the most part), but it was the triumvirate of *Rigoletto, Trovatore,* and *La Traviata* that sent Verdi into the stratosphere. Because of arias like "Questa o quella" and "La donna è mobile" from *Rigoletto,* which demonstrate the composer's impressive ability to write hooks (he'd be a great pop songwriter today), it's easy to forget that the opera wasn't just a series of hit songs but was considered somewhat scandalous—a harsh criticism of Italian court life. Similarly, *La Traviata*'s sympathetic portrait of a Paris courtesan came out at a time that predates by more than a hundred years the hooker-with-a-heart-of-gold plotline that seized Hollywood in the twentieth century. Back in 1853, the story of Violetta was shocking stuff. I'm not crazy about *Aida* (the inevitable procession of horses and the faux glamour of the pyramids are distracting), but it's such a monumental crowd pleaser that I'd be nuts to exclude it. There are plenty of other Verdi operas that deserve inclusion in this roundup, especially *Don Carlo* and *Falstaff,* which fall into the impressive late-Verdi, Wagneresque music-drama period (*Don Carlo* came out a little earlier, but it nonetheless shares characteristics of Verdi's last two operas). To represent this era of Verdi's oeuvre, I've included *Otello,* which, with its well-constructed libretto (courtesy of sometime composer Arrigo Boito) and sublime music, is not only Verdi's greatest opera, but, to my mind, among the top five of all time.

Rigoletto

Libretto by Francesco Maria Piave, based on *Le Roi s'amuse* by
   Victor Hugo

Premiere: Teatro La Fenice, Venice, 1851

Scene: Mantua in the sixteenth century

ACT I SCENE I The Duke of Mantua is having a party. In the midst of the revelry, he pulls aside his friend Borsa to inform him that he's all horned up for some chick he sees around town. He doesn't even know her name, but that won't stop him from plotting to have her. He sings an aria ("Questa o quella") that indicates his belief that, essentially, booty is booty. The Duke may have his eye on the mystery girl, but for the time being he's content to keep himself occupied dancing with the Countess Ceprano. This doesn't sit particularly well with the Countess's husband, who is presently teased by Rigoletto, the Duke's hunchback court jester. Count Ceprano's mounting anger becomes old news at the entrance of Count Monterone, who comes in bitching that the Duke has seduced his daughter. Instead of apologizing or denying the charge, the Duke simply has the poor guy arrested. Rigoletto turns his taunts on Monterone, who replies by placing a curse on the hunchback.

SCENE 2 Rigoletto is on his way home from the party. Monterone's curse has genuinely freaked him out. He becomes further agitated when confronted by Sparafucile, the town hit man. He needs work; does Rigoletto need anyone taken care of? Not at the moment, thank you. The thug leaves, and Rigoletto becomes morose, bemoaning the pointlessness of his job. He finally arrives home, where he's met by his daughter, Gilda, who's the apple of his eye. Gilda's mother has died and the girl is pretty much all Rigoletto has. An overprotective father, he doesn't let her out of the house and makes sure his maid, Giovanna, watches over the girl when he's not around. Sure enough, the nameless girl that the Duke has the hots for is Gilda. In disguise, the Duke has snuck over to the house to try and woo her; Rigoletto hears sounds of an intruder and goes to check it out. The Duke hides in the garden, slipping Giovanna a stack of cash as incentive to cover for him. Rigoletto exits, and the Duke reappears. Giovanna turns a blind eye as the Duke and Gilda flirt. The Duke says that he's a student, one Gualtier Maldè by name. He takes his leave momentarily as Borsa and Count Ceprano are heard outside, having come to get revenge from Rigoletto for ridiculing them at the party. Gilda sings her first big aria ("Caro nome"), in which she rhapsodizes over the young man's rather peculiar name. Borsa and Ceprano enter secretly, not realizing that Gilda is the hunchback's daughter; they think she is his lover. When Rigoletto comes back, the two men blindfold him, assuring him it's part of a Duke-sponsored intrigue. With the jester thus compromised, they seize Gilda and carry her off. When he hears his daughter's screams and realizes that she's been kidnapped, Rigoletto is convinced of the power of the curse.

ACT II The Duke is unaware that Gilda has been abducted. All he knows is that when he returns to the house, she is gone. He returns to his palace and, alone, sings of his genuine affection for the girl. Borsa and Ceprano enter with the news that they have captured Rigoletto's ladyfriend. The Duke knows instantly that it is Gilda and rushes off to see her. Rigoletto wanders in, devastated by his daughter's capture and determined to get to the bottom of things. He tries to put on a happy face to keep up appearances but soon is lamenting the loss of his daughter. Borsa and Ceprano can't believe it. Daughter? Gilda all of a sudden runs in, having managed to escape the Duke's clutches. Gualtier Maldè is not the man she thought he was. Rigoletto vows to exact revenge from his employer, although Gilda—still harboring feelings for the guy—begs her father not to be too harsh.

ACT III The Duke is back on the prowl. Disguised as a soldier, he's chilling in an inn with his buddy Sparafucile. He sings the famous aria "La donna è mobile" about how fickle all women are. Rigoletto, meanwhile, has a plan. He's brought Gilda with him to the inn; the two of them peer in the window so that the girl can get the full picture of the Duke's immorality. She observes as the nobleman flirts with Sparafucile's sister, Maddalena. The Duke is unaware, however, that Sparafucile has been retained by Rigoletto. The tough guy goes outside to confer with the hunchback, who instructs his daughter to go home, disguise herself as a boy, and decamp to Verona, where she will be safe. He pays Sparafucile and arranges things so that Rigoletto himself will be able to dispose of the body. He leaves and Sparafucile goes inside. His sister has found herself attracted to the Duke and begs her brother not to kill him. Why don't you just kill someone else and give Rigoletto the wrong body? He probably won't notice. Sparafucile agrees, asserting that the next guy to enter the inn is a dead man. Gilda has returned (in boy's clothing) just in time to hear this scheme. She's heartbroken by the Duke's lack of devotion but loves him nonetheless. She decides to sacrifice herself to save the lecher and enters the inn. Sure enough, Sparafucile kills the girl and puts her corpse in a bag. Rigoletto promptly returns, grabs the body bag, and heads to the river to throw in what he believes to be the Duke's cadaver. All of a sudden, though, he hears from a distance the upbeat strains of "La donna è mobile" and recognizes the Duke's voice. He opens the bag to discover Gilda at death's door. She apologizes for her rash act and expires. Rigoletto, horrified, once again cries out about the curse that has taken his daughter.

Il Trovatore
Libretto by Salvatore Cammarano and Leone Emanuele Bardare
Premiere: Teatro Apollo, Rome, 1853
Scene: Spain in the fifteenth century

ACT I SCENE 1 The Count di Luna's guardsman, Ferrando, sets the scene of the opera by regaling a group of palace soldiers with the story of the Count's younger brother. Years ago, the gypsy Azucena, horrified by the burning at the stake of her mother and seeking revenge, kidnapped the infant child and threw him into the fire. No one was able to recover the kid's body, and some think he may still be alive.

SCENE 2 In a palace garden, Leonora, a noblewoman, is confiding in her girlfriend Inez about the troubadour who appears regularly under her balcony to serenade her. She's madly in love with the man, but she doesn't know his name. The tête-à-tête is interrupted by the arrival of the Count, who wants Leonora for himself. He's about to make a move on the woman when the sound of the troubadour singing is heard from outside. Leonora runs to the troubadour. So does the Count, who's ready for a fight. The singer introduces himself as Manrico. He and the Count argue and make preliminary plans for a rumble.

ACT II SCENE 1 Manrico is hanging out with his mother, Azucena, and the rest of the gypsies at their campsite. Azucena is feeling melancholy, and she launches into an aria ("Stride la vampa") about the time her mother was burned at the stake. She then lets it slip that she accidentally threw her own kid into the fire rather than the Count's younger brother. This bit of news stops Manrico dead in his tracks. Is he not actually Azucena's son? She deflects the question, and suddenly Manrico recalls how, in his duel with the Count a few months back, he couldn't bring himself to kill his opponent. Something had told him he should hold back. Suddenly, a messenger bursts in with the news that Leonora, having been misinformed that Manrico was dead, has decided to go into a convent. He better get up to the palace—and fast—if he wants to see the girl again.

SCENE 2 Leonora has made it to the convent and is about to take her vows of chastity. Manrico is on his way, but the Count has beaten him there. He sings of his love for the girl, and when she appears, he emerges from hiding with his henchman. He's about to seize Leonora when Manrico rushes in. Manrico and his homies defeat the Count in a rumble, and the troubadour exits with Leonora in tow.

ACT III SCENE I Manrico and Leonora are inside the Castellor fortress. Outside, the Count and his platoon prepare to attack. Nutty Azucena wanders in, searching for Manrico. The Count recognizes her as the baby killer of long ago, not to mention as the mother of his enemy. He decides the gypsy should share the same fate as her mother, and prepares for her to be burned.

SCENE 2 Inside the castle, meanwhile, Manrico and Leonora are trading words of love and getting ready for their imminent marriage ceremony. A messenger arrives with news of Azucena's capture. Hearing that she's going to be burned at the stake, Manrico prepares a rescue mission, and sings his big number ("Di quella pira") expressing his anger.

ACT IV SCENE I Well, the rescue mission didn't go so well, and Manrico is now imprisoned with his mother in the Count's palace. Leonora is determined to save her man; she sneaks in and sings of her love ("D'amor sull'ali rosee"). Chanting in the distance indicates that Manrico is not long for this world. The Count walks in and is shocked to see Leonora. She begs him to release Manrico, even going so far as to offer herself in marriage if he just lets the guy go. This sounds good to the Count, and he agrees to the arrangement. When the Count isn't looking, Leonora ingests some poison that she'd hidden inside her ring.

SCENE 2 In their cell, Manrico and Azucena try to keep their spirits up in the face of impending death. Leonora, weak and near death, comes in and informs Manrico of the deal. He's furious at the arrangement, but there's no time for a fight. Leonora confesses her suicide mission—undertaken entirely to save the man she loves. The Count walks in as Leonora dies. Well, with no wife on the horizon, the Count returns to his decision that Manrico should be killed. The troubadour is led to the executioner, who promptly beheads the man as the Count and Azucena watch through a window. The deed done, Azucena gleefully informs her captor that he has just murdered his own brother. Finally, the gypsy's long-dead mother is avenged!

La Traviata

Libretto by Francesco Maria Piave, based on *La Dame aux Camélias* by Alexandre Dumas fils
Premiere: Teatro La Fenice, Venice, 1853
Scene: Paris in the mid nineteenth century

ACT I Violetta is the life of the party. The courtesan is hosting a ball at her well-appointed Paris apartment and everyone is having a grand old time. Violetta's current boyfriend and benefactor, Baron Douphol, is there; so are her best friend, Flora, and their buddy Gastone. Gastone has brought a new friend, Alfredo Germont, who has had a crush on Violetta for some time, even though they have never met until now. Alfredo sings a toast (the rousing and famous brindisi), and the whole crowd joins in. At the conclusion of the toast, everyone hastens to another room, where a band is striking up some dance music. Violetta, however, remains behind to get over a coughing fit. Alfredo has witnessed the scene and is worried. He confesses to Violetta that he loves her, but she rebuffs him, saying she's not the kind of girl he should get involved with. Nevertheless, she tells him he can visit her again sometime soon. The party soon dies down; the guests leave, and Violetta is left alone. She cannot quite get thoughts of Alfredo out of her mind. She sings a long aria ("È strano . . .") about her mixed emotions. Her soliloquy is periodically interrupted by the sounds of Alfredo serenading her from outside her window. Violetta's soul-searching moment concludes with the decision that she should not be tied down to this one man. She must be free!

ACT II SCENE I A few months later, Violetta and Alfredo are living together just outside the city. Alone in the drawing room, Alfredo sings about how happy he is with his newfound domesticity. What he doesn't realize is that living in a chic country house doesn't come cheap: Violetta's maid, Annina, enters and informs Alfredo she has been dispatched by the woman to go into town and sell some of her jewelry. Alfredo feels sick to his stomach. How could he have been so thoughtless?

He immediately dashes off to Paris to figure out a new financial arrangement. Violetta enters, having just received an invitation to one of Flora's parties, which she intends to skip. To Violetta's surprise, Alfredo's father is announced, and the old man enters screaming bloody murder about how Violetta has driven his son into poverty. What is he talking about? Violetta demands. She's paying for virtually everything. Germont softens a bit, but nonetheless makes a distressing request. His daughter is engaged, but the wedding has been called off by the groom's side of the family. It seems that Alfredo's relationship with a courtesan has scandalized society and ruined the family's good name. Violetta is horrified. How could she possibly give up the man she loves? However, when Germont describes his lovely daughter and her despair at the situation, Violetta sadly resigns herself to breaking things off with Alfredo in order to save his family. Despite the tension of the meeting, there is a deep mutual regard between Violetta and Germont, who takes his leave with words of thanks and a strong impression of the girl's character. Suddenly single, Violetta decides to go to Flora's party after all. She writes a note to Alfredo, explaining that it's over, but without mentioning the visit from his father. She's barely done writing when Alfredo himself enters. An agitated Violetta tells her man she loves him and rushes out to her carriage. Alfredo is confused, but a moment later, when a servant enters with Violetta's note, he realizes he's been dumped. Germont returns and offers his sympathy (although he withholds the true cause of Violetta's departure). Alfredo is convinced that his girlfriend must be with Baron Douphol. He notices Flora's party invite and determines to show up that night.

SCENE 2 Flora's party is reminiscent of the revelry that opened the opera, but even more spectacular. She's got fortune-tellers, bullfighters, and all manner of party diversions. Alfredo walks in and immediately hits the gambling tables. He's doing well. Violetta enters with, of course, Douphol. The men are almost immediately at each other's throats. Violetta pulls Alfredo aside and begs him to leave before Douphol does something rash. Alfredo is livid. When a group of guests reenters the room, Alfredo publicly humiliates the woman; claiming he can finally repay her, he throws a handful of cash directly at Violetta, an act of aggression that sends the crowd into a tizzy. Old man Germont has arrived in time to witness his son's rudeness, and he publicly excoriates miserable Alfredo. Violetta is hysterical and about to pass out. As the curtain closes, she murmurs that she does indeed still love Alfredo.

ACT III A few weeks have passed, and tubercular Violetta's health has rapidly declined. She's back at her Paris apartment. Everyone seems to have forgotten the poor woman except her maid, Annina, and her physician, Dr. Grenvil. A letter arrives from Germont, explaining that Alfredo has finally learned the reason for Violetta's departure and is en route to her house. Violetta knows she's at death's door, and she sings sadly about what might have been. Alfredo finally bursts in, despondent and offering promises of a life together outside Paris once Violetta gets well. But Violetta knows that's not going to happen. She doesn't think she can last much longer, and sends Annina out to get the doctor. They return posthaste with Germont, who has come to pay his respects. Selflessly, Violetta urges Alfredo to find another woman and to settle down and be happy—just please remember to honor her memory and tell his new wife about the woman who once loved him. Everyone is moved beyond words. Suddenly, unaccountably, miraculously, Violetta starts to feel a little better. Could it be? She's going to recover?! She gets out of bed and joyfully announces that she feels fine, only to fall to the ground dead a moment later.

Aida

Libretto by Antonio Ghislanzoni
Premiere: Opera House, Cairo, 1871
Scene: Ancient Egypt

ACT I SCENE I Egypt is at war with Ethiopia. Inside the royal palace of Memphis, the soldier Radames is informed by the high priest Ramfis that he must lead the Egyptians to victory. The goddess Isis has declared it. The man is committed to the fight but, left alone, admits that he's in love with an Ethiopian slave girl, Aida. Aida is in the personal employ of Princess Amneris, who suddenly approaches Radames. She wants the soldier for herself. Aida enters and it's clear that there's chemistry between her and Radames, a fact that irritates Amneris no end. She manages to keep from revealing her suspicions of the attraction between the Egyptian object of her affection and the Ethiopian slave. Amneris's father, the King, enters with Ramfis and other advisors. The group learns from a messenger that the Ethiopian king, Amonasro, has had success in battle and is on the verge of conquering Thebes. Aida may be just a slave in Egypt, but in Ethiopia she's a princess—Amonasro's daughter, in fact. Her true identity is a secret, however, and to keep it that way, Aida joins in the group's call for victory. It is decreed that Radames will lead the army into battle. Everyone leaves except Aida, who prays to somehow keep her sanity amid the confusion of her conflicted feelings for Radames and for her homeland.

SCENE 2 In the Temple of Vulcan, Ramfis and a priestess lead a prayer for the Egyptian army. They bless Radames's sword and send the young man off to fight.

ACT II SCENE 1 Radames has won the battle, and back at the palace Amneris is getting ready to give him a very special and personal victory present. Slave girls do her hair and makeup as she waits for the hero to return. Aida enters. Amneris figures she can make the girl admit her feelings for Radames, and tells her that he died on the battlefield. Aida is beside herself and can't contain the fact that she loves Radames passionately. Amneris admits she was lying and lays into the girl for secretly desiring someone she herself clearly has eyes for. Amneris exits, and Aida prays.

SCENE 2 At Thebes, the Egyptians are singing in triumph and enjoying a celebratory parade. The King and Amneris offer Radames whatever riches he can think of. The Ethiopian prisoners are brought in, among them Amonasro, whose identity escapes everyone except Aida, who nonetheless keeps silent. Without revealing who he is, Amonasro begs the Egyptians to spare their lives. The Egyptian King is not as hard-hearted as some of his advisors; he agrees to free all the prisoners except Amonasro and Aida. He then "rewards" Radames with his daughter's hand in marriage. Aida and Radames are silently distraught.

ACT III Ramfis and Amneris arrive at a temple on the banks of the Nile, where she intends to pray for a successful marriage. Aida appears, unseen, and yearns for her former life in Ethiopia. She's waiting for Radames to arrive (they've planned a secret rendezvous), but her father, Amonasro, gets there first. The old man is dead set on revenge, and he instructs his daughter to elicit military secrets from Radames. By what route are the Egyptians planning their next attack? Aida is hesitant to go ahead with the plan, but Amonasro says it's for the good of Ethiopia, and she agrees. The old king scurries off, and Radames enters. He's got good news and bad news: The bad news is that there's going to be another battle. The good news is, if he wins, he will get whatever he wants, and he intends to ask for Aida. Why don't they just run off together then and there? Aida begs. And, oh yeah, by what route are the Egyptians planning to attack? Radames reveals the battle secret just as Amonasro returns from hiding. Radames is mortified by the slipup, and the two Ethiopians implore him to run away with them. Just then, Amneris and Ramfis come out of the temple to witness the bizarre conference. Radames, a traitor? Arrest him, the princess cries. Aida and her father manage to escape as Radames is seized by authorities.

ACT IV SCENE 1 Amneris may have ordered Radames's capture, but she still can't help but love him. She has the man brought before her, and informs him that she can ensure his survival if he agrees to renounce Aida and marry her. But Radames refuses to say anything against Aida. Amneris is livid and sends him off to a panel of judges who will decide his fate. It's determined that Radames should be buried alive. This is more than Amneris can bear and she begs them to change their minds, but to no avail.

SCENE 2 Back in the Temple of Vulcan, Radames has been sealed in an underground crypt. He is shocked to discover Aida in the tomb with him. She learned of the guy's fate and snuck into the crypt when no one was looking, so that they could die together. They sing a love duet in preparation for death. Amneris, above them in the temple, prays for Radames's salvation.

Otello

Libretto by Arrigo Boito, based on Shakespeare's *Othello*
Premiere: La Scala, Milan, 1887
Scene: Cyprus in the late fifteenth century

ACT I A huge crowd of Cypriots waits at the seaport for their army's general, Otello, to return from a battle with the Turks. A storm is raging, and so far there's no sign of the Moor's ship. Finally, it comes into view and shortly thereafter sails into the harbor, to the endless relief of the citizens. Otello disembarks and sings a tremendously difficult victory statement ("Esultate!"). There are only two people who don't join in the jubilation: Iago, a friend, colleague, and confidant of Otello, who nonetheless hates the man for bestowing a promotion on his rival, Cassio; and Roderigo, a Venetian gentleman who's in love with Otello's wife, Desdemona. Otello goes off to his wife, and wily Iago leads the crowd in a drinking song and toast. He sees to it that Cassio has a bit too much to drink, and instructs Roderigo to pick a fight with the guy. All hell breaks loose, and when the respected former officer Montano tries to break things up, he is injured by a blow from Cassio. Iago calls for Otello, who enters with Desdemona, both of them annoyed by this interruption of their reunion. Otello sees that Cassio is in the middle of the dispute and fires him on the spot, to Iago's profound glee. Everyone leaves except the Moor and his wife, who sing words of love to each other before returning to the bedroom.

ACT II Shortly thereafter, in the castle, Iago approaches Cassio and suggests that he turn to Desdemona for help in getting back on Otello's good side. Good idea! thinks not-so-bright Cassio. He exits and Iago is left alone to continue plotting to break up Otello and Desdemona. It becomes clear through his "Credo" aria that Iago is pure evil; there doesn't seem to be much rhyme or reason behind his meanness. With Iago observing from a distance, Cassio approaches Desdemona to seek her counsel. Otello wanders in, and Iago points out that his wife seems to be embroiled in a tête-à-tête with Cassio, cleverly planting the seeds of jealousy. Otello observes as a group of townsfolk greet Desdemona and bring her presents. He goes to his wife, who immediately asks about giving Cassio his job back. The Moor becomes tense; the woman gives him a handkerchief so he can wipe himself down. He takes the hanky and throws it to the ground, startling Desdemona. Her maid, Emilia, who is also Iago's wife, picks it up and hands it over to the villain at his insistence. Desdemona is concerned about her troubled husband, but he demands that everyone leave him in peace. Otello is irritated that Iago has brought up the sore subject of Cassio and Desdemona, but he still trusts the guy and asks if he truly suspects any infidelity. Iago concocts a tale of having heard Cassio talking in his sleep about Desdemona. He also says (planning a few steps ahead) that he's seen the man with one of her handkerchiefs. Otello is irate and vows to get revenge.

ACT III Otello is in the great hall of the castle, where he is visited by a messenger with news that some political types are on their way from Venice. Iago enters to get Otello riled up, but cuts the meeting short when Desdemona enters. Otello tries to keep his cool, but Desdemona insists on bringing up that damn Cassio. Otello asks for Desdemona's handkerchief, but she says it's back in their quarters. She once again directs the conversation to the subject of Cassio, and Otello loses it, accusing his wife of having an affair. Desdemona is thunder-struck and instantly denies the charge. Otello refuses to believe her and tells her to get out of his sight. Otello sees Iago on his way back in with Cassio and hides so that he can eavesdrop on the conversation (Iago's idea, of course). Iago and Cassio are talking about noth-ing in particular, but Iago throws in a few remarks, within Otello's hearing, that make it seem like Desdemona is the primary topic. Earlier that day, Iago had planted Desdemona's handkerchief in Cassio's room. The unwitting pawn now

Renée Fleming and
Plácido Domingo in *Otello*

produces the item, which sends Otello over the edge. Suddenly, the visi-tors from Venice are announced. Cassio leaves and Otello confers with Iago about killing Desdemona. The Venetian officials enter, led by Lodovico, who gives Otello an edict from government headquarters. Otello reads the note aloud. It seems he's being called back to Venice; Cassio will take his place running things on Cyprus. The promotion of Cassio incenses Otello and he takes it out on his wife, pushing her to the ground in front of everyone and screaming bloody murder. Everyone is stunned—except Iago, whose plan is working better than he could have hoped. Otello kicks them all out of the hall. Only Iago remains to watch as Otello passes out, overcome by the stress of the day's proceedings.

ACT IV Desdemona is alone in her bedroom with Emilia. She's devas-tated by the situation with Otello and senses that her life is in danger. She sings the famous Willow Song lament, sends Emilia away, and kneels to pray ("Ave Maria"). She subsequently falls asleep, but Otello enters and wakes her. He brings up the familiar Cassio accusations, and Desdemona once again insists she's innocent. Otello has by now truly gone over the deep end, and he smothers the woman in her bed. Emilia reenters to deliver the news that Cassio has killed Roderigo. She can't believe her eyes when she sees Desdemona on the verge of death. Otello indicates that it was her husband, Iago, who gave him the information of Desde-mona's infidelity. Emilia cannot believe he would take the word of her evil spouse. Iago, Cassio, and Montano enter. Iago tells his wife to button her lip, but she refuses and manages to persuade Otello that the whole story came out of Iago's mean-spirited head. Despondent, Otello whips out his sword and falls on it, kissing his dead wife one last time before dying himself.

RICHARD WAGNER 1813–1883

Trying to condense the career of Richard Wagner into a couple of paragraphs is like trying to sit through *Die Meistersinger von Nürnberg* without dozing off now and again. There simply has been no other composer of equal influence or commitment to advancing the form of opera. Wagner himself would be the first to assert his importance; the man was a ferocious egomaniac who wasn't shy about pointing out his achievements. Wagner was a devotedly nationalistic German (born in Leipzig), and his operas (thirteen of them in total) focus on German mythology, much of it Wagner's own creation. The composer's advancements were many, including the heavy use of leitmotiv (musical themes that reappear throughout a piece to represent specific characters or concepts); the implementation of a through-composed technique (no more recitatives connecting arias but, rather, full start-to-finish orchestration that seldom lets up); and the establishment of his own theater in Bayreuth, where he was able to stage his works using various theatrical innovations he'd dreamed up (dimming the lights in the audience, hiding the orchestra in a pit under the stage, etc.). But Wagner's ultimate legacy is probably the idea of the *Gesamtkunstwerk*, or total work of art. Folks had been wrangling with the words-versus-music problem since opera's origins in the late sixteenth century, but Wagner saw that opera encompassed more than just these two elements. Music, poetry, drama, sets, costumes, lighting, and dance all had to be joined in a seamless whole. Opera, or the "artwork of the future," as he called it, was the ultimate multidisciplinary art form, and none of its components could suffer at the hands of another.

Wagner didn't start out so deeply committed to the *Gesamtkunstwerk* concept, though. Indeed, for the early part of his career, he was the quintessential (and best) German Romantic composer, with *Tannhäuser* and *Lohengrin* proving to be his greatest achievements in this arena. Because

Wagner is so indelibly associated with the *Ring* cycle and with a certain progressiveness, it's easy to dismiss these two operas because they're not revolutionary. But I find *Tannhäuser* to be the man's most musically appealing work, and, along with *Lohengrin*, it offers up actual arias, which makes it more agreeable to the newcomer who may need such set pieces to help guide him through a work. These arias, or numbers, were dropped in *Tristan und Isolde*, a harmonically advanced work that was also Wagner's first foray into the through-composed style of orchestration he would favor for the rest of his life. *Tristan* was followed by the *Ring* series, a tetralogy that would take more than twenty-five years to produce and that necessitated the construction of the Bayreuth theater to accommodate its technical demands. No other operatic endeavor in history has been so ambitious, and I think it's safe to say that *Der Ring des Nibelungen*—all sixteen or so hours of it—is one of the greatest accomplishments in all the arts. Wagner followed up the *Ring* with *Parsifal*, which was meant to be heard only by his friends at Bayreuth, but which inevitably made its way into the international standard repertory.

Tannhäuser

Libretto by Richard Wagner
Premiere: Hoftheater, Dresden, 1845
Scene: Thuringia in the thirteenth century

ACT I SCENE 1 The opera opens in the Venusberg, the mountaintop domain of the goddess of love, where a nonstop orgy essentially runs in perpetuity. As one of Venus's habitual bacchanals starts to wind down, Tannhäuser, who has been there for about a year, admits to Venus that, believe it or not, he's starting to get a little bored of the constant action. Maybe he ought to go back to the real world. The woman is not pleased with Tannhäuser's no-place-like-home conversion, but he cannot help but desire to go back to reality. He prays to be released, invoking the Virgin Mary. He's barely uttered the second syllable of "Mary" when the Venusberg and its proud and beautiful namesake vanish into thin air.

SCENE 2 Tannhäuser is back in Thuringia. A shepherd boy wanders by, singing a folk song, followed by a group of pilgrims. Suddenly, Hermann, the landgrave of Thuringia, enters with his entourage, of which the minstrel Tannhäuser was once a member. It only takes a moment for Wolfram von Eschenbach, another singer, to recognize the man. The group implores Tannhäuser to rejoin them, but he was fixing to join the pilgrims. When they drop the name of Elisabeth, however, Hermann's niece and Tannhäuser's former flame, he decides to return with his old friends to Wartburg Castle.

ACT II Elisabeth has heard that Tannhäuser has come home, and she opens this act with a rousing aria in the music hall of the castle—a room she has refused to enter since Tannhäuser jumped ship. Wolfram and Tannhäuser enter together, and the wayward minstrel immediately begs Elisabeth for forgiveness. She wants to know where he's been all this time, but he dodges the question and they rekindle their love with a duet. Wolfram, meanwhile, is upset over the probability that he will never get to have Elisabeth for himself. Hermann enters. It's been a long time, but now he wants to stage another of the song contests in which Tannhäuser has historically performed so admirably. And today, love songs only, please. An audience arrives, and Wolfram kicks things off with a number about pure love. Contestant number two, Walther von der Vogelweide, sings a similar ditty, with zero carnal content. Finally, Tannhäuser steps up to the mike, and, having studied under Venus herself for a while, launches into a defense and endorsement of physical love. Everyone is appalled, especially the knight Biterolf, who pulls out his sword and challenges the minstrel. Hermann manages to break it up and restore order, but Tannhäuser, swept up in memories of the Venusberg pleasures, keeps right on singing, this time invoking the name of the goddess he's studied under. This is more than the women in the audience can bear; they swarm out of the hall as the men move to seize Tannhäuser. Elisabeth, however, intercedes, and begs the crowd to give Tannhäuser a chance to redeem himself. The man finally comes to his senses and apologizes. Hermann decrees that Tannhäuser must join the next group of pilgrims to come through and head to Rome. He agrees and rushes off to seek the pope.

ACT III Outside the castle, Elisabeth prays for Tannhäuser's safe return. He's been away for several months, and the woman is starting to worry. Wolfram joins her and they look for their friend in a crowd of returning pilgrims walking past. Tannhäuser, however, is nowhere to be seen. Elisabeth sings an aria of prayer and heads back to the castle, leaving Wolfram behind (she wants to be alone). Solitary Wolfram soliloquizes on his love for the woman. Suddenly, Tannhäuser enters, looking like hell. The trip to Rome didn't go so well, and now he wants to go back to Venus. Wolfram exhibits his customary kindness and patience, and Tannhäuser explains that the pope simply refused to absolve anyone who's had a dalliance with Venus. Tannhäuser is about as likely to be saved as the pope's staff is to sprout flowers. He calls out to the goddess, who appears before him in a vision. Wolfram begs the man to keep his wits about him: He doesn't want to get involved with that woman again. A group of mourners enters with the news that Elisabeth, in despair over Tannhäuser's absence, has died; her funeral procession is right around the corner. The image of Venus disappears, apparently defeated by the power of dead Elisabeth's pure, selfless love. As Elisabeth's coffin is wheeled by, Tannhäuser is overcome and he falls dead. Another group of pilgrims comes by, praising the miracle that has occurred in Rome: The pope's staff has bloomed. Tannhäuser is redeemed.

Lohengrin

Libretto by Richard Wagner
Premiere: Grossherzogliches Hoftheater, Weimar, 1850
Scene: Antwerp in the tenth century

ACT I The duchy of Brabant is in a state of disarray. King Heinrich of Germany is about to lead his people into battle with the Hungarians, but first he needs to recruit soldiers from nearby Brabant. What is the cause of the internecine warfare that's tearing everyone apart? Count Friedrich of Telramund steps forward with his wife, Ortrud, and speaks. It seems that Telramund had been engaged to the now-dead duke's daughter, Elsa, whose brother, Gottfried, was placed under his care. He hasn't got any proof, but the consensus among Telramund and his cronies is that Elsa murdered her brother. Needless to say, Telramund was not interested in marrying a murderess, so he took Ortrud instead. Still, he's determined to take over the dukedom that would have been his had he gone through with the marriage to Elsa. Furthermore, his wife, Ortrud, is a princess; doesn't that entitle him to a little power? King Heinrich calls in Elsa and asks for her side of the story. Elsa is a weird chick, and instead of denying the charges, she recounts a recurring dream of hers, in which a mysterious knight comes to her defense. Yeah, but what about your dead kid brother, Elsa? The woman refuses to provide any information, waiting instead for her imaginary friend to show up. Telramund asserts that he's willing to throw down with anyone who'll come forward on Elsa's behalf. Heinrich calls for someone to represent Elsa, but no one steps forward.

Finally, someone notices in the distance a swan pulling a boat behind it. Everyone is stunned. The swan approaches, a man gets out of the boat, and offers his services. He'll defend Elsa, but she has to agree to marry him and promise never to ask what his name is. Fine with Elsa; this is the man of her dreams, after all. The strange knight (Lohengrin, if you haven't figured it out by now) and Telramund put up their dukes. Lohengrin kicks Telramund's ass but decides not to kill him. Elsa is euphoric. Telramund and Ortrud are livid.

ACT II Outside the Antwerp cathedral, Ortrud and Telramund are licking their wounds. Telramund momentarily turns on his wife, blaming her crazy witchcraft for their troubles. Ortrud ignores him, already plotting their revenge. She pounces on Lohengrin's comment that Elsa is forbidden from asking his name. The secret to defeating Elsa and her new fiancé depends on them convincing the girl to demand her husband's name. This is going to be easy. Elsa's palace is right across the street, and she just then walks out onto her balcony to thank the heavens for sending the knight to her rescue. Telramund steals away, and Ortrud approaches, offering a truce: Their husbands may hate each other, but there's no reason they themselves can't be friends. Half-wit Elsa thinks this sounds great and comes downstairs to chat with her new girlfriend. Ortrud can't believe what easy prey Elsa is, and calls on the gods to help her. Elsa enters and the two strike up a conversation. Crafty Ortrud plants the seeds of doubt in Elsa's head. Gosh, what's it like not even knowing your husband's name? Aren't you afraid he'll just up and leave as suddenly as he came? They exit together, and Telramund reenters for a just a moment. The sun is coming up, and he can hear Heinrich's officials on their way in. He knows they're planning to kick him out of the kingdom, so he hides. Sure enough, the king's Herald announces to the growing assembly of noblemen that Telramund is out and Swan Boy is in. Not everyone is keen on this idea; a few of the nobles actually like Telramund, who emerges from hiding to consult with them. Suddenly, a group of pages enters to announce that Elsa is ready and her wedding procession is about to start. A huge crew of people marches solemnly into the cathedral to witness Elsa's wedding. Ortrud follows her "friend," helping her with the train of her dress. But as they are about to enter the cathedral, Ortrud loses it. She can't take it anymore. Damn it, Elsa, *I* should be running this kingdom, not you! Don't you even want to know your fiancé's name, for God's sake! A catfight is about to break out. Elsa is shocked but manages to keep her cool and retort that she has complete trust in her man. Worried about the holdup, Lohengrin and the king come up from their place at the back of the procession. Lohengrin scolds Ortrud, and things get moving again. But just for a moment: This time Telramund runs in and brings things to a standstill. How do they know this guy isn't some evil magician? he demands. Everyone is ill at ease (except the nasty couple, whose plan is in motion). Elsa confesses to herself that, frankly, she would like to know the name of the man she's about to exchange vows with. Nevertheless, once Ortrud and Telramund have been kicked off the premises, they all continue into the cathedral to go through with the wedding.

ACT III SCENE I The chorus sings Wagner's famous Bridal Chorus and prepares the wedding suite for the arrival of the happy couple. Elsa and Lohengrin enter and are left alone to get busy. They sing about their happiness with each other, but it doesn't take long for Elsa to start having those damn nagging feelings about her husband's identity. She tries to suppress her desire to flat out ask Lohengrin's name, but to no avail. Tell me, please! I won't tell a soul! Lohengrin begs her to forget about it, but once she's asked, she's determined to get at the answer. All of a sudden, Telramund and his henchman burst into the bedroom, ready to rumble. Lohengrin grabs his sword and kills Telramund on the spot. The men remove his body, and Lohengrin tells Elsa to get dressed. Since she must know (and since she's essentially destroyed their chance at happiness), he'll reveal his name at a meeting with the king.

SCENE 2 The time has finally come for that battle with the Hungarians folks were mumbling about in the first act. Lohengrin is expected to lead the troops alongside King Heinrich. Everyone has assembled by the river to head off to fight when the corpse of Telramund is brought in. Elsa follows in a moment. Lohengrin informs the king that he cannot go to war. Elsa has broken her promise and he has killed Telramund. Finally, he reveals his identity: Lohengrin, son of Parsifal and a knight of the Holy Grail. His secret exposed, he must now go back to the fold. Elsa is distraught and on the verge of fainting. Everyone begs Lohengrin to stay, but it's too late: The swan he rode in on is on its way back. Lohengrin is about to get into the swan's boat when Ortrud enters with the giddy announcement that the swan is in fact Elsa's brother, Gottfried, whom Ortrud had turned into a swan by means of her witchcraft. Only Lohengrin would have been able to return Gottfried to his rightful physiognomy, but he's made that impossible by saying his own name. Ortrud's triumph, however, is interrupted by the appearance of a dove invested with power from the Holy Grail. The swan turns back into Gottfried; Ortrud is hysterical; Elsa drops dead; and Lohengrin is led off by the dove. Everyone else sings praise to Gottfried, who can now resume his position as duke.

Tristan und Isolde

Libretto by Richard Wagner
Premiere: Königliches Hof- und Nationaltheater, Munich, 1865
Scene: A boat en route to Cornwall and Cornwall proper in
    mythic times

ACT I The Irish princess Isolde is on a ship with her friend Brangäne en route to Cornwall to meet her husband-to-be. From the deck above, one of the sailors can be heard singing, a fact that irritates Isolde—who's steaming mad to begin with. It seems she's been chosen to be the new wife of King Marke of Cornwall. The king's nephew, Tristan, has been entrusted with the job of transporting the girl to her new home. Angry Isolde sends her friend to fetch Tristan, whom she thinks hasn't been sufficiently attentive to her during the journey. Tristan is polite but he doesn't want to go to Isolde. His friend Kurwenal, however, goes in his place and makes clumsy statements about Tristan not owing the woman a visit

PHOTO BY GARY SMITH, SEATTLE OPERA

Tristan und Isolde

and about Isolde's dead fiancé, Morold, who was killed in battle by Tristan. Tristan is mortified by Kurwenal's lack of judgment and he scolds the young man. Isolde gives Brangäne a little background about her relationship with her captor. During his hand-to-hand combat with her fiancé, Tristan was wounded and came to Isolde using an alias (Tantris) to seek medical care. Not knowing she was administering to the man who killed her beloved, Isolde, who inherited her mother's gift for magic, nursed him back to health, falling in love with him at the same time. And now, the man whom she brought back from the brink of death is delivering her to his uncle to become his bride. Isolde is pissed. Brangäne reminds her that she's going to be a queen—it's not the end of the world. But Isolde, despite her captivity, still loves Tristan. She and Brangäne start talking about Isolde's vast knowledge of potions and such. Brangäne suggests mixing an elixir that will cause Isolde to fall in love with King Marke. But instead, Isolde orders her friend to make the one that causes death. Kurwenal enters the cabin and reports that land is in sight; the two ladies should get ready for their arrival. Isolde informs the fellow that she categorically refuses to get off the damn boat until Tristan comes to see her. He exits, and Isolde urges Brangäne to hurry with the death potion. Tristan enters and Isolde offers him a cup from Brangäne. Why don't they drink a toast to an end to their dispute? Isolde suggests. Tristan is no dummy; he can guess Isolde's scheme. But he, too, loves the girl and is despondent over her imminent nuptials to his uncle. If she wants to poison them both, that's fine by him. They drink together, and are instantly seized with powerful feelings of love for each other. Crafty Brangäne actually gave them the love potion, and the two are head over heels.

ACT II Isolde has been installed in King Marke's castle. Marke is off on a hunting trip, and Isolde waits for Tristan to arrive for a rendezvous. Brangäne is concerned that one of Marke's knights, Melot, is acting as a spy, and she warns Isolde to be wary of him. Whatever, says Isolde. Just send word to Tristan to get over here. Tristan finally shows up, and the lovebirds sing the praises of nighttime—the only moment of the day when they are able to be together. Brangäne warns them from the next room that this assignation is not safe; they're sure to be discovered. But Tristan and Isolde ignore her. Kurwenal enters to support Brangäne's words of warning. It's too late to hide, however. Marke and Melot enter. Melot is angry, but Marke more hurt than anything else. His own nephew cuckolding him! Tristan doesn't know what to say to this and asks Isolde if she would be willing to die with him. Guess what? She would. Melot pulls out his sword and stabs Tristan, injuring but not killing him. Kurwenal comes to his friend's assistance as the curtain falls.

ACT III Tristan has gone home to his family estate in Brittany, where loyal Kurwenal tends to him. A local shepherd boy ambles by, playing his pipe. He asks Kurwenal how Tristan is doing. Not well, the man replies. He wishes Isolde could somehow visit and cheer Tristan up. The shepherd has been playing a sad song on his pipe, but he promises to launch into an upbeat number if he sees any ships approaching. Tristan wakes up, but he's unwell. He mumbles something about having dreamed he visited the land of death. He sees Kurnewal and expresses his appreciation for his friend's steadfastness. Delirious, he rambles on about Isolde, whom he imagines is on her way. Finally, the shepherd's song takes a turn; Isolde's ship really is sailing into the harbor. Tristan is out of his head. Throwing caution to the wind, he rips off his bandages as Isolde races to his side. The moment they are reunited, Tristan drops dead in his loved one's embrace. But Isolde's is not the only ship to arrive on Brittany's shores. King Marke and Melot arrive momentarily, and Kurwenal angrily attacks the knight. He manages to kill Melot, but others of Marke's retinue return the favor and Tristan's faithful friend falls dead. Marke is devastated by the turn things have taken; his nephew's death has shattered him. Isolde, meanwhile, intends to join her man in death. She sings her famous Liebestod ("Mild und leise") about her imminent reunion with Tristan. Brangäne tries to shake her out of it, but it's no use. She dies, collapsing onto Tristan's body as the onlookers observe in horror.

DER RING DES NIBELUNGEN

Das Rheingold

Libretto by Richard Wagner
Premiere: Königliches Hof- und Nationaltheater, Munich, 1869
Scene: The Rhine and thereabouts in mythical times

SCENE I Three Rhinemaidens are frolicking in their namesake river, not paying attention to the task of guarding the invaluable Rhinegold that's kept underwater. The dwarf Alberich, one of the Nibelung race of little people, ambles by and tries to hit on the three lovely ladies. Needless to say, none of them is interested in the dwarf and they mercilessly tease the poor thing. Alberich is annoyed, but he suddenly becomes fixated not on the women but on the Rhinegold, which he can see glimmering in a rock on the riverbank. He asks the women what it is. The maidens explain that whoever obtains the gold and fashions it into a ring will rule the world. The only drawback is that person, despite his power, will never be able to experience love. Alberich quickly assesses his situation: He's an ugly little dwarf who's never going to get with the ladies. Why not steal the gold? He races over to the rock, pulls out the mass of gold, and rushes off, as the Rhinemaidens, horrified, chase after him.

SCENE 2 The leader of the gods, Wotan, is chilling outside Valhalla, his mountaintop palace, with his wife, Fricka. The construction of Valhalla has recently been completed; the palace serves as a residence and all-purpose HQ for the gods. It has been built by two giants, Fafner and Fasolt, who are expecting payment for their services. Fricka is concerned, because instead of money, Wotan has promised the giants his wife's sister, Freia, as a prize for their labors. Freia dashes in with the giants in hot pursuit. Can't Wotan help her? The god tells Fafner and Fasolt that he wasn't serious when he said they could take his sister-in-law. Surely there's something else they'd rather own. Freia's brothers, Froh and Donner, show up to help extricate their sister from the tricky circumstances. Wotan calls on Loge, the god of fire, for additional aid. Loge reports that the only thing he can think of that might serve as a suitable substitute for Freia is the Rhinegold that the dwarf Alberich has made into a supremely powerful ring. In fact, the Rhinemaidens have asked Loge to request that Wotan help them get the gold back. Perhaps he could procure the ring and give it to the giants in return for Freia. Fafner and Fasolt like this idea, but Wotan is not so sure. He's all for stealing the ring from Alberich. But handing it over to the giants? He'd rather keep it for himself. Fafner and Fasolt lead Freia off; she's under their custody until the ring is produced. Wotan and Loge, meanwhile, head down to earth together to locate Alberich.

SCENE 3 Alberich and his brother, Mime, are in their underground cave, finishing up the ring. Mime is the metalworking expert, and he has also concocted a golden helmet (or Tarnhelm) that can both make the wearer invisible and able to change his form (Wonder Twin–style). Alberich puts on the Tarnhelm, disappears, and cruelly kicks his brother's ass for sport before exiting. Wotan and Loge walk in and confront Mime, who says he can't take his brother's abuse much longer. Alberich comes back in and warns Wotan and Loge of his ring-inspired power. The gods have no sway over him any longer, and he intends to fight them for world

A B C D E F G H I J K L M N O P Q R S T U V W X Y Z

dominance. Wily Loge is determined to get some information out of the cocky dwarf, and he inquires about the ring and the helmet. Alberich explains the helmet's powers, and turns himself into a dragon to prove the thing's abilities. Loge is impressed. Can you turn into something small, like, say, a toad? Sure! replies Alberich. Foolishly, he transforms himself into the creature, allowing Wotan and Loge to seize the helmet and, when he returns to midget form, arrest the dwarf.

SCENE 4 Back at the mountaintop, Loge and Wotan demand that Alberich hand over all the Rhinegold. He agrees to give them the unforged gold, but demands to keep the ring and the helmet. No deal. They summon Alberich's Nibelung kinsmen, who dutifully show up with the gold. Alberich is holding back with the ring, so Wotan simply tears it off his finger. Alberich is so angry about the loss of his power that he curses the ring and all who come into contact with it before heading back to his cave. Having heard about the mass of gold that Wotan has procured to exchange for Freia, Fafner and Fasolt show up to claim their booty. The thing is, they've grown to like Freia and don't want to lose her. In fact, they'll only return the goddess if the pile of gold rises so high that it hides her from view. The unforged gold doesn't quite make it high enough, so Loge yields the helmet. All they need now is to put the ring on the pile and Freia will be restored. But Wotan refuses to part with the ring; he's too greedy for the power that accompanies it. Suddenly, Erda, the goddess of the earth, appears and warns Wotan to relinquish the ring; it'll only bring heartbreak and misery. Wotan is annoyed, but is persuaded to throw the ring onto the pile. The giants are jubilant and immediately start divvying up their treasure. But they cannot agree on who gets to keep the ring and launch into a tremendous argument. Fafner ends up killing his brother in order to obtain the ring—an indication that Alberich's curse has already kicked into gear. The gods, meanwhile, with Freia back in the fold, decide to head back to Valhalla, but with mixed feelings. They walk along a rainbow bridge to their new home and ponder the recent events.

Die Walküre

Libretto by Richard Wagner
Premiere: Königliches Hof- und Nationaltheater, Munich, 1870
Scene: A mountainous region in mythical times

ACT I An exhausted Siegmund stumbles into an empty forest hut, built around a massive tree trunk, to escape a storm outside. He's scarcely dis-

Die Walküre

cerned that no one's home before passing out in front of the fire. Sieglinde, the lady of the house, enters and sees that the young intruder is exhausted and in need of care. Siegmund wakes up and accepts a drink of water from his hostess, who informs him that her husband, Hunding, will be home soon. Immediately, there is a profound connection between these two that neither can put his or her finger on. Hunding enters and notes the resemblance of this strange person to his wife. Siegmund says his name is Wehwalt (which can be roughly translated as "full of woe"), and accepts Hunding's rather reluctant offer of a meal and a bed for the night. Wehwalt delivers a personal bio to his hosts, relating that his parents are both dead and that he hasn't seen his twin sister for years. His father somehow vanished during a battle with the Neidings. Siegmund is now on the run, having been involved in fatal combat with another tribe. As it turns out, Hunding is a member of this last group; Wehwalt is his mortal enemy. Hunding informs Siegmund/Wehwalt that he can stay the night (as custom in this region dictates), but he better be ready for a fight tomorrow morning. Hunding goes to bed, and Sieglinde accompanies him to tuck him in and give him something to drink before bedtime. Siegmund is concerned about the next day's battle. He recalls that his father once told him that, in a time of need, a supremely powerful sword would make itself available to him. Gosh, he sure could use that sword right about now. Sieglinde reenters with the news that she slipped a little something into Hunding's drink, which should buy Siegmund a little time as he prepares to fight. It's Sieglinde's turn to tell her own tale of woe: She explains that, after her forced wedding to Hunding, an old man arrived at the hut and plunged a sword into the trunk of the tree in the center of the room. No one has been able to pull the thing out. Siegmund can't believe what he's hearing. He's sure it's the sword of his father's tale. He and Sieglinde cannot contain their passion any longer. They sing a long duet in which they proclaim their devotion to one another, and Siegmund reveals that his father's name was Wälse (who was, incidentally, actually Wotan in disguise). Sure enough—you guessed it—Siegmund and Sieglinde are long-lost twins, a turn of events that doesn't stop them from jumping each other's bones. Siegmund approaches the sword in the tree, miraculously pulls the thing out of the confines of the trunk, and dubs it Nothung (or Needful). Siegmund and Sieglinde kiss, and the curtain falls.

ACT II The impending battle between Siegmund and Hunding has taken on an added dimension now that Sieglinde has sided against her husband. Up in the mountain domain of the gods, Wotan tells his daughter Brünnhilde (one of nine Valkyries, daughters of Wotan) to watch over Siegmund and help him win the fight if need be. Wotan's wife, Fricka (the goddess of marriage), enters to remind her husband that Hunding and Sieglinde are married and that their vows should be respected: Siegmund has broken up the couple and should die in the battle. Her argument is persuasive, and Wotan finally relents. Fricka leaves and Brünnhilde returns. Wotan is miserable over the troubles that damn ring has caused. He sadly retracts his instructions to Brünnhilde to protect Siegmund. The man must die, and she should side instead with Hunding. If he doesn't begin to set some things right, the very infrastructure of Valhalla is in danger. Brünnhilde begs her father to let Siegmund win, but he stands firm. She must help Hunding in the battle. They exit, clearing the stage for Siegmund and Sieglinde, who are running from Hunding. Sieglinde is a nervous wreck, and her agitation is made worse by the arrival of Brünnhilde, who announces to Siegmund the predestined fact that he's going to die at Hunding's hand. Siegmund mulls it over. Okay, but can Sieglinde be sacrificed and come to Valhalla, too? Sorry, you're going solo; but Brünnhilde will be sure to keep an eye on Sieglinde and the twins' unborn child. Siegmund cannot stand the idea of parting from his sister and tells Brünnhilde he's going to kill them both. The Valkyrie is fond of Siegmund, and decides to defy Wotan and protect her half-brother in combat. Hunding appears, and he and Siegmund are at each other's throats in moments. Brünnhilde shields Siegmund from Hunding's blows, but Wotan soon enters, very pissed. He destroys Nothung, allowing Hunding an opportunity (which he seizes) to kill Siegmund. Fearing her father's wrath, Brünnhilde grabs Sieglinde and they race off together. Wotan has done what he had to do, but he can't stand the fact that Hunding has killed his son. He strikes Hunding dead, and prepares to look for Brünnhilde, whom he plans to punish mightily.

ACT III Brünnhilde returns with Sieglinde to Valhalla, accompanied by the strains of Wagner's Ride of the Valkyries (sometimes known as "Kill the Wabbit"). The other Valkyries worry about helping Sieglinde in defiance of Wotan's wishes. Sieglinde doesn't even care to be helped; she'd rather die. But when Brünnhilde informs her that she's pregnant with Siegmund's child, she reconsiders. Brünnhilde hands the woman the shards of Siegmund's ruined sword. Sieglinde must keep the pieces for her son to reforge into another powerful weapon. Wotan approaches, and Sieglinde rushes off. The king of the gods is steaming mad, and informs his daughter that she is to lose her powers and be consigned to a rock in the mountains, where she will remain asleep until someone finds her. She begs him to reconsider the punishment. Wotan loves his daughter, and the last thing he wants to do is take away her powers, but at this point it's beyond his control. Brünnhilde has just one request: She doesn't want to be claimed by the first schmuck to walk by; if she's going to be mortal, at least let her marry a hero. Wotan consents to surrounding the sleeping ex-Valkyrie by a wall of fire. That way, only someone really brave will be able to get to her. He says good-bye, puts her to sleep, and summons Loge to build the fire. He walks off, devastated over the loss of his daughter.

Siegfried

Libretto by Richard Wagner
Premiere: Festspielhaus, Bayreuth, 1876
Scene: A mountainous region in mythical times

ACT I Sieglinde died in childbirth, and her son, Siegfried, has been reared by the dwarf Mime, Alberich's brother. The little fellow has been toiling relentlessly at putting Nothung back together again, but he hasn't had much success. Siegfried is a cocky young man, and he isn't always as polite with the little dwarf as he should be. He enters the cave with a bear he's caught, scaring poor Mime witless. Siegfried sends the bear away and demands to try out Mime's latest sword. Of course, the weapon breaks the moment Siegfried swings it. The young man excoriates the dwarf, who responds by demanding a little respect; after all, it was he who saved infant Siegfried and treated him like a son. Siegfried couldn't care less. Who were his real parents? he demands to know. Mime recounts the tale of how, years earlier, he came across an ailing Sieglinde mid-delivery. All the woman could explain before dying was that the child was to be called Siegfried, his father had died in battle, and the pieces of the sword must somehow be resoldered. Siegfried sends Mime back to work on redoing the sword and exits as Wotan, in disguise as a Wanderer, walks in, asking for shelter. Mime is hesitant to allow a stranger into the house, but the Wanderer presents a bargain: They will exchange three trivia questions each, and whoever replies correctly to all three gets the other's head as a prize. Mime figures he can stump the guy, and demands to know who lives in each of the three regions of the world: underground, on the earth's surface, and in the heavens. Needless to say, this is easy for Wotan, and he turns the tables on Mime. The dwarf gets two out of three, but is unable to answer the question about who has the ability to repair the sword, Nothung. Poor Mime has no idea. Not him, that's for sure. The Wanderer tells Mime not to worry; he's not going to cash in on his prize. The answer, though, is the person who fears nothing. Wotan leaves, and Siegfried reenters, and it occurs to Mime that this is a man who truly does not comprehend the concept of fear. He sets Siegfried up in the forge, and the young man gets to work repairing Nothung. Mime's got a plan. Once the sword is finished, he'll lead Siegfried to the giant Fafner, whom Siegfried should have no trouble disposing of with his new and improved sword. Once Siegfried has taken the ring, Mime will poison his ward and take Alberich's beloved Rhinegold for himself! Siegfried finishes his work on Nothung. Testing it out, he splits an anvil in half with one swift blow. Nothung is back and better than ever. Mime is anxious.

ACT II The Wanderer pays a visit to Alberich, who is hanging out near Fafner's place. The dwarf is not fooled by Wotan's disguise, and the two fall into their familiar bickering. Wotan informs Alberich that a young hero is on his way, and he has the goods to kill Fafner. What's more, this fellow is working with Mime, who has his eyes on the ring. Wotan turns his attention to Fafner, warning the giant that trouble is on the way. Fafner, who has used the Tarnhelm to assume the form of a dragon, ignores the Wanderer's words: He's never met a human he couldn't take care of. The Wanderer exits, Alberich hides, and Mime and Siegfried arrive. Siegfried tells Mime to wait outside, and whimsically sets about trying to imitate the sounds of the bird who happens to be flying by at that moment. He wakes Fafner by blowing his horn. Within minutes, Siegfried has successfully used Nothung to kill Fafner, although some of the giant's blood manages to get into the hero's mouth. By ingesting Fafner's blood, Siegfried acquires the power to interpret the song of the bird, which was apparently trying to direct him toward the ring. He goes into the cave to retrieve the ring and the helmet as Alberich emerges and starts arguing with Mime. Siegfried comes out of the cave with the booty, and the brothers hide. Mime returns momentarily, bearing a cup of poison that he offers to the hero. The bird, however, has warned Siegfried of Mime's duplicity. It has also told him of the sleeping Brünnhilde, who's just waiting for a man like Siegfried to claim her. Siegfried kills Mime, and, with the ring and the Tarnhelm in hand, heads off to find Brünnhilde.

ACT III SCENE 1 Wotan is monumentally concerned with the havoc the ring has wreaked. Siegmund and Sieglinde are dead; Brünnhilde is a perpetually sleeping mortal; and Wotan is worried that the whole system of rule at Valhalla could collapse at any moment. He calls for the earth goddess, Erda, to give him some insight as to how he should proceed. Erda has nothing to say. Wotan has chosen Siegfried as the man who'll reclaim the ring and rule humanity. There's nothing Erda can say to alter that path. She disappears and Siegfried enters, coming face to face with the Wanderer for the first time. They chat briefly, and Wotan is happy that Siegfried seems so capable, intelligent, and fearless. But he's also cocky, and quickly becomes annoyed with the strange old man who's occupying his time. He moves to leave, but Wotan blocks his path by holding up his supernatural spear. It was this same spear that destroyed Nothung back when it was in Siegmund's possession. In its present incarnation, however, Nothung is unstoppable. Siegfried draws the weapon and destroys Wotan's spear in a flash. The king of the gods is stunned. It looks like his power is truly starting to wane. Siegfried proceeds to the place where the fire-imprisoned woman (Brünnhilde) lies sleeping.

SCENE 2 Siegfried has finally made it to Brünnhilde's resting place. He rushes through the fire and moves to the woman's side. She's wearing her full warrior gear, and Siegfried cannot at first tell if it's a man or a woman. For the first time in his life, he's afraid, and he invokes his mother, Sieglinde, to help him. Gazing on Brünnhilde, he's struck, finally, by how sexy she is. He kisses her, and, Sleeping Beauty–like, she wakes up. Brünnhilde is beside herself, and cannot keep herself from launching into the vivid tale of her history and of her relationship with Siegfried's parents. Siegfried is a little freaked out by this nutty lady, who appears alternately thrilled to have been released from sleep and devastated over her loss of power. But mostly, he feels love for the former Valkyrie, and she returns that love in spades. They voice their feelings for each other, kiss, and the curtain falls.

Götterdämmerung
Libretto by Richard Wagner
Premiere: Festspielhaus, Bayreuth, 1876
Scene: A mountainous region and the Rhine in mythical times

PROLOGUE Erda's three daughters, the Norns, recap the events of the three previous *Ring* operas as they weave a rope that represents fate. When they mention the Rhinegold, the rope suddenly breaks, signaling the Norns' imminent destruction. They vanish, foreshadowing the loss of power of the rest of the gods. Brünnhilde and Siegfried enter, singing about their mutual affection. But Siegfried is a born adventurer, and he needs to go out into the world and get some experience under his belt. Brünnhilde hates the idea of a separation from her man, but she understands his proverbial need for speed. Siegfried hands his wife the ring for safekeeping and heads off. The flames that surrounded Brünnhilde while she slept return to protect her while her husband is away.

ACT I SCENE I This scene introduces the Gibichungs, another of the various tribes and races that live near the Rhine. Gunther is the Gibichung chief; he is just now conversing with his half-brother, Hagen, who happens to be Alberich's son (and thus half Nibelung). The brothers share Siegfried's lust for adventure, and they plot to get some action. Hagen thinks that Gunther should occupy himself by trying to attain Brünnhilde for himself. In fact, what would be ideal is for them to somehow rig it so that Siegfried marries Gunther's sister, Gutrune. Hagen schemes to slip Siegfried a love drug that will make the man forget Brünnhilde and fall for Gutrune. Who should arrive momentarily but Siegfried himself. Gutrune gets to work quickly, giving the man a laced drink. Right away, it's "Brünnhilde who?" and "Hello, Gutrune!" Gunther confides in his new friend that he's got a thing for sexy Brünnhilde behind the wall of flame. He wishes he could somehow get to her. Don't worry, says Siegfried. He'll just don the Tarnhelm, transform himself into a replica of Gunther, and walk through the flames as a substitute for Gunther. Gunther and Hagen's plan couldn't be going more smoothly. Siegfried and Gunther stage a brief blood-brotherhood ceremony and head off to claim Brünnhilde. Gutrune stays behind with Hagen, who figures that with Siegfried on his team he's got a shot at obtaining the ring.

SCENE 2 Waltraute, one of the Valkyries, comes to visit her sister, Brünnhilde, on the rocky mountain. Waltraute knows that Brünnhilde is guarding the ring, and she's come with a request from Wotan. Brünnhilde must return the ring to the Rhinemaidens, otherwise all of the gods of Valhalla will be destroyed. The curse of the ring is more powerful than Wotan and all his godly sidekicks combined. But the ring is a gift from Siegfried, and Brünnhilde's man is more important to her than anything else. She will not part with the ring. Waltraute leaves in despair. In a moment, Siegfried arrives through the flames, disguised (by means of the Tarnhelm) as Gunther. Brünnhilde cannot believe that anyone other than Siegfried could make it through the fire, but there's little she can do to deny "Gunther's" claim on her. She hands over the ring, and the curtain falls.

ACT II Back at home with the rest of the Gibichungs, Hagen is visited by a vision of Alberich, who instructs his son to obtain the ring at all costs. Siegfried shows up momentarily, followed separately by Gunther and Brünnhilde. Hagen calls an assembly to witness the marriage of Siegfried and Gutrune. Brünnhilde is already in the hall when Siegfried enters with his new bride. Needless to say, when she sees Siegfried accompanied by some other chick and with the ring on his finger, she goes apeshit. How can he not recognize her? How does he possess the ring when she just gave it to Gunther earlier that day? Brünnhilde charges that Siegfried is her husband and that he has perpetrated the ultimate act of betrayal. Siegfried truly does not remember Brünnhilde and denies the charges. Hagen's plan to conquer Siegfried is moving ahead; now he and Gunther have Brünnhilde on their side. How can they defeat the hero? they ask the former goddess. Go at him from behind, she suggests. His back is his one vulnerable spot. Gutrune is understandably upset, but everyone else agrees that Siegfried must be killed. The Gibichungs are going hunting the next day; they can get Siegfried then, amid the confusion of the expedition.

ACT III Scene 1 The three Rhinemaidens have barely had a moment's peace since Alberich stole their gold. The curtain rises on the women swimming along the Rhine and praying that Siegfried will return the gold. The hero arrives at the waterfront and the girls immediately try the flirtation tactic, hoping that will persuade Siegfried to give back the gold. He considers giving them the ring, but decides to keep it when they allude to the curse. Siegfried is damned if he's going to let some dumb curse dictate his actions. The girls swim off, and Hagen enters with Gunther and the group of hunters. Among "friends," Siegfried recounts Nothung's history, as well as his own adventures with the dragon, Wotan, etc. The time has come to refresh Siegfried's memory, and Hagen presents the man with the antidote to the forgetfulness elixir. His story subsequently turns to the subject of Brünnhilde and their rapid-fire courtship. Hagen has kept Gunther in the dark about Siegfried's relationship to Brünnhilde, and the poor man is mortified by the current revelation. Hagen, however, desires the ring with a ferocious single-mindedness, and when Siegfried isn't looking, he comes up from behind and stabs him in the back. Siegfried dies slowly, all the while singing of Brünnhilde, the love of his life. Hagen is gleeful, but the others show respect for the dead hero, bearing his corpse aloft and taking it away to be buried.

Scene 2 Back at the Gibichung castle, Gutrune has been having nightmares portending Siegfried's death. She becomes hysterical when the group returns, carrying Siegfried's dead body. Naive Gunther explains to his sister that it was all Hagen's fault. Hagen denies nothing, and when Gunther moves to take the ring from Siegfried's finger, Hagen kills him. Hagen subsequently moves to procure the ring himself, but when he gets close, Siegfried's hand miraculously resists him. Brünnhilde walks in, mad as hell, and takes over the scene. She commands that a funeral pyre be built near the river. She sings in praise of her dead husband and takes the ring from his finger. Valhalla and the gods are not long for this world, and Brünnhilde is heroically taking their necessary destruction into her own hands. She invokes Wotan to witness the proceedings and sends word to Loge to burn down the mountaintop palace of the gods. Once Siegfried's body has been placed on the pyre, she sets it on fire. With her horse at her side, Brünnhilde then marches stoically into the flames to follow her husband into death. The fire rages out of control, but the Rhine suddenly overflows, putting out the fire and washing the ring off Brünnhilde's finger and back into the hands of the Rhinemaidens. Hagen dives in after the ring, but the Rhinemaidens drown him in the river. From afar, Valhalla can be seen burning to the ground, the gods perishing within its walls.

Parsifal

Libretto by Richard Wagner
Premiere: Festspielhaus, Bayreuth, 1882
Scene: Monsalvat, Spain, in the Middle Ages

ACT I SCENE I It's dawn, and old Gurnemanz, one of the knights of the Holy Grail, confers with two younger knights about their ailing leader, Amfortas. Amfortas has a serious (but unspecified) injury, which requires that he bathe regularly in healing waters. This treatment is not going so well, but Amfortas is on his way to take a dip in the lake nonetheless. Crazy Kundry (who's sort of a quasi-witch) arrives with a salve that she thinks just may do the trick. Amfortas is carried in momentarily by an entourage. He has prophesied that only an as-yet-unnamed "fool" will be able to save him. Gurnemanz gives the old fellow Kundry's ointment. He takes the stuff, thanks the woman, and heads into the water. Some of the younger knights aren't so sure about this Kundry character, but Gurnemanz assures them that she's on the up-and-up. He then reminisces about the formation of the Holy Grail knighthood. Old Titurel, Amfortas's father, founded the group to guard the Grail, as well as the Holy Spear, which had at one time been used on Christ. Everything was going fine until nasty Klingsor, a wizard, stole the spear, conjuring up a field full of hot chicks to distract Amfortas while the magician absconded with the spear—though not before stabbing Amfortas with it. The only way to heal the old man is to recover the spear that wounded him, which can only be done by said "fool." Gurnemanz's lengthy song of exposition finally comes to a close as the group notices that a swan on the lake has been shot by some strange young man. You simply do not mess with the knights' swans, and the man is seized. The young man apologizes for shooting the swan, but is unable to reveal anything of his identity. He knows neither his own name nor that of his father. Kundry, however, recognizes the guy as Parsifal, the son of Gamuret, who was killed in battle. She also mentions that his mother is dead, which inexplicably incenses Parsifal. Gurnemanz intercedes just as Parsifal is about to eject Kundry.

SCENE 2 Back in the Castle of the Holy Grail, ancient, wizened Titurel calls for the Grail to be brought out before the assembly. Having been wounded and disgraced by Klingsor, Amfortas no longer cares for these official rituals, but Titurel insists that he go on with the ceremony. The Grail is revealed, and it is a splendid, glowing thing. The knights all sing in praise. Amfortas cannot stand it; his wound flares up. Parsifal observes the proceedings at Gurnemanz's side, but doesn't appear to really get what's going on. Gurnemanz determines that vacuous young Parsifal must be some kind of fool, and the curtain falls.

ACT II SCENE 1 The scene changes to the castle of the sorcerer Klingsor, who has noticed Parsifal and plans to kidnap the fellow before the others become hip to his fool's powers. It seems that Kundry is in Klingsor's employ. The woman wants desperately to go straight (which is why she hangs with the knights so often), but Klingsor's got secrets on her, which require that she do his bidding. Klingsor and Kundry argue ferociously, but ultimately the woman cedes to the magician's demand that she seduce Parsifal and bring him to the castle.

SCENE 2 Parsifal stumbles onto a garden filled with gorgeous girls (presumably, the same ones who distracted Amfortas years before). He cannot believe his eyes. These girls are hot! And they're flirting with him! Kundry has assumed the form of one of the maidens and approaches Parsifal, telling him that she knew his parents. She regales him with the story of his mother's death, for which Parsifal has always felt partially responsible. Kundry kisses Parsifal, but instead of pleasure, he feels the same sharp pain that Amfortas experienced when he was stabbed. Parsifal senses that this woman is up to no good; he senses that he is about to follow in Amfortas's footsteps and be consigned to a life of pain if he isn't careful. Abandoning her disguise, Kundry begs Parsifal to help her: Ever since she taunted a dying Christ, she has had to endure a horrible curse. Can't Parsifal deliver her from the torture of her existence? He can help her, but not by sleeping with her, as she insists. Kundry is by now damn near out of her mind; she lays a curse on Parsifal and summons Klingsor. The magician appears and throws the spear at Parsifal (just as he did at Amfortas), but the spear miraculously stops dead in midair before it reaches the boy. Parsifal seizes the spear and makes the sign of the cross. Klingsor's castle and garden instantly disappear. Parsifal exits, after bidding Kundry a quick farewell.

ACT III SCENE 1 Several years have gone by since Parsifal went head to head with Klingsor, and things have changed. Gurnemanz is now living as a hermit, and, when the curtain rises, he comes across a near-dead Kundry, who has renounced her magic arts. Gurnemanz administers to the ailing woman and sends her into his hut, at which point he sees an unknown man come forward. At first, Gurnemanz doesn't recognize Parsifal, who is decked out in full head-to-toe black armor. It is Good Friday, and the two men pray together, after which Gurnemanz realizes who the visitor is. Parsifal tells Gurnemanz how he won the spear from Klingsor; he explains that he has spent the intervening years searching desperately for the Castle of the Holy Grail so that he could reunite the chalice with the spear. Gurnemanz sure is glad he made it: It seems that things haven't been going so well for the knighthood. Amfortas refuses to let anyone look upon the Grail, and Titurel is dead. It's all very depressing to the rest of the knights, who will be happy to install Parsifal as their new leader. Kundry washes Parsifal's feet, and in return he baptizes her. Everyone notes what a beautiful day it is. Gurnemanz guides Parsifal back to the castle.

SCENE 2 Amfortas and the rest of the knights are mourning the death of Titurel, who lies in a coffin in the center of the room. Please, the knights beg, let us look on the Grail, but Amfortas refuses to uncover it. The pain of his wound has been unending, and now he just wants to die. Parsifal enters and, before Amfortas knows what's going on, touches the old man's wound with the spear. Amfortas is instantly cured; all of a sudden, he feels like a million bucks. Parsifal insists that the Grail be exposed. He picks up the glowing chalice and a white dove appears, flapping its wings above Parsifal's head. Kundry has finally achieved a measure of salvation, and she drops dead onto the floor, while the rest of the group kneels before their savior, Parsifal.

Appendix I
Starting Your Record Collection

Most of the operas mentioned in this book have been recorded numerous times by a multitude of different conductors, singers, and orchestras. I'd hate to think how many *Madama Butterfly* LPs are lying around virtually forgotten as newer renditions crop up year after year. Other operas, like *Einstein on the Beach,* are more recent compositions and can claim just one or two studio efforts. There are budget recordings, deluxe box sets, obscurities on vinyl, shorter highlight CDs—all available at various outlets and yearning to be made part of your collection. The recordings I've listed below are all classics. You may find you want a more recent recording with artists you're more likely to actually hear performing these days. But in the early stages of buying opera CDs, it's wise to stick to the tried and true. You can't go wrong with any of these fifteen titles.

Alban Berg. *Lulu*. Deutsche Grammophon 15489. Teresa Stratas, soprano; Pierre Boulez, conductor; Paris Opera Orchestra.

Georges Bizet. *Carmen*. RCA Victor 39495. Leontyne Price, soprano; Mirella Freni, soprano; Franco Corelli, tenor; Robert Merrill, baritone; Herbert von Karajan, conductor; Vienna Philharmonic.

Benjamin Britten. *Peter Grimes*. London Classics 14577. Peter Pears, tenor; Claire Watson, soprano; Benjamin Britten, conductor; Royal Opera House Covent Garden Orchestra.

Gaetano Donizetti. *Lucia di Lammermoor*. EMI Classics 56284. Maria Callas, soprano; Tullio Serafin, conductor; Philharmonia Orchestra.

Philip Glass. *Einstein on the Beach*. Sony Classics 38875. Michael Riesman, conductor; Philip Glass Ensemble.

Wolfgang Amadeus Mozart. *Le Nozze di Figaro*. EMI Classics 63266. Elisabeth Schwarzkopf, soprano; Anna Moffo, soprano; Fiorenza Cossotto, mezzo-soprano; Giuseppe Taddei, bass; Carlo Maria Giulini, conductor; Philharmonia Orchestra.

Jacques Offenbach. *Les Contes d'Hoffmann*. Deutsche Grammophon 27682. Plácido Domingo, tenor; Edita Gruberova, soprano; Seiji Ozawa, conductor; Orchestre National de France.

Giacomo Puccini. *La Bohème*. London Classics 21049. Mirella Freni, soprano; Luciano Pavarotti, tenor; Herbert von Karajan, conductor; Berlin Philharmonic.

Giacomo Puccini. *Tosca*. EMI Classics 56304. Maria Callas, soprano; Giuseppe di Stefano, tenor; Tito Gobbi, bass; Victor de Sabata, conductor; Milan Teatro alla Scala Orchestra.

Gioacchino Rossini. *Il Barbiere di Siviglia*. Deutsche Grammophon 457733. Teresa Berganza, mezzo-soprano; Hermann Prey, baritone; Claudio Abbado, conductor; London Symphony Orchestra.

Richard Strauss. *Der Rosenkavalier*. EMI Classics 56113. Elisabeth Schwarzkopf, soprano; Christa Ludwig, mezzo-soprano; Herbert von Karajan, conductor; Philharmonia Orchestra.

Giuseppe Verdi. *Aida*. RCA Victor 6198. Leontyne Price, soprano; Plácido Domingo, tenor; Grace Bumbry, mezzo-soprano; Sherrill Milnes, baritone; Erich Leinsdorf, conductor; London Symphony Orchestra.

Giuseppe Verdi. *Otello*. RCA Victor 63180. Jon Vickers, tenor; Leonie Rysanek, soprano; Tito Gobbi, bass; Tullio Serafin, conductor; Rome Opera House Orchestra.

Giuseppe Verdi. *La Traviata*. London Classics 30491. Joan Sutherland, soprano; Luciano Pavarotti, tenor; Richard Bonynge, conductor; National Philharmonic Orchestra.

Richard Wagner. *Der Ring des Nibelungen*. London Classics 455555. Birgit Nilsson, soprano; Christa Ludwig, mezzo-soprano; Wolfgang Windgassen, tenor; Dietrich Fischer-Dieskau, baritone; Sir Georg Solti, conductor; Vienna Philharmonic Orchestra.

Appendix II
Further Reading

Abbate, Carolyn. *Unsung Voices: Opera and Musical Narrative in the Nineteenth Century*. Princeton University Press, 1991.

Bagnoli, Giorgio. *The La Scala Encyclopedia of the Opera*. New York: Simon & Schuster, 1993.

Blackmer, Corinne E., and Patricia Juliana Smith. *En Travesti: Women, Gender Subversion, Opera*. New York: Columbia University Press, 1995.

Clément, Catherine. *Opera, or The Undoing of Women*. Minneapolis: University of Minnesota Press, 1988.

Dellamora, Richard, and Daniel Fischlin, eds. *The Work of Opera: Genre, Nationhood, and Sexual Difference*. New York: Columbia University Press, 1997.

Dizikes, John. *Opera in America: A Cultural History*. New Haven: Yale University Press, 1993.

Freeman, John W. *The Metropolitan Opera Stories of the Great Operas*. New York: W. W. Norton, 1984.

Glass, Philip. *Music By Philip Glass*. New York: Da Capo Press, 1995.

Grout, Donald Jay. *A Short History of Opera*. New York: Columbia University Press, 1965.

Hoelterhoff, Manuela. *Cinderella and Company: Backstage at the Opera with Cecilia Bartoli*. New York: Alfred A. Knopf, 1998.

Jacobs, Arthur, and Stanley Sadie. *The Wordsworth Book of Opera*. London: Wordsworth Editions, 1996.

Kerman, Joseph. *Opera as Drama*. New York: Alfred A. Knopf, 1956.

Koestenbaum, Wayne. *The Queen's Throat: Opera, Homosexuality, and the Mystery of Desire*. New York: Vintage Books, 1993.

Lindenberger, Herbert. *Opera: The Extravagant Art*. Ithaca: Cornell University Press, 1984.

———. *Opera in History: From Monteverdi to Cage*. Stanford University Press, 1998.

Littlejohn, David. *The Ultimate Art: Essays Around and About Opera*. Berkeley: University of California Press, 1992.

MacMurray, Jessica M., and Allison Brewster Franzetti, eds. *The Book of 101 Opera Librettos*. New York: Black Dog and Leventhal, 1996.

Matheopoulos, Helena. *Diva: Great Sopranos and Mezzos Discuss Their Art*. Boston: Northeastern University Press, 1991.

Mordden, Ethan. *Opera Anecdotes*. New York: Oxford University Press, 1985.

Osborne, Charles. *The Complete Operas of Richard Strauss*. New York: Da Capo Press, 1988.

———. *The Complete Operas of Richard Wagner*. New York: Da Capo Press, 1993.

Peyser, Ethel, and Marion Bauer. *How Opera Grew: From Ancient Greece to the Present Day*. New York: G. P. Putnam's Sons, 1956.

Schonberg, Harold C. *The Glorious Ones: Classical Music's Legendary Performers*. New York: Times Books, 1985.

Till, Nicholas. *Mozart and the Enlightenment: Truth, Virtue and Beauty in Mozart's Operas*. New York: W. W. Norton, 1992.

Acknowledgments

As with opera itself, putting together a book like this is a collaborative effort. I'd like to give shout-outs to (in no particular order) my editor, Paul Schnee, and everyone else at Pocket Books; my agent, Elizabeth Sheinkman; everyone at Universal Music, especially Albert Imperato, Wende Persons, Jayme Burzette, and Glenn Petry; Joseph Volpe, Peter Clark, and Francois Giuliani at the Metropolitan Opera; and John Pennino at the Metropolitan Opera Archive. I also received help and materials from a number of opera houses around the country; thank-yous are in order to Leo Boucher at the Houston Grand Opera; Speight Jenkins and Tina Ryker at the Seattle Opera; Peter Hemmings and Mary Kane at the Los Angeles Opera; William Mason and Susan Mathieson at the Chicago Lyric Opera; and Andy Higgins, formerly of the New York City Opera. I had a personal staff of supporters, editors, and friends who helped me with the book. In alphabetical order, they are: Alex Ceglia, Ondine Cohane, Tisa Heads, Kippy Joseph, Sidaya Moore, Carole O'Hara, Allyson Pimentel, Tom Samiljan, and Lara Spotts. I'd also like to mention the opera-loving matriarchs of my family, O'ma and Grandma Ceil. And, finally, the very patient and not-quite-opera-obsessed Charles Runnette.

KGM STUDIOS

MATT DOBKIN is a former classical music editor at *Time Out New York,* where his work continues to appear regularly. In addition to working as a freelance music, technology, and travel writer, Matt writes and records original rock music.